High-Pop

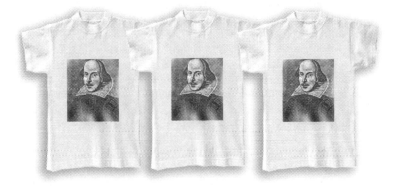

High-Pop

Making *Culture* into Popular Entertainment

EDITED BY

Jim Collins

Blackwell Publishers

Copyright © Blackwell Publishers Ltd 2002; editorial introduction and arrangement
copyright © Jim Collins 2002

First published 2002

2 4 6 8 10 9 7 5 3 1

Blackwell Publishers Inc.
350 Main Street
Malden, Massachusetts 02148
USA

Blackwell Publishers Ltd
108 Cowley Road
Oxford OX4 1JF
UK

Library of Congress Cataloguing-in-Publication Data has been applied for.

ISBN 0-631-22210-3 (hardback); 0-631-22211-1 (paperback)

British Library Cataloguing in Publication Data

A CIP catalogue record for this book is available from the British Library.

Typeset in 11/13 on 26 pt Bembo
by Best-set Typesetter Ltd, Hong Kong
Printed in Great Britain by MPG Books Ltd, Bodmin, Cornwall

This book is printed on acid-free paper.

For

Stephanie

Contents

List of Illustrations ix

List of Contributors xi

Acknowledgments xiii

High-Pop: An Introduction 1
Jim Collins

1 "Expecting Rain": Opera as Popular Culture? 32
John Storey

2 Signature and Brand 56
John Frow

3 From Brahmin Julia to Working-Class Emeril:
The Evolution of Television Cooking 75
Toby Miller

4 "Tan"talizing Others: Multicultural Anxiety and
the New Orientalism 90
Kim Middleton Meyer

5 Class Rites in the Age of the Blockbuster 114
Alan Wallach

6 Museums and Department Stores: Close
Encounters 129
Carol Duncan

7 Which Shakespeare to Love? Film, Fidelity, and
the Performance of Literature 155
Timothy Corrigan

Contents

8 No (Popular) Place Like Home?   182
    Jim Collins

9 Style and the Perfection of Things   201
    Celia Lury

Index   225

Illustrations

Plate 0.1   The cover of the Holiday 2000 catalogue from the
            Museum of Modern Art, New York.   12
Plate 5.1   Facade, Metropolitan Museum of Art, New York,
            July 2000, with banner announcing Chardin
            exhibition. Author's photograph.   115
Plate 5.2   Facade, National Gallery of Art, Washington,
            DC, June 2000, with three-part banner for
            "The Impressionists at Argenteuil." Author's
            photograph.   116
Plate 6.1   International Exhibition of Ceramic Art, view of
            English section, Newark Museum, 1929. Collection
            of the Newark Museum.   145
Plate 6.2   Exhibit of ceramics at Hahnes Department Store,
            1929. A placard links the display to the Exhibition
            of Ceramic Art running concurrently in the
            Newark Museum. Collection of the Newark
            Museum.   146
Plate 6.3   Examples of hardware from the Design in Industry
            Exhibition, Newark Museum, 1929. Collection of
            the Newark Museum.   147
Plate 6.4   Examples of glass and ceramics from the
            Inexpensive Objects Exhibition, 1929. Also called
            the 10c Exhibition. Collection of the Newark
            Museum.   147
Plate 6.5   Case of glass and black and white textile from the

Inexpensive Objects Exhibition, 1929. Collection
of the Newark Museum.   148

Plate 7.1   Joseph Fiennes as *Shakespeare in Love* (Miramax
Films, 1998). Museum of Modern Art Film Stills
Archive.   156

Plate 8.1   The Crate and Barrel flagship store on Michigan
Avenue in Chicago.   188

Contributors

Jim Collins is Associate Professor of Film, Television, and English at the University of Notre Dame. He is the author of *Uncommon Cultures: Popular Culture and Postmodernism* and *Architectures of Excess* and co-editor of *Film Theory Goes to the Movies*.

Timothy Corrigan is currently chair of the Graduate English Program at Temple University. He is the author of *Film and Literature*, *A Cinema Without Walls*, *Writing About Film*, and *New German Film: The Displaced Image*.

Carol Duncan is Professor of Art History, Ramapo College of New Jersey. She is the author of *The Pursuit of Pleasure: The Rococo Revival in French Romantic Art* and *The Aesthetics of Power: Essays in the Critical History of Art*, translated into Italian as *L'Estetica del Pottere* with a preface by Angela Vettese. Her most recent book is *Civilizing Rituals: Inside Public Art Museums*, Chinese translation by Wang Ya-Ke.

John Frow is Regius Professor of Rhetoric and English Literature at the University of Edinburgh and Director of the Institute for Advanced Studies in the Humanities. He is the author of *Marxism and Literary History*, *Cultural Studies and Cultural Value*, *Time and Commodity Culture*, and (with Tony Bennett and Michael Emmison) *Accounting for Tastes*.

Celia Lury is a Reader in Sociology at Goldsmiths College, University of London. She has written widely on cultural theory, the culture industries, and consumer culture. She teaches a course called "A sociology of objects" and is writing a book on *Brands: The Logos of the Global Economy*.

Kim Middleton Meyer is presently a graduate student in the English Department at the University of Notre Dame. Her current project investigates sites at which Asian American identity signifies in American culture and methods of performing ethnicity.

Toby Miller is Professor of Cultural Studies and Cultural Policy at New York University. He is the author of *The Well-Tempered Self: Citizenship, Culture, and the Postmodern Subject*, *Contemporary Australian Television*, *The Avengers*, *Technologies of Truth: Cultural Citizenship and the Popular Media*, and (with Alec McHoul) *Popular Culture and Everyday Life*, edited *SportCult*, and co-edited (with Robert Stam) *A Companion to Film Theory* and *Film and Theory: An Anthology*. He is the editor of the journals *Social Text* and *Television and New Media*.

John Storey is Professor of Cultural Studies and Director of the Centre for Research in Media and Cultural Studies, University of Sunderland, UK. His publications include *Cultural Studies and the Study of Popular Culture*, *What is Cultural Studies? A Reader*, *Cultural Theory and Popular Culture: A Reader*, 2nd edn, *Cultural Consumption and Everyday Life*, and *Cultural Theory and Popular Culture: An Introduction*, 3rd edn.

Alan Wallach is Ralph H. Wark Professor of Art and Art History and Professor of American Studies at the College of William and Mary. In 1994 he was co-curator of the exhibition "Thomas Cole: Landscape into History," which was seen at the National Museum of American Art, the Wadsworth Atheneum, and the Brooklyn Museum, and co-editor of the accompanying catalogue. He is the author of *Exhibiting Contradiction: Essays on the Art Museum in the United States*.

Acknowledgments

I would like to express my appreciation to the Museum of Modern Art and the Newark Museum for their permission to reprint images used in this volume. I would also like to thank Willam Saunders and Nancy Levinson at *Harvard Design Magazine* for their advice and editorial assistance in the preparation of the essays by Alan Wallach and this author in the collection. For his patience and meticulous work in the production of this volume, I'd like to thank Jack Messenger at Redshoes Cooperative.

It is difficult to convey the extent of my gratitude to Jayne Fargnoli at Blackwell Publishers. Without her insight and encouragement this collection would have never appeared. She is, in every way, an exemplary editor, as well as a continual delight to work with in every context.

I want to thank my family for their limitless support, especially my parents, Virginia and William, and my daughters, Ava, Nell, Sophia, and Gabriela (my select advisory committee on quality consumerism).

My wife Stephanie deserves my profoundest appreciation because she was instrumental in conceptualizing the collection and did a great deal of the most significant fieldwork. Her enthusiasm for this project was a constant source of inspiration. I also need to thank her for being the great love of my life.

High-Pop: An Introduction
Jim Collins

Recently a great deal of attention has been paid to tabloid television, gangsta-rap, and violent video games as examples of a popular culture now seen as a destructive social force, appealing to only the basest instincts as it dumbs down its audiences. Yet emergent forms of *high-pop* are becoming increasingly ubiquitous, all around the town – out at the mall in superstore bookshops like Barnes and Noble complete with on-site Starbucks cafes; down at the multiplex where literary adaptations by Miramax now compete head-to-head with high-concept action films; and in our own mail-boxes, since we can now count on a daily delivery of high-style design in the form of Pottery Barn and Crate and Barrel catalogues which allow us to transform our homes into tasteful environments, with, perhaps, the advice of Martha Stewart, available on-line, on television, in magazine and catalogue formats, as well as over at the local K-Mart store, . . . which is right next to Target, another discount store, now featuring its new Michael Graves collection. . . .

The popularization of good taste – or more precisely, how to get it – is a manifestation of consumer culture but it is also a complex phenomenon which complicates many of the basic assumptions about how "taste," whether it be popular or elite, is recognized as such in contemporary cultures. High-pop is, in large part, a reaction against the sordidness of aggressive mass-marketing and blockbuster entertainment, yet its high-profile visibility depends on the incorporation of marketing techniques borrowed directly from that world. This has led to unprecedented developments in which institutions and tastes which were formerly thought to be mutually exclusive have become commonplace – *good design* chain-stores, *blockbuster* museum shows, *high-concept* literary adaptations. This merger of the previously antagonistic is exemplified by a recent exhibition devoted to painter John Singer Sargent. Once the veritable court painter of the British and American elite, full-page ads for the Sargent show at the Museum of Fine Arts in Boston and the National Gallery in Washington appeared in the *New York Times* alongside ads for the biggest summer movies, like *Notting Hill* (in which a famous Hollywood star falls desperately in love with the owner of a struggling little bookshop, of all things). Between the two museums, nearly 800,000 people viewed the Sargent paintings, a painter whose chief virtue was, according to Michael Kimmelman, his ability to "encapsulate most precisely the era's operative notion of luxe" (Kimmelman, 1999). Both blockbusters, the museum show and the romantic-comedy-of the-year, suggest that the relationship between capital and "cultural capital" appears to be going through a period of mutual revaluation.

The essays in this collection investigate specific high-pop phenomena in film, television, literature, opera, fashion, interior design, and museum exhibition. The investigation of narrative texts, material culture, and cultural institutions is essential because the boundaries between those categories have grown ever more difficult to maintain now that museums exhibit art treasures but also do multi-million dollar business selling exhibition- and collection-related merchandise, now that material objects come either fully narrativized or brimming with narrative potential, or now that narrative texts seem to grow ever more dependent on material decoration, i.e., the right sort of art direction for all those words. In the now legendary airplane shot which opens and closes Anthony Minghella's *The English Patient* (1996) the characters come from Ondaatje's novel but the gleaming silver bi-plane is Air Pottery Barn. This interpenetration of narrative and material texts could hardly be more visible than in the "Ernest Hemingway Furniture Collection" unveiled at the annual International Furnishings Market in North Carolina in 1998, featuring 96 pieces for living, dining and bedroom furniture and a host of accessories (Hamilton, 1998). The print advertisements that have appeared in shelter magazines such as *Metropolitan Home* feature a leather-bound club chair with matching ottoman, upon which sit two leather-bound volumes and an antique typewriter. The copy within the advertisement, printed to resemble an old-fashioned typewriter face, reads, "Sure, you can get Hemingway in paperback. But wouldn't you rather own the leather-bound edition?" The print beneath the picture concludes, "Simple, bold statements wrought in wood, metal, stone, and leather. As unique and durable as Hemingway's writing."

Taken together, these essays share a larger project – to trace the development of a new stage in the ever-shifting relationship between "high art" and popular culture. In this introduction, I describe the agendas of the individual chapters and elaborate on their points of contact, but I will also present a set of revised theoretical paradigms for understanding taste in contemporary cultures. This investigation of taste formations involves, by necessity, another component – to re-examine the efficacy of cultural studies, which has always been un-comfortable with the question of cultural evaluation and avoided any examination of *Culture* as *popular* culture. One of the most troubling blind spots that has developed within cultural studies has been the implicit assumption that *legitimate* culture was being tended to by the rest of the academy, and it was the sort of thing best left to the old guard because it didn't really address itself to anyone but them anyway. But "high culture" didn't stay put, living out its days as some sort of hot-house plant in the greenhouse of the academy. It has become popular culture – Shakespeare's in love, with a vengeance.

Making *Culture* into Popular Entertainment: The Backstory

I want to begin by locating high-pop within a meaningful historical context, which in this case means situating it in regard to two different historical trajectories. The first is the history of the mass culture/high art relationship within which high-pop marks the beginning of a fourth phase. In the first phase, usually delimited as the first half of the nineteenth century, new forms of popular culture were developing as the industrial revolution generated the two essential preconditions for mass entertainment: mass production and a mass audience. During this period, popular and high art texts were encountered in the same venues; concerts included arias as well as the popular songs of the day without any sense that the latter were somehow inappropriate for the proceedings. Museums included both European masterpieces and stuffed exotic animals in a diverse spectacle of visual delights. The

second phase, which might be called for shorthand purposes the Sacrilization of Culture, begins in the second half of the nineteenth
century, according to social historians such as Paul Dimaggio (1991)
and Lawrence Levine (1988), with the bifurcation of culture into
popular and elite arenas. Dimaggio traces the ways in which Brahmins
gravitated toward not-for-profit cultural organizations as a means of
framing culture according to their own tastes and sensibilities, gaining
control of museums, opera houses, and concert halls by taking them
out of the marketplace which catered to a grand public (i.e., the immigrant classes possessed of decidedly different sensibilities). Led by entrepreneurs like Henry Lee Higginson, the Brahmins became cultural
gatekeepers, their symphony societies and museum boards securing
hegemonic control over cultural life in Boston when they were facing
a steady loss of political control. By situating it outside the marketplace, culture could be administered, made manageable by the proper
guardians of public virtue. In a glowing appreciation of Higginson
which appeared in a salute to the 100th anniversary of Boston's Symphony Hall, Joseph Horowitz (2000) argues that the portrait of Higginson as cultural autocrat is "overdrawn" because "when it came to
audiences Higginson was a considerable democrat," instituting work-
ingman's concerts and opening the balcony to women, students, and
other non-subscribers. But the point is not whether the working classes
were allowed to attend. The Brahmins could exercise hegemonic
control over what it meant to be cultured only by inviting in a public
that was expected to observe the proper protocols and thereby learn
an invaluable lesson – to be cultured was to do as the Brahmins did
(and the Brahmins didn't *do* popular culture). Rather than monopoliz-
ing culture, they corralled it in hopes of taming the immigrant masses
who threatened their very existence, a point made abundantly clear by
a letter from Higginson to a relative requesting a donation: "Educate,
and save ourselves and our families and our money from the mobs!"
(quoted in Dimaggio, 1991: 393).

John Storey examines the fate of opera during this period in his
essay in this collection, " 'Expecting Rain': Opera as Popular Culture?"
He stresses that the recent popularization is not, as such, a new phenomenon because "the key thing to understand historically about opera
is that it did not become unpopular, rather it was *made* unpopular." He
points to the broad-based appeal that opera enjoyed before this great
bifurcation, invoking Janet Wolf's contention that a "parallel process of

differentiation had also been occurring in England, where the pre-industrial cultural pursuits, enjoyed on a cross-class basis, were gradually replaced by a class-specific culture" (Wolf, 1989). For Storey, opera had to be made unpopular as it was enclosed within the realm of legitimate culture, an institutional relocation that was accompanied by ideological justification for a new hierarchy of taste. Dimaggio describes this justification as a process of legitimation:

> as long as cultural boundaries were indistinct, "fashionable taste," far from embodying cultural authority, was suspect as snobbish, trivial, and undemocratic. Only when elite taste was harnessed to a clearly articulated ideology embodied in the exhibitions and performances of organizations that selected and presented art in a manner distinct from that of commercial entrepreneurs . . . did an understanding of culture as hierarchical become both legitimate and widespread. (Dimaggio, 1992: 22)

Storey makes the essential point that this legitimation process, like any effective ideological maneuver, *naturalized* this hierarchy of tastes, making the historically contested into the-way-things-have-always-been. Storey quotes Levine most effectively on this naturalization of the rituals needed for the proper appreciation of high culture: "what was invented was the illusion that the aesthetic products of high culture were originally created to be appreciated in precisely the manner late nineteenth century Americans were taught to observe: with reverent, informed, disciplined seriousness" (Levine, 1988: 229).

This hierarchy of tastes remained relatively stable until the late 1950s, when a third phase emerged in this evolving relationship between high and popular culture – the Pop Art era – which signaled a profound dissatisfaction with that great bifurcation as well as a growing contempt for the sacrilization of culture. According to Dick Hebdige, the Pop phenomena that appeared first in Great Britain revealed the "loaded arbitrariness" of those binary oppositions (Hebdige, 1989). The dissatisfaction was generated by a period of prosperity that followed the relative austerity of the postwar economy. Historian Christopher Booker has said of this period: "For never again would so many English families be buying their first car, installing their first refrigerator, taking their first continental holidays. Never again could such ubiquitous novelty be found in that dawn of the age of affluence" (quoted in Hebdige, 1989: 99). This burst of exuberant

consumerism inaugurated a "drama of possessions" in which the acquisition of commodities rapidly became inseparable from the formation
of personal identity. Within this drama, which Lawrence Alloway (1959)
argues is a key dynamic in both American and British Pop, the taint
of the commercial sector did not fade away as much as it was countered by a growing fascination with commercial imagery. The admiration for popular iconography exemplified by Richard Hamilton's "*Just
what is it that makes today's homes so different, so appealing?*" (1956) and
Hommage a Chrsysler (1957) was part of a through-going rejection of
British "good taste" still advocated by, for example, the BBC, which
tried to continue its cultural gatekeeper role in the midst of this taste
crisis. For Hebdige, "Pop challenged the legitimacy of validated distinctions between the arts and the lingering authority of pre-War taste
formations. The 'lessons' inscribed in Pop's chosen objects – Americana,
'slick graphics,' pop music – matched BBC didacticism point for point
and turned it upside down. Where the BBC counseled discrimination
and sobriety, pop recommended excess and aspiration" (Hebdige, 1989:
88).

The desacrilization of culture which fueled the Pop Art movement
in both the UK and the US challenged the allegedly timeless distinctions between the artistic and the commercial, but the attack took
a very particular direction, namely the determination to move the
popular into the world of legitimate culture. The high-pop phenomena that began to appear in the 1990s involve a significantly different
dynamic, a fourth phase in that complicated history. This is not to
suggest that the advent of high-pop marked a unilateral change, or that
vestiges of earlier forms of both sacrilization and desacrilization didn't
continue to thrive in the 1990s. If the Pop Art period was, to a great
extent, a matter of academy-trained artists taking forms of popular
iconography into the rarefied realm of museum art, high-pop represents the reversal of that flow by transforming *Culture* into mass entertainment. While the appropriation of popular culture was also one of
the defining characteristics of the postmodern texts of the 1980s, the
popular often remained within quotation marks, and as such, functioned as a critique of the orthodoxy of modernist sensibilities. High-
pop depends on the appropriation of elite cultural pleasure without
quotation marks, an appropriation not just of specific icons or canonical
texts but entire protocols for demonstrating taste and social distinction.
Warhol may have taken Campbell's soup cans into the gallery scene

with all the requisite irony, but Martha Stewart promises to deliver the scene at her Connecticut homestead to your local discount store, without a trace of irony in those cans of paint. The Pop era was born of affluence, a time when consumerism was in search of style and legitimation as unprecedented numbers of people began to acquire homes, automobiles, and a host of big-ticket appliances. The high-pop phase is also the result of economic prosperity, but the terms of the resulting taste crisis are fundamentally different, if for no other reason than it comes at a later stage in the history of consumerism when all of the grand new consumer items of the postwar period have been commonplace for generations, when the relationship between identity and consumer choice must be articulated by more sophisticated commodities and far more semiotically complicated transactions in order to be considered meaningful.

One could also situate high-pop in reference to another historical trajectory, the one formed by the various forms of "middlebrow" culture that have appeared since the end of the nineteenth century. Yet I believe it is a serious mistake to conceive of the current popularization of elite cultural pleasures as simply the most recent incarnation of middlebrow aesthetics. Joan Shelby Rubin's *The Making of Middlebrow Culture* (1992) and Janice Radway's study of the Book-of-the-Month Club, *A Feeling for Books* (1997) have provided richly detailed histories of the formation of institutional frameworks which brought culture and commerce together in extremely profitable forms. They both explore the cultural preconditions for these hybrid combinations, placing special emphasis on the ways in which notions of self-education were promoted. It is in regard to what Rubin calls "self-culture" that high-pop phenomena might be productively compared to middlebrow culture, because it throws into sharp relief what that self-education now consists of, both in terms of primary ingredients and in terms of the underlying notions of good taste which animate the imperative to acquire that education. Rubin and Radway detail the heterogeneity of middlebrow entertainment, but both their books also delineate the separateness of middlebrow, that it depended on a certain kind of intellectual experience that was demonstrably not of the highest order in terms of cultural prestige. Dwight Macdonald expressed the official intellectual's disdain for middlebrow culture of the post-World War II period, condemning *midcult* as just one more manifestation of the dreaded mass culture, a great watering down process resulting in the "tepid ooze of midcult" (Macdonald, 1960: 609). Russell Lynes offered a typology of high-, middle-, and lowbrow cultures in *Harper's Magazine* in February 1949 which was followed by an article in *Life* magazine two months later (April 11) featuring an elaborate chart drawn by designer Tom Funks, complete with the appropriate illustrations of each taste culture's preferences. Both concluded that each "brow" was defined by a relatively self-contained set of tastes, e.g., highbrows were drawn to Eames chairs, red wine, and the ballet, while middlebrows preferred Empire chairs, martinis, and the theater.[1] In her analysis of the selections made by the Book-of-the-Month Club (one of the definitive middlebrow institutions demonized by Macdonald) Radway identifies a comparable distinctiveness, arguing that while the club offered a variety of different titles, the appeal to the "general reader" as opposed to the "academic reader" led to the promotion of books that were decidedly non-canonical, e.g., *To Kill a Mockingbird*, *Marjorie Morningstar, Gone with the Wind*. Reflecting on her own reading history, she defends these club selections that made such an impression on her at the time, despite the fact that they had no place in her college English classes, where "the only female authors I read were the Bröntes, Jane Austen, Emily Dickinson, and Edith Wharton" (Radway, 1997: 349).

This passage crystallizes the key difference between middlebrow culture of the postwar era and the high-pop of the 1990s. Where the Book-of-the-Month Club promoted books that had little or no status within the academy, preferring to cultivate another kind of "good read," Miramax and Sony Classical have enjoyed enormous success since the early 1990s through their lavish adaptations of the most highbrow academic titles, delivering classical authors like Austen and Shakespeare to audiences far broader than any ever contemplated by the Book-of-the-Month Club. Literary adaptations have been a Hollywood staple for decades, but by the late 1990s the adaptation had become a phenomenon so expansive that Hollywood producer Lynda Obst insisted that "There are no more classics left to film – they're all in production." Middlebrow entertainment continues to find a receptive audience in the form of singers like Andrea Bocelli and Charlotte Church, big voices singing light and pseudo-classical, heavy on the Ave Marias with extra helpings of "Amazing Grace." Opera stars like Roberto Alagna and Angela Gheorghiu, on the other hand, are the soul of high-pop, promoted like pop stars but singing the classical repertoire in best-selling recordings like "Verdi per Due" or connoisseurs' operas like Puccini's *La Rondine*. Reproductions of anonymous period furniture *à la* Pennsylvania House define the essence of middlebrow tastefulness; knock-offs of Jean-Michel Frank couches at Restoration Hardware are high-pop. Both represent massification of a certain notion of tastefulness, but the latter rests on a designer auteurism which assumes, as *practically* common knowledge, a sophisticated design literacy formerly possessed by only the sort of people who could afford interior decorators (and the sort of one-of-a-kind furniture that they offered).

Just as directors went from anonymity to celebrity in the 1960s when popular film critics began to identify *auteurs* possessed of identifiable personal styles, the names of designers, architects, and chefs began to acquire a high degree of visibility in the 1990s. Articles in lifestyle publications like *Vanity Fair, Gentleman's Quarterly*, and the *New York Times Magazine* now refer to Philippe Starck, Frank Gehry, or Alice Waters with the expectation that their readerships have accumulated the requisite taste literacy to be in on the conversation. The expansion of *auteur* status by borrowing the prestige of the literary author as celebrity, is epitomized by a feature on chef Mario Batali in *Bon Appétit*. We learn that his restaurant, *Babbo*, is a Greenwhich Village hot spot but still humble, "Even with the high-wattage celebrity – *Wasn't that Salman Rushdie?* – *Babbo* welcomes all" (Chapman, 2000: 142). The representative celebrity isn't one of the movie or television stars who frequent the place; Batali's other restaurant, *Po*, was in fact featured on an episode of *Seinfeld*. The coupling of Batali and Rushdie, rather than Batali and Seinfeld, reveal a great deal about the framing of the *auteur*-chef, associated not with just a mere media star but a literary lion who, in this context, apparently has greater star power.

Signature, Literacy, Value; or the Coming of Emeril

In chapter 2 of this collection John Frow argues that this promotion of the signature is the result of a "convergence of, on the one hand, the commercial branding of aesthetic goods, and, on the other, the aesthetic valorization of commercial goods." For Frow, the conflation of the systems responsible for the maintenance of signature and brand name exemplifies post-Fordist marketing which makes the signature effect a way of targeting niche consumers, but:

At the same time – and this is the point of convergence – high art has become entirely a component of large-scale industrial production; no longer a craft, it finds its place as a niche market amongst others in a world of mass production. To say this is not to say anything one way or the other about the quality or value of work produced at this convergence: it is only to say that it is no longer possible in good faith to oppose an "authentic" aesthetics of the signature to a "commercialized" aesthetics of the brand.

This convergence has had a profound effect, for example, on the relationship between what used to be called the design *industry* and the art *world*. According to the *New York Times*, "To judge by the buzz, design is *the* hot topic right now – it's got its own vodka-sponsored events, its own young fashionable audience pushing into the openings at stores. 'I'm watching the art world of the 1980s take shape in the design community,' said Tony Whitfield, chairman of the product design department of Parsons School of Design" (Hamilton, 2000: B1). What used to be considered the culmination of a designer's career – a distribution deal with a boutique firm like Alessi, Herman Miller, or Cappellini – is now generally considered to be a stepping stone, an association which might lead to a contract with the Target Corporation, the discount chain-store which has recently added a product line by Philippe Starck to its massively successful Michael Graves Collection, both of which are displayed in the stores with photos of the designer and museum-style explanatory plates. According to Peter Stathis, head of the design department at Cranbrook Academy of Art, "It was an invisible profession," but that has changed because "Kids, youth culture exist with design in a way they never have before" (ibid: B12).

High-pop depends on the expansion of the system of the signature into formerly anonymous realms of cultural production that coincides with the proliferation of audiences that subscribe to that system. Where middlebrow culture could be characterized in terms of a specific demographic according to age, race, gender, and economic class, the appeal of high-pop defies any such homogeneity. While Jane Austen adaptations and Jean-Michel Frank sofas appeal to a largely postgraduate audience, the system of the signature now dominates upscale marketing in youth culture, normally considered to be an entirely different taste culture, one that would, if anything, be openly antagonistic to the *sophistication* required for the enjoyment of nineteenth-century novels and interior design. But sophisticated taste, expressed in terms of a knowledge of the appropriate signatures, now pervades a wide variety of target audiences, including teenage girls. In another article covering the current style scene in the *New York Times*, this one focusing on the upscale teenage market, an 18-year-old describes her wardrobe in this way: "I own a Prada messenger bag, I have two Kate Spades, a Gucci belt and a Prada belt, several pairs of Sisley jeans . . ." (La Ferla, 2000: B8). While brand mania has defined teenage taste for decades, the conflation of the systems of the signature and brand name signal a profound shift from the fetishizing of a particular type of item – bell bottoms, baggies, slap bracelets, etc. – to an appreciation of the *auteur*-designer, a change made possible by the increase in disposable income but also in what the *Times* refers to as the "enormous information base" these teenagers now possess. The extension of this designer literacy into an even earlier form of "youth culture" is also underway. The Pottery Barn Kids catalogue regularly features knock-offs of modernist classics like Arne Jacobson chairs (called, appropriately enough, "Copenhagen chairs") and the Holiday 2000 catalogue from the Museum of Modern Art features on its cover a dollhouse designed by photographer Laurie Simmons and architect Peter Wheelwright, "reminiscent of Gerrit Reitvald's Schroeder House (1925)," to be filled with furniture custom-designed by the likes of Dakota Jackson, Ron Arad, and Karem Rashid, complemented with paintings by Peter Halley and photographs by Cindy Sherman (see plate 0.1). Most importantly, the dollhouse is not just a museum-shop stunt; it is also being offered simultaneously by a number of upscale toy catalogues. Larry Mangel, founder of Bozart Toys and the original developer of this concept, hopes it "will bring design to a whole new group of people. It walks that fine line between toys and grown-up things" (Vlades, 2000: 58).

The ability to deliver the goods, namely the goods that were once the stuff of elite cultural pleasures, reflects a massive increase in the volume of production and the breadth of audiences, but that expanding knowledge base is the result of profound changes in delivery systems and the cartography of taste. In chapter 3 Toby Miller charts the evolution of the food program from Julia Child to Emeril Lagasse, arguing that when Child's *The French Chef* first aired in the 1960s on PBS, French cuisine was indeed considered to be an important educational experience for its small, but highly educated, viewership. With

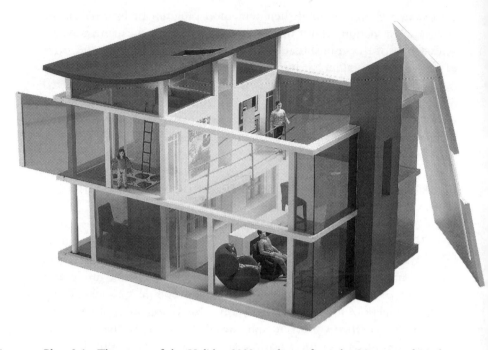

Plate 0.1 The cover of the Holiday 2000 catalogue from the Museum of Modern Art, New York.

the advent of cable and satellite technologies, food programming has escaped the public television ghetto, as both the Food Network and the Carleton Network have made chefs into national celebrities, a point epitomized by Emeril's appearance during celebrity guest week on *Who Wants to Be a Millionaire?* The same issue of the *New York Times* that detailed the hotness of the design scene includes a full-page ad from William Morrow Books: "Congratulations EMERIL on more than two million books sold! Coming to a town near you this fall!" (B14). That the coming of Emeril should be advertised on this scale is due to the fact that Emeril has already come into our homes in the form of his television program and his bestselling cookbooks. Where the notoriety of chefs used to depend primarily on restaurant reviews read by a very particular audience, and the "experience" of their mastery was possible only by actually going to their restaurants, chef–*auteurs* now come to *your* house and fans can *know* the celebrity chef's cuisine by simply watching their television program or by performing it themselves at home with the cookbooks. In much the same way, the celebrity of the architect is due to media coverage beyond the orbit of the architectural press, but it depends on bringing that signature home, into your own cultural space through the popularly priced design-lines which bear their names, i.e., you may not be able to have Richard Meier design your home, or even be able to travel to see the Getty Museum, but you can drink out of his old-fashioned glasses.

Cultural Studies and the Ritualization of Resistance

These changing relationships between the aesthetic and the commercial, in terms of the volume of production, the sophistication of delivery systems, and proliferation of unprecedented taste formations, seems especially ripe for analysis, but cultural studies has, up to this point, expressed little interest in the popularization of what were formerly considered elite cultural pleasures. This omission is attributable to two interdependent problems: the avoidance of questions concerning aesthetic value and the valorization of marginality within cultural studies, to the point where certain forms of cultural expression, no matter how popular, either don't appear on theoretical maps, or do so only as some vast dark continent labeled "official culture." The original project of cultural studies, as it was articulated at the Birmingham Centre for Contemporary Cultural Studies, was the study of culture, as Raymond Williams had defined it – as a *whole way of life*. The determination to pursue a more ethnographic approach to culture (i.e., descriptive but not evaluative, inclusive but not exclusive) was an essential step in justifying the study of the popular, primarily because it introduced a paradigm shift which allowed the popular to fall within the purview of academic research by obviating the need to demonstrate its "quality" according to evaluative criteria which were axiomatically opposed to it.

One of the most far-reaching contributions of cultural studies was its critique of *the Aesthetic*, conceived of in terms of transcendent, universal values and intrinsic artistic characteristics. By arguing that aesthetic judgments were always contingent upon material circumstances, always imbricated in a web of interlocking power relations in which no *purely* aesthetic judgments were ever possible, the "Birmingham

school" established a mode of *cultural* analysis which didn't begin and
end with evaluation. Yet the need to demolish *the Aesthetic* as a magical
category also produced a kind of infrastructural weakness within cultural studies, namely an avoidance of texts which insisted upon their
aesthetic *superiority* according to the very hierarchies that cultural
studies sought to dismantle. In other words, the mystification of *the
Aesthetic* as transcendent, and the specification of the ways in which
aesthetic textuality operates within the broader realm of cultural production, are fundamentally different projects and the rejection of the
former should not preclude the pursuit of the latter. Evaluation may
never be purely aesthetic but, on the other hand, aesthetic evaluation
is a specific mode of differentiation, a regime of value that has become
increasingly ubiquitous when so many popular texts make the *remysti-
fication* of the aesthetic the basis of their appeal as something other than
mere popular culture.

While the bracketing of evaluation may have been necessary for the
discipline, that avoidance has put cultural studies at a distinct disad-
vantage in terms of providing the "thick description" of the various
forms of cultural production it explores, because it remains somehow
above the fray. John Frow has identified this resistance as one of the
principal limitations of cultural studies:

> To refuse the question of value is not, however, to escape it. . . . The
> dilemma flows from the methodological necessity of suspending per-
> sonal judgment, pleasure, and position in the objectification of a cul-
> tural terrain. But that moment of suspension, of separation from the
> object, thereby deprives it of all its interactive force and meaning, since
> culture is by definition, a realm of uses and of circulating energies. (Frow,
> 1995: 2)

To reduce those energies to mere commodity fetishism, or to simply
cover them over with a thick coat of Bourdieu, rather too casually
applied, only distances cultural studies from the feverish evaluation that
is one of the greatest pleasures derived from popular texts, at least for
non-academic audiences. There is perhaps no more succinct description of the primacy of value determinations and of the need to demonstrate taste distinctions as a way of establishing identity at the most
primary level than the formulation made by the narrator in Nick
Hornby's (1995) novel, *High Fidelity*. During a discussion of courtship

rituals he says: "what really matters is what you like, not what you *are* like." His friend at the record store suggests compiling a questionnaire to give to prospective partners which would cover all the "music/film/TV/book bases." Rob advises against this but admits: "there was an important and essential truth contained within the idea, and the truth was that these things matter, and it's no good pretending that any relationship has a future if your record collections disagree violently, or if your favorite films wouldn't even speak to each other if they met at a party" (ibid: 117).

The other reason that cultural studies has failed to address the popularization of *Culture* is the inability to escape from the ghetto of self-imposed marginality. The desire to study forms of cultural production that have been ignored by the academy has led to an unfortunate counter-extremism. By the late 1990s cultural studies had become the critical-approach-of-choice for dealing with anything subcultural or any subcultural dimensions of canonical works, but was generally considered inappropriate for much of anything else – hardly the glorious culmination of a project devoted to the study of culture as a whole way of life. Tony Bennett, one of the key figures in the formation of the seminal Open University unit on popular culture, has been especially critical of this foreclosure, particularly "the view that the aim of teaching cultural studies should be to nurture more politically correct forms of resistance" (Bennett, 1996: 149). Since cultural studies was instrumental in developing a robust theoretical framework for defining the formation and functioning of working-class *subcultures*, it is hardly surprising that it should have become so quickly applied to the study of ethnic and racial subcultures in the United States within English, Media, and American Studies departments. That cultural studies provided a theoretical armature for the affirmation of identity politics within the academy has been, for many scholars, its single most significant contribution. Yet Bennett's critique exposes one of the drawbacks of this development. If cultural studies was initially a project which set out to investigate the various ways that culture was institutionalized, circulated, and made sense of by specific audiences, that agenda has indeed transmogrified into an amorphous mass of vaguely "sociological" approaches, too often taking the form of a celebration of ethnic difference through descriptive content analysis of representative multicultural texts, i.e., readings which seem indistinguishable from the traditional American Studies "thematic" approach to "the American

Experience." The domination of the marginal and subcultural within the field of cultural studies is understandable as a function of professional legitimation, particularly during the "culture wars" that beset the American academy in the early 1990s. Yet the continuing obsession with marginality as the only legitimate subject matter for cultural studies leaves vast realms of cultural production untouched and produces only a distorted, self-deluding perspective if it fails to come to terms with the unavoidable fact that voices that were once silenced or marginalized are now among the most widely heard in popular culture.

In chapter 4 Kim Middleton Meyer focuses on exactly this development, specifically that multicultural novels have become bestsellers, among the most popular choices of reading groups in search of a "quality read." She begins by describing the successful institutionalization of multiculturalism within the academy, and then turns to the construction of Asian/American-ness within reading-group culture, arguing that gaining a more expansive understanding of the New Orientalism necessitates going outside the realm of the academy to assay the "market value of difference." In order to trace the appeal of these novels as a form of upscale popular fiction, Middleton Meyer first discusses the Amy Tan phenomenon before moving on to more detailed analyses of two novels which have enjoyed enormous success with readings groups, David Guterson's *Snow Falling on Cedars* (1995) and Arthur Golden's *Memoirs of a Geisha* (1997). Utilizing Bennett's notion of *reading formation*, she details the interaction between Vintage Books and this audience through a meticulous examination of the advertising, websites, and the readers' guides devoted to these books. Middleton Meyer's analysis of the reading group stresses the self-education process that animates this particular type of reading. Vintage's Reading Group Guides labor to make good on the promise made by these book jackets – that readers will learn vital information, that they will acquire lessons in cultural literacy outside the academy which has somehow lost its *love* of books.

Popular Culture as "Finishing School"

This need to acquire the right sort of cultural education, outside the academy, has generated a host of authorities available through a variety of delivery systems. The affluence of the Clinton years has made upscale consumerism possible, but the availability of disposable income without the information necessary to make the appropriate choices is attributable to the lack of a *proper* education. Dominique Browning, the editor of *House and Garden* magazine, formulates this lack most tellingly:

> Okay, I'm ready to sign myself up, and eager to enroll about 50 people I can think of just off the top of my head. I think it is time to admit we got a little confused, a few decades back, when we decided that higher education should not include instructions in, well, what do we even call it? How to appreciate the finer things in life? How to behave like the one of the finer things in life? It's time to bring back finishing school. (Browning, 2000: 20)

She goes on to condemn the vulgarity of the beneficiaries of "big and instant money" because they fail to appreciate that "the sense of the value of a thing – quite distinct from its cost – does matter. Much of the making of a home has to do with the making of a soul."

Browning's assessment of the problem reveals the key operative assumptions that animate this taste crisis – that the acquisition of taste, unlike money, is a matter of the right education, that no one receives those lessons in how to live tastefully from a secondary or university education anymore, but that knowledge has to be found *elsewhere*, specifically from various forms of popular culture which provide the goods and, just as crucially, the information needed to translate consumer decisions into the expression of one's inner being. The notion that popular culture has offered not just the prospect of entertainment but some sort of life lessons is, of course, hardly new. As I have argued elsewhere, popular texts in a wide variety of media have presumed to provide a kind of ad hoc, alternative education, epitomized by Bruce Springsteen's lyric, "We learned more from a three-minute record baby, than we ever learned in school" (Collins, 1989). The song posits a clear-cut dichotomy in which popular music offers lessons in love and desire that have greater resonance than anything that might be gained from psychology class or the study of Romantic poetry. But the sort of "finishing school" provided by popular culture in the form of the celebrity taste mavens, style magazines, or food channels, doesn't offer strictly speaking an *alternative* education as such because there is no dichotomy – the academy no longer provides taste lessons except implicitly in terms of the setting of curricula which validate certain texts as worthy of study. That the chief objective of a higher education should be the acquisition of taste has been rejected by the academy, which considers any such notion of *refinement* to be at best antique and at worst ideologically repugnant because it carries vestiges of an educational system intended to maintain the hegemony of upper-class values. By insisting that taste distinctions have everything to do with the making of a soul, *House and Garden* posits an educational agenda which bears an uncanny resemblance to the vision of a college education advocated by Harvard moral philosophers such as William Ellery Channing, Joseph Stevens Buckminster, and Andrews Norton in the 1850s. Joan Rubin identifies this philosophy of education as the foundation of "self-culture," a pedagogy dedicated to the enhancement of aesthetic and moral judgment. This notion of self-refinement was challenged, according to Rubin, by another theory of education postulated by John Dewey, whose conception of *self-realization* advocated "not a conscious quest for personal growth but a sense of selfhood arising out of moral action undertaken to benefit society as a whole" (Rubin, 1992: 24). Taste distinctions are hardwired into the academy through a host of institutional protocols but they remain *implicit*, articulated in terms of educational objectives that eliminate the category of personal taste in favor of social responsibility.

By making personal taste an *explicit* value in a philosophy of consumer education which reinstates self-cultivation as the ultimate priority, high-pop doesn't just return the repressed – it brings it back with a roar. Where the academy has abandoned taste as an antiquated concept, popular taste brokers have repositioned it as a thoroughly contemporary value by conceiving of taste as the ability to make informed personalized choices out of a sea of consumer options. Within this new evaluative dynamic a higher education is judged essential but incomplete, in need of the finishing that only high-end popular culture authorities can now provide as they make taste into a process of converting one's stored cultural literacy into registers of personal preference articulated by the proper consumer choices. The self-culture advocated by Channing and company was envisioned as a profoundly moral one, set in direct opposition to what they perceived to be the rampant materialism of the industrial revolution. *House and Garden*'s notion of a soul may be a far more secularized one than that of the Unitarians at Harvard over a century ago, but the commercial sector, here in the form of taste-making shelter magazines, claims a higher moral ground by condemning the excesses of a materialism without taste, demonizing it as consumerism without a soul.

This conflict between the academy and the taste educators of popular culture regarding the nature of the proper *finishing* of the individual makes one thing abundantly clear: *cultural capital*, as defined by Pierre Bourdieu and widely applied within cultural studies to a variety of cultural phenomena, no longer operates as a unitary gold standard of cultural evaluation. Within the past decade several studies have questioned the near universal application of Bourdieu's analysis. John R. Hall has identified the limitations of Bourdieu's "holistic value theory" which results in a class-reductionism. Arguing along similar lines, Bennett, Emmison, and Frow assert that the "key untested assumption in Bourdieu's work is that there is a single powerful and universally binding scale of cultural legitimacy." Their analysis of cultural fields in Australia in the 1990s revealed a "plurality of scales of value, in many of which age or gender or regional location, rather than social class, play a dominant role" (Bennett, Emmison, and Frow, 1999: 269). I have also argued elsewhere that cultural authority has not disappeared in postmodern cultures, only the cultural *sovereignty* of any one standard of cultural capital because no unitary hierarchy of values renders all cultural distinctions somehow commensurate (Collins, 1993). Yet that very plurality suggests that within specific arenas, particularly those which labor to maintain traditional forms of cultural distinction, Bourdieu's work might provide a powerful theoretical framework for understanding certain forms of upscale popular culture. In chapter 5 of this volume Alan Wallach makes a compelling case for the relevancy of Bourdieu in regard to the museum blockbuster phenomenon.

Wallach argues that despite attempts to reach a broad popular audience with the blockbuster show, museums continue to reinforce the sacrilization of culture. Those record-breaking crowds may be increasing in volume but they remain homogeneous. Wallach begins by invoking Bourdieu and Darbel's *The Love of Art* (1969) because it had such a profound effect on the development of "critical museum studies." In this study of European art museums and their publics, Bourdieu contended that the homogeneity of that audience was attributable to the level of formal education, but class affiliation still remained the key determining factor because the museum-goers most likely to attend museums on a regular basis were those who came from families which encouraged museum attendance on a regular basis. Wallach argues that the situation remains the same to a very great extent and offers as confirmation Michael Schuster's *The Audience for American Art Museums* (1991), a statistical analysis of museum attendance that also identifies education as the most important predictive variable. For Wallach, the homogeneity of the audience remains stable because most art museums remain the temples of the arts they were intended to be when they were built during the age of philanthropic benefactors. The need for the non-profit world of *genuine* culture to maintain the proper distance from the marketplace was formalized by a Greco-Roman form vocabulary (which defamiliarized as it sacrilized) and by a set of rituals which, in much the same way, estranged art from day-to-day life by establishing the proper relationships between art and its public. No matter how museums may now try to move back toward the marketplace with a host of outreach strategies, Wallach contends that the museum experience remains an alienating one for audiences without the previously acquired art education necessary to make the museum truly user-friendly.

In chapter 6 Carol Duncan maintains that the mandate for museums to keep a distance from, and even deliberately oppose what was considered commercial and popular has not always been the case since the great sacrilization of art began in the latter half of the nineteenth century. The relationship between cultural capital and financial capital is generally thought to have been remarkably stable for nearly a century, from the time when philanthropists moved art out of the marketplace until the past decade when museums have been aggressively moving back toward the commercial sector with the merchandizing of the museum experience. Duncan insists that there are important precedents for the convergence of the museum experience and the consumer experience. She begins her history of their interconnectedness with the founding of the Victoria and Albert Museum in 1857, which was inspired by the success of the first world's fair, the Great Exhibition in the Crystal Palace in London in 1851. She points to the shared cultural functions of the world's fair, the department store, and the museum of decorative arts during this period: to promote the culture of consumerism and introduce notions of good taste to a broad middle class. As such, there was a clear-cut delineation in Britain

between the art *gallery* which descended from the princely or aristocratic collection of pictures, and the museum of decorative arts which
was closely associated with a manufacturing economy. According to
Duncan,

> The Americans who founded the nation's major art museums in New
> York, Boston, and Chicago in the decade of the 1870s were enthralled
> by the V&A's much vaunted power to improve and civilize the working
> classes, but they were also dazzled by the old master collections in the
> Louvre Museum and other impressive European art galleries. Their com-
> bined gallery of fine art/museum of applied arts became the template
> for almost all later American museums.

Given this combination of contradictory ideals, it is no surprise that
there have been precedents for the recent convergence between the
museum and marketplace. Duncan points to the attempts made by
museum professionals and department stores in the 1920s and 1930s
to develop what we would now call a synergistic relationship. She sees
John Cotton Dana, Director of the Newark Museum, as a paradigmatic
example of a willingness to establish a "museum of service" which
might work in conjunction with, rather than in outright disdain for,
the commercial sector. Dana and the department-store magnate Louis
Bamberger collaborated closely throughout the 1920s, a time when
Bamberger's department store sometimes functioned as an extension of
the Newark Museum. Duncan refers to a specific exhibition in 1929
of ceramic art at the museum when Bambergers featured a similar
display, complete with a museum-style catalogue with academic entries
about the works. During this period art museum personnel moved back
and forth freely, lecturing at other department stores, most visibly at a
three-day symposium held in the auditorium at Macy's (then the largest
department store in the world). According to Duncan, the place where
Dana's approach really took hold was the Design Department of the
Museum of Modern Art in New York under the guidance of Alfred
Barr, a devoted admirer of Dana.

Duncan's chapter provides a crucial historical framework for understanding the contemporary convergence of the museum store and
department store experiences. At the time of writing, the catalogues
from that same Museum of Modern Art, as well as the Art Institute of
Chicago and the Metropolitan Museum of Art in New York, all include

substantial sections devoted to Frank Lloyd Wright merchandise. The
Marshall Fields department store at my local mall has just added an
elaborate display of Wright bookends, lamps, cards, and magazine racks
and their Sunday advertising insert in the local newspaper features a
Wright pattern on its cover and a photograph of the man himself,
complete with a text which explains his significance in museum catalogue style (before it gives way to the standard images of waffle-irons,
coffeemakers, and pizza ovens). The very fact that Wright is the subject
of this merchandising is, in and of itself, a factor which complicates
the history of the relationship between the commercial and cultural,
since Wright argued, contra William Morris, for the beneficial potential of the machine in mass-producing aesthetic objects before World
War I (Wright, 1901) and became the first self-styled celebrity architect when the profession was still anonymous except for a coterie audience of patrons and critics. For all these institutions, department stores,
and museums (modern and otherwise) this is obviously the *wright stuff*,
for those consumers who want to furnish their homes with items
drawn from museum collections. The Marshall Fields advertising insert
says it best: "We're pleased to offer you the opportunity to bring the
timeless vision of America's greatest architect into your home." Yet
what does this desire to bring the museum home suggest about the
relationship between taste and contemporary consumerism?

Apart, Yet Somehow So Accessible: Consumerism as *Recreation*

Conceiving of high-pop phenomena as just one more manifestation of
a consumerism which seemingly knows no bounds, or more specifically, a consumerism which ignores the bounds which once distinguished the marketplace from genuine cultural experience, fails to
address the complexity of consumerism itself as a form of cultural
practice. Within the past decade a growing body of work, sometimes
referred to as "new consumer theory," has challenged many of the most
hidebound assumptions concerning the nature and function of consumerism, particularly in regard to how this activity compares to "real
culture."[2] According to Ann Bermingham the first thing to be rejected
is "modernism's master narrative of culture," which has

obscured the early history of consumption and its relationship to other social and cultural forms, substituting in its place a history of culture focused on artistic production, individualism, originality, genius, aestheticism and avant-gardism. This would help to explain why critics of postmodernism like Fredric Jameson, nostalgic for a more "authentic" culture, see consumer society as part of a superficial, schizophrenic "logic" of late capitalism. Indeed, it is only by operating outside the limits of modernism that we can see a consumer society that is nearly four hundred years old. (Bermingham, 1995: 3)

Bermingham makes the essential point that the sort of aestheticism we associate with conservative denunciations of the commercialization of mass culture – that culture should remain a place somehow "apart" from the marketplace – also served as the foundation for Marx's notion of aesthetic production. For Bermingham, it is most revealing that Marx's example of unalienated labor is John Milton, who he insists "produced *Paradise Lost* as a silkworm produces silk, as the activation of his own nature." She argues:

> Marx remains wedded to the idealist notion of artistic creation in which the space of artistic production is imagined apart from that of commerce and alienated labor. Thus he projected a utopian future that was a recapitulation of a prelapsarian past – a time before alienation – in the form of the Romantic artist. . . . Thus the *cordon sanitaire* drawn by Kant, Schiller, and Arnold is not cut by Marx. (Ibid, 9)

The status of the modernist narrative of culture, in which commodity fetishism is paired in yin-yang fashion with the fetishism of the Romantic artist, becomes especially complicated in the case of high-pop, since phenomena like the Miramax adaptation, the museum blockbuster show, the opera singer as pop star, all depend on the vestigial force of that narrative as a kind of mythology that is still subscribed to, even as it is rewritten into a new taste ideology in which the aesthetic experience is *apart* but thoroughly *accessible*. When Miramax advertises *An Ideal Husband* as the "perfect antidote to the summer blockbuster" the dichotomy between art and commerce is retained, but reconceived as Miramax cashes in on the force that narrative has enjoyed as received opinion, even as its aggressive promotion of the Wilde adaptation would seem only to disprove the veracity of that master narrative. As such, it is a neat reconciliation between availability and rarity as evaluative modalities. In her seminal work on the television program *Dallas*, Ien Ang (1985) identified two distinct taste ideologies which viewers used to evaluate the program: the "ideology of mass culture" (which allowed viewers to reject the program outright as a product of the commercial culture industry), and the "populist ideology" (which allowed viewers to justify their love of the program on the basis of "there's no accounting for taste"). Between these two diametrically opposed taste formations she found a third – the ironical viewing attitude – which "makes a reconciliation possible between the rules of the ideology of mass culture ("I must find *Dallas* bad") and the experiencing of pleasure ("I find *Dallas* amusing *because* it's so bad"). Here Ang identifies the basis for the guilt-free ironic delights which television watching provides for so many viewers, but this reconciliation is fundamentally a camp gesture, a latter-day Pop art taste formation in which the mass cultural experience must remain safely bracketed in quotation marks to be pleasurable.

The reconciliation between ease of access and rarity of expression serves as the foundation of the popular connoisseurship which comes after the Pop art moment; it insists on the *apartness* of genuine aesthetic expression, but at the same time promises to deliver that experience to a mass audience, an evaluative maneuver made possible by redefining the delivery system *vis-à-vis* content. Where the standard form of the ideology of mass culture made mass distribution an evil unto itself, the mode of transmission precluding the possibility of genuine art as the content of that widely disseminated message, the taste ideology that authorizes the pleasures of high-pop distinguishes between the two, uncoupling the Modernist pairing of rarefied content and exclusivist delivery system, by insisting that knowledge, rather than money, is the only thing required in order to appreciate the *apartness* of the object, even as it becomes ever more widely available.

The work of Arjun Appadurai (1986) is especially useful in describing the contours of this transformation. Appadurai argues that value is determined within consumer societies by *regimes of value* that establish the customary *paths* by means of which a given commodity circulates. Within a given path an entire network of institutional frameworks and protocols maintains the value cohesiveness of that particular regime. The value of commodities can change fundamentally through what Appadurai calls *diversions*, in which objects begin to circulate in different orbits. An example of this sort of diversion, according to Appadurai, is the way that objects which function as tools within one path (Masai spears, Dinka baskets, etc.) become *objets d'art* through a very specific form of aesthetic diversion. His description of the category of luxury goods depends on a special register of consumption rather than a special class of thing.

> The signs of this register are (1) restriction, either by price or by law, to elites; (2) complexity of acquisition, which may or may not be a function of real "scarcity"; (3) semiotic virtuosity, that is, the capacity to signal complex social messages; (4) specialized knowledge as a prerequisite for their appropriate consumption, that is, register by fashion and (5) a high degree of linkage of their consumption to body, person, and personality. (Ibid: 38)

This list of interdependent signs provides a neat framework for delineating the massification of elite cultural pleasures, since high-pop phenomena represent an emergent regime of value, one which depends on a very precise diversion of paths. This regime retains the latter three characteristics – semiotic virtuosity, specialized knowledge for appropriate consumption, high degree of linkage to personality – but makes restriction a matter of knowledge more than price, and makes a virtue of the ease, rather than the complexity, of acquisition (see chapter 1 of this volume for John Storey's analysis of the proliferation of "Opera Homework" books where one can gain that knowledge).

But, as Appadurai insists, "diversions are meaningful only in relation to the paths from which they stray" (Appadurai, 1986: 28). It is precisely because good design, *haute cuisine*, designer fashion, grand opera, carry with them the vestiges of a previous path, the path of elite, rarefied pleasure, that they can now be desirable, as well as accessible. The skillful activation of that previous path is one of the common strategies employed by high-pop texts, as effective in regard to literary adaptations and cooking programs as it is in museum shows and interior design. Appealing to a grand overarching hierarchy of taste has become unnecessary; the status of elite taste can be signified simply through the evocation of an earlier moment in that text's history, thereby allowing for the return of prestige without the taint of outright snobbery.

The binary opposition between consumerism and genuine cultural experience which Bermingham considers largely mythological has been complicated even more profoundly by the work of Colin Camp-bell, who insists that modern consumerism actually begins with the Romantic theory of artistic creation. He acknowledges that it was the Romantics who first articulated a version of the mass culture critique that became the basis for the Modernist master narrative of culture. Yet he is struck by the fact that this theory of artistic creation "places almost as much emphasis upon the 'recreative' abilities of the reader as upon the original creative faculties of the poet. . . . The reader is also, in that sense, assumed to be a creative artist, capable of conjuring up images which have the power to 'move' him" (Campbell, 1987: 189). Through this unprecedented ethical authorization of the pursuit of per-sonal pleasure for both artists and their readers, "Romanticism provided that philosophy of 'recreation' necessary for a dynamic consumerism: a philosophy that legitimates the search for pleasure as good in itself" (ibid: 201). Campbell complicates the Modernist narrative of culture, not by exploding the category of Romantic artist, but by expanding it, recognizing that both artist and audience enjoy the privileges that come with the cultivation of a *personal* sensibility.

In his analysis of "blockbuster adaptations," Tim Corrigan (chapter 7) sees the reassertion of the personal as one of the distinguishing fea-tures of recent film production, arguing that "the problem for cultural studies today may be that the cult of the author and embedded agency have replaced the text with more power than ever, so that what con-temporary film culture offers is the experience of authorship as a par-ticipatory engagement or performance." The cultivation of the personal operates at the level of author, performer, and the viewer simultane-ously, exemplifying what Campbell saw as the blurring of the creative and the *recreative*. The names of classical authors are foregrounded through a variety of strategies, nowhere more visibly than in making the name part of the title: *William Shakespeare's Romeo and Juliet, Emily Brönte's Wuthering Heights, Bram Stoker's Dracula, Shakespeare in Love*. For Corrigan, Kenneth Branagh embodies the new aesthetic of adaptation that alters the relationship between Shakespeare, adapter, and viewer in terms of an expansive all-encompassing personalization: "With Branagh, Miramax has found an *auteur* like Tarantino who, instead of reauthorizing pulp fiction and blaxploitation films, draws viewers back to Shakespeare's plays by remaking them through a performative per-sonality that marks and absorbs the history of Shakespeare on film as a singular performance." The viewer is a co-participant in this circuit of performativity. Corrigan makes the crucial point that due to the vast library of adaptations now available on video and DVD,

> fidelity has become a fully archaic aesthetic measure, except as one can be faithful to one's own self, desires, tastes, imagination, and inclinations . . . what the activity of technological browsing describes is how viewers have acceded to positions somewhere between a critic and a performer who might seek to spot the original text in the film, to compare film versions, or engage in a variety of other "performative" interactions. Films no longer realize or rewrite texts, viewers select and measure versions of adaptations as participatory agents.

Corrigan's emphasis on *selection* as a vital part of the performance of one's taste reveals a great deal about the dynamics of the blockbuster adaptation, but I think it also provides a particularly apt description of the ways in which taste is expressed in the arena of material culture. The need to make one's home one's own, to realize the interdependency of decorating a home and fashioning a soul, depends on a remarkably similar articulation of taste as selection, the same conflation of the creative and the recreative in the pursuit of a personal *mise-en-scène* conceived out of a vast array of available design options. The appeal to potential subscribers of a new shelter magazine entitled *dwell* sums this up quite neatly. The name of the magazine itself ("dwell" rather than "dwelling") suggests the performative nature of taste – a home is not a site but an active performance of living tastefully. It insists that "Compared to most people, you have a very different idea of home: You want your home to work for you, not some design diva. Rules and fads are irrelevant. You're creative, independent and flexible and you want a place that helps you live that way" (*dwell*, 2000). The creativity referred to here represents the fusion of Romantic sensibility and consumer desire, a *recreative* auteurism in which individual dwellers' relationships to their homes is like Branagh before Shakespeare, a process of adaptation in which the author's signature is an end in itself, but also the instigation for the formation of another personal signature, the basis for demonstrating the *apartness* of the tasteful consumer.

This apartness depends on the development of what would have been seen previously to be oxymoronic: popular connoisseurship. In an article entitled "The Educated Eye" in the Home Design section of

the *New York Times Magazine*, David Rimanelli presents a useful if
incomplete history of connoisseurship. He identifies three main stages
in its evolution: the eighteenth century, when dilettante aristocrats like
Sir William Hamilton cultivated their knowledge of antiquities; an early
modern period when Bernard Berenson turned a gentleman's hobby
into a profession as an adviser to the industrial rich; and the modern
period when anti-elitism, embodied by Andy Warhol, became a form
of anti-connoisseurship resisted now only by a few who, like Harold
Bloom, choose to "take the high road." In my contribution to this collection (chapter 8) I pursue another form of connoisseurship, one built
on the reassertion of taste distinctions but without a commonly agreed
upon hierarchy of taste, when Berenson has been replaced by Conran
and Stewart and their clients have become a heterogeneous mass
audience rather than the industrial rich, when the "high road" has
become a multimedia, superhighway of delivery systems that runs right
through that domestic space we like to call home. One of the chief
concerns of this essay, then, is what happens to taste categories when
good design becomes accessible to a mass audience convinced that interior design should be as much an expression of self-image as personal
wardrobe.

Both my essay and Celia Lury's (chapter 9) address what she calls
the *disorganization of taste* that has occurred within the past decade.
Using George Simmel's distinction between subjective and objective
culture as her point of departure, she argues that as a result of the
increase in the sheer number of objects and the degree of specialization of the objects themselves, "there has been a shift in the manner
in which objects present themselves." One of the highest priorities in
contemporary design is the almost unlimited potential transmutability
of form. According to Lury,

> the status of many objects is no longer understood in terms of the
> quality of the body of a product, but rather as a system of relations, a
> set of performances . . . a complex, somehow informational logic comes
> to structure the designed object such that its properties are understood
> by both producers and consumers in terms of an autonomous ability to
> communicate.

Within this world of hyperstylization Lury finds the traditional vocabulary of taste insufficient, preferring a term like *virtuosity* that takes into

account "the ability to make use of the *degree of play* afforded by the ensemble of objects."

If one of the defining principles of cultural studies has been, since its inception, the need to distinguish between *Culture* defined as rarefied forms of artistic expression, and culture as a whole way of life, the essays in this collection focus on a historical moment when *Culture* has become, metaphorically and quite literally, part of the fabric of day-to-day life. The goal of this collection, then, is not just to produce a series of detailed case studies that will yield a better understanding of upscale popular culture. By focusing on the changing relationship between elite and popular entertainment, in regard to the volume of their production, the sophistication of their delivery systems, the kind of education necessary to appreciate them, and the sort of consumer dynamics which factor into their acquisition, the ultimate goal of this book inevitably becomes a redefiniton of just what the category of popular culture might still mean at the turn of the twenty-first century.

Notes

1   For a more detailed overview of this period see Michael Kammen, *American Cultures, American Tastes* (New York: Knopf, 1999).
2   For incisive discussions of this work see Celia Lury, *Consumer Culture* (Cambridge: Polity Press, 1996) and John Storey, *Cultural Consumption and Everyday Life* (London: Arnold, 1999).

References

Alloway, Lawrence (1959). "The Long Front line of Culture." In *Cambridge Opinion*, Cambridge: Cambridge University Press.

Ang, Ien (1985). *Watching Dallas.* London: Methuen.

Appadurai, Arjun (1986). "Introduction: Commodities and the Politics of Value." In *The Social Life of Things*, Cambridge: Cambridge University Press.

Bennett, Tony (1996). "Out in the Open: Reflections on the History and Practice of Cultural Studies," *Cultural Studies*, 10 (1).

Bennettt, Tony, Emmison, Michael, and Frow, John (1999). *Accounting for Tastes: Australian Everyday Cultures.* Cambridge: Cambridge University Press.

Bermingham, Ann (1995). "Introduction." In Ann Bermingham and John Brewer, eds., *The Consumption of Culture 1600–1800: Image, Object, Text*, New York: Routledge.

Bourdieu, Pierre and Darbel, Alain (1969) [1990]. *The Love of Art: European Art Museums and Their Publics*, trans. Caroline Beattie and Nick Meeriman. Stanford, CA: Stanford University Press.

Browning, Dominique (2000). "Anything But the Eighties!" *House and Garden*, May.

Campbell, Colin (1987). *The Romantic Ethic and the Spirit of Modern Consumerism*. Oxford: Blackwell Publishers.

Chapman, Susan (2000). "Making the Scene," *Bon Appétit*, September.

Collins, Jim (1989). *Uncommon Cultures: Popular Culture and Postmodernism*. New York: Routledge.

Collins, Jim (1993). *Architectures of Excess: Cultural Life in the Information Age*. New York: Routledge.

Dimaggio, Paul (1991). "Cultural Entrepreneurship in Nineteenth Century Boston: The Creation of an Organizational Base for High Culture in America." In Chandra Mukerji and Michael Schudson, eds., *Rethinking Popular Culture*, Berkeley: University of California Press.

Dimaggio, Paul (1992). "Cultural Boundaries and Structural Change: The Extension of the High Culture Model to Theater, Opera, and the Dance, 1900–1940." In Michele Lamount and Marcel Fournier, eds., *Cultivating Differences: Symbolic Boundaries and the Making of Inequality*, Chicago: University of Chicago Press.

Frow, John (1995). *Cultural Studies and Cultural Value*. Oxford: Clarendon Press.

Hall, John (1992). "The Capital(s) of Cultures: A Non-holistic Approach to Value Status Situations, Class, Gender, and Ethnicity." In Michele Lamount and Marcel Fournier, eds., *Cultivating Differences: Symbolic Boundaries and the Making of Inequality*, Chicago: University of Chicago Press.

Hamilton, William (1998). "Americans are Being Branded Where They Sit," *New York Times*, October 10.

Hamilton, William (2000). "Young Designers Learn They Can't Live By Buzz Alone," *New York Times*, September 21.

Hebdige, Dick (1989). "In Poor Taste." In Paul Taylor, ed., *Post-Pop Art*, Cambridge, MA: MIT Press.

Hornby, Nick (1995). *High Fidelity.* New York: Riverhead Books.

Horowitz, Joseph (2000). "A Home with a Sense of Place," *New York Times*, October 8.

Kimmelman, Michael (1999). "Sargent's Dazzling Sensuality," *New York Times*, February 19.

La Ferla, Ruth (2000). "Teenage Shoppers (Purses By Brinks)," *New York Times*, September 11.

Levine, Lawrence (1988). *Highbrow/Lowbrow: The Emergence of Cultural Hierarchy in America*. Cambridge, MA: Harvard University Press.

Macdonald, Dwight (1960). "Masscult and Midcult," *Partisan Review*, spring, 203–33.

Radway, Janet (1997). *A Feeling for Books.* Chapel Hill: University of North Carolina Press.

Rimanelli, David (1997). "Accounting for Taste," *New York Times Magazine*, Home Design, October 5.

Rubin, Joan Shelby (1992). *The Making of Middlebrow Culture*. Chapel Hill: University of North Carolina Press.

Schuster, Michael (1991). *The Audience for American Art Museums*. National Endowment for the Arts, Research Report Division 23. Washington, DC: Seven Locks Press.

Vlades, Pilar (2000). "Welcome to the Dollhouse," *New York Times Magazine*, Home Design, Part II, fall, October 8.

Wolf, Janet (1989). "The Ideology of Autonomous Art." In Richard Leppert and Susan McClary, eds., *Music and Society: The Politics of Composition, Performance and Reception*, Cambridge: Cambridge University Press.

Wright, Frank Lloyd (1901). "Art in the Age of the Machine." In Bruce Brooks Pfeiffer, ed., *Frank Lloyd Wright: Collected Writings*, New York: Rizzoli.

1

"Expecting Rain": Opera as Popular Culture?
John Storey

For many people opera represents (whether this is understood positively or negatively) the very embodiment of "high culture." Yet lately there have been signs that its status is changing, as opera becomes more and more a feature of everyday cultural life.[1] What I want to explore in this chapter is whether these changes have now made it possible to describe opera as popular culture.

Inventing Opera as "High Culture"

In order to fully understand what has been happening to opera in recent years, I think it is first necessary to examine something of the history of opera. Traditionally, opera is said to have been invented in the late sixteenth century by a group of Florentine intellectuals known as the *Camerata*.[2] However, according to musicologist Susan McClary,

> Despite the humanistic red herrings proffered by Peri, Caccini [members of the Camerata], and others to the effect that they were reviving Greek performance practices, these gentlemen knew very well that they were basing their new reciting style on the improvisatory practices of contemporary popular music. Thus the eagerness with which the humanist myth was constructed and elaborated sought both to conceal the vulgar origins of its techniques and to flatter the erudition of its cultivated patrons. (McClary, 1985: 154–5)

Although there may be some dispute over the intellectual origins of opera, there is general agreement about its commercial beginnings.

Significantly, the opera house was the "first musical institution to open its doors to the general public" (Zelochow, 1993: 261). The first opera house opened in Venice in 1637: it presented "commercial opera run for profit . . . offering the new, up-to-date entertainment to anyone who could afford a ticket" (Raynor, 1972: 169). By the end of the century Venice had sixteen opera houses open to the general public. Interestingly, as Henry Raynor observes, "The Venetian audience consisted of all social classes" (ibid: 171). Bernard Zelochow argues that this remained the case throughout the next two centuries.

> By the late eighteenth century and in the nineteenth century the opera played a preeminent role in the cultural life of Europe. The opera was enjoyed and understood by a broad cross-section of urban Europeans and Americans. The opera house became the meeting place of all social classes in society. . . . The absence of the concept of a classical repertoire is an index of the popularity and vigor of opera as a mode of communication and entertainment. (Zelochow, 1993: 262)[3]

By the nineteenth century, then, opera was established as a widely available form of popular entertainment consumed by people of all social classes. As Lawrence W. Levine explains, referring specifically to the US (but also the case in most of Europe), opera was an integral part of a shared public culture, "performed in a variety of settings, [it] enjoyed great popularity, and [was] shared by a broad segment of the population" (Levine, 1988: 85).[4] For example, on returning to the United States in the late 1860s from England, where he had been American Consul, George Makepeace Towle noted how "Lucretia Borgia and Faust, The Barber of Seville and Don Giovanni are everywhere popular; you may hear their airs in the drawing room and concert halls, as well as whistled by the street boys and ground out on the hand organs" (quoted in Levine, 1988: 99–100).

To turn opera into "high culture" it had to be withdrawn from the everyday world of popular entertainment, especially from the heterogeneous dictates of the market and the commercial reach of cultural entrepreneurs. Bruce A. McConachie argues that between 1825 and 1850 elite social groups in New York developed three overlapping social strategies which gradually separated opera from the everyday world of popular entertainment. The first was to separate it from theater by establishing buildings specifically for the performance of opera.

Second, they "also worked to sharpen and objectify a code of behavior, including a dress code, deemed proper when attending the opera.
Finally, upper-class New Yorkers increasingly insisted that only foreign-
language opera could meet their standards of excellence – standards
upheld by behavior and criticism employing foreign words and
specialized language impenetrable to all but the cognoscenti"
(McConachie, 1988: 182). As he explains,

> In 1825 theater audiences from all classes enjoyed opera as a part of the
> social conventions of traditional playgoing behavior. By the Civil War
> [1861–5] the elite had excluded all but themselves and spectators from
> other classes willing to behave in ways deemed "proper" according to
> upper-class norms. (Ibid)[5]

Levine, however, maintains that it is only at the end of the nineteenth
century that opera can be said to have been effectively isolated from
other forms of entertainment. It is only then, he argues, that there
begins to be a growing social acceptance of the "insistence that opera
was a 'higher' form of art demanding a cultivated audience" (Levine,
1988: 102). For example, in 1900 the Metropolitan Opera, New York,
had completed its season with a production of four acts from four different operas. This had been a common practice throughout most of
the nineteenth century. But times were changing and music critic
W. J. Henderson, writing in the *New York Times*, was quick to remind
his readers of the new dispensation: "There were people who had never
heard 'Carmen' before. There were people who had never heard of 'Il
Flauto Magico.' There were people who had never heard 'Lucia.' . . .
There were people who did not know any one of the three ladies in
'The Magic Flute.' This was an audience there only to hear 'the famous
singers.' What they got was 'a hotch-potch . . . of extracts . . . a program
of broken candy.' " In producing such a show, the Metropolitan Opera
had, according to Henderson, removed "all semblance of art in the
opera house" (quoted in Levine, 1988: 103). Henderson's words no
longer signaled a threatened elitism, as they might have done fifty years
earlier. On the contrary, Henderson was articulating what would
become the commonplace attitudes of the culture of twentieth-century
opera. Opera was no longer a form of living entertainment; it was
increasingly a source of "Culture" with a capital C – a resource of both
aesthetic enlightenment and social validation.[6] As Levine explains:

What was invented in the late nineteenth century were the rituals accompanying the appreciation [of high culture]; what was invented was the illusion that the aesthetic products of high culture were originally created to be appreciated in precisely the manner late nineteenth-century Americans were taught to observe: with reverent, informed, disciplined seriousness. (Ibid: 229)

The success of the invention can be seen in Oscar Hammerstein's confident claim (made in 1910) that

grand opera [is] . . . the most elevating influence upon modern society, after religion. From the earliest days it has ever been the most elegant of all forms of entertainment . . . it employs and unifies all the arts. . . . I sincerely believe that nothing will make better citizenship than familiarity with grand opera. It lifts one so out of the sordid affairs of life and makes material things seem so petty, so inconsequential, that it places one for the time being, at least, in a higher and better world. . . . Grand opera . . . is the awakening of the soul to the sublime and the divine. (Quoted in DiMaggio, 1992: 35)

Like Levine, Paul DiMaggio argues that "The distinction between high and popular culture, in its American version, emerged in the period between 1850 and 1900 out of the efforts of urban elites to build organizational forms that, first, isolated high culture and, second, differentiated it from popular culture" (DiMaggio, 1998: 454). With particular reference to Boston, DiMaggio argues that

To create an institutional high culture, Boston's upper class had to accomplish three concurrent, but analytically distinct, projects: entrepreneurship, classification and framing. By entrepreneurship, I mean the creation of an organizational form that members of the elite could control and govern. By classification, I refer to the erection of strong and clearly defined boundaries between art and entertainment, the definition of a high art that elites and segments of the middle class could appropriate as their own cultural property; and the acknowledgment of that classification's legitimacy by other classes and the state. Finally, I use the term framing to refer to the development of a new etiquette of appropriation, a new relationship between the audience and the work of art. (Ibid: 457)

DiMaggio differs from Levine and McConachie in his insistence that although there is clearly a "shift in opera's social constituency during the nineteenth century . . . issues of opera's definition, sponsorship, merit, and legitimacy were [not] resolved by the turn of the century" (DiMaggio, 1992: 49). He argues that it is only in the 1930s, when opera adopts "the non-profit educational form" ("trustee-governed non-profit organizations"), that opera's "legitimacy" as high culture is finally secured (ibid: 40, 37). He cites the head of classical repertoire at RCA Victor, who wrote in 1936: "While in former years [opera] generally attracted large audiences primarily as a form of entertainment, today opera is commanding the attention of both layman and serious musician as an important and significant art form" (ibid: 37).[7]

McConachie, Levine, and DiMaggio do not claim that before the establishment of opera as high culture there had not existed a visible connection between cultural taste and social class. What had changed – and what I mean by the invention of opera as high culture – was the institutionalization of this connection. Removing opera from the heterogeneous demands of the market ensured that differences in taste could be marked by, and be indicative of, clear social boundaries. As DiMaggio makes clear:

> as long as cultural boundaries were indistinct, "fashionable taste," far from embodying cultural authority, was suspect as snobbish, trivial, and un-democratic. Only when elite taste was harnessed to a clearly articulated ideology embodied in the exhibitions and performances of organiza-tions that selected and presented art in a manner distinct from that of commercial entrepreneurs . . . did an understanding of culture as hier-archical become both legitimate and widespread. (Ibid: 22)

Opera as "high culture" is therefore not a universal given, unfolding from its moment of intellectual birth; rather, it is an historically spe-cific category institutionalized (depending on which cultural historian you find most convincing) by the 1860s, 1900s, or 1930s. Although these accounts may differ in terms of periodization, what each demon-strates is how elite social groups in the major American cities began the process of constructing a separate social space in which opera could be self-evidently high culture. Similarly, as Janet Wolff argues,

> A parallel process of differentiation had also been occurring in England, where the pre-industrial cultural pursuits, enjoyed on a cross-class basis,

were gradually replaced by a class-specific culture, the high arts of music, theatre and literature being the province of the upper-middle and middle classes, and the popular cultural forms of music hall, organized sport and popular literature providing the entertainment of the lower classes. (Wolff, 1989: 5–6)

The key thing to understand historically about opera, then, is that it did not become unpopular, rather it was *made* unpopular. That is, it was actively appropriated from its popular audience by elite social groups determined to situate it as the crowning glory of their culture, i.e., so-called "high culture." In short, opera was transformed from *entertainment* enjoyed by the many into *Culture* to be appreciated by the few. As Levine points out, well-meaning arguments (made in the 1980s) that opera might "finally be extended to the masses *for the first time*, betrays a lack of historical memory or understanding of the contours of culture in nineteenth-century America [and most of Europe]" (Levine, 1988: 241).

"Opera Homework"

The active removal of opera from the world of popular entertainment was not just an organizational accomplishment, it also involved the introduction of a particular way of seeing opera – what Pierre Bourdieu calls the "aesthetic gaze" (Bourdieu, 1984, 1993). Moreover, to redefine opera as art "is tantamount to saying that a certain education is necessary to understand it at all: which is a convenient way of policing culture, and making sure it is kept as the property of an elite" (Tambling, 1987: 108). Although opera once again attracts a popular audience, it now confronts this audience as *art that can be entertaining*. In order to unlock the entertainment in the art, the new popular audience must do its "opera homework." It should, therefore, come as no surprise that the reemergence of opera as popular entertainment has been accompanied (and no doubt promoted) by the many introductory textbooks[8] which have been published in the 1990s offering to "educate" the reader in what is required in order to be able to appreciate opera (even as entertainment). The fact these books have to exist at all speaks volumes about the success of the project to invent opera as high culture.

In order to reintroduce opera into the everyday world of popular entertainment, all the introductory textbooks I have read deploy three discursive strategies: (1) a welcoming irony; (2) an insistence that opera is a special kind of entertainment called art; and (3) a tactical anti-elitism.

Irony

The cover blurb of *Opera: A Crash Course* asks: "Is the word opera always preceded by the word soap to you? Have you an uneasy suspicion that *La Donna e Mobile* does not really mean "my girl's got a cellphone"? . . . Opera: A Crash Course is for you". Similarly, the cover blurb of *Opera for Dummies* asks: "Do you have trouble telling the difference between a tenor and soprano or a mezzo and mozzarella?" Under a section called "Who You Are" the book observes: "For starters, you're an intelligent person. We can sense it, and we're never wrong about these things. After all, you picked up this book, didn't you?" (Pogue and Speck, 1997: 1).

Art

Opera: A Crash Course alerts readers to the difficulties ahead: "One word of warning. Don't expect opera simply – or always – to entertain you. Opera, like all art, should provide a way into the human spirit. If a work seems difficult and long, try your damnedest not to walk out. Tell yourself that someone out there – the composer – has agonized long and hard about how to say something. Try to enter this world, a world that is also an important corner of yours" (Pettitt, 1998: 9). *Teach Yourself Opera* suggests that "An opera is rather like a beautiful painting. Each time you return, you should find something new to enjoy" (Sutherland, 1997: xii). *Getting Opera: A Guide for the Cultured but Confused* declares: "It takes work to appreciate an opera – work that many aren't willing to put in given the fact that watching TV or going to a movie is so easy. Well, this book is intended to give you all the workout you need to start getting opera. . . . You don't need a degree in musicology to appreciate opera. All you need is to do the basic groundwork" (Dobkin, 2000: 8–9).

Anti-elitism

Opera: The Rough Guide is aware that "opera remains off-putting for too many people. Partly this is due to the social exclusivity cultivated by many opera houses" (Boyden, 1999: ix). *Opera: A Crash Course* promises "to help you penetrate the miasma of social snobbery that envelops opera everywhere except Italy." It also reassures the reader: "And you will find out how to comport yourself in an opera house." According to the cover blurb, "*Teach Yourself Opera* opens the door allowing *everyone* to step through and follow the fascinating path leading from 1600 to the present day" (my italics). Inside, the reader is told: "This is not intended to be an exhaustive, or an exhausting study, but a tasty appetizer that leads you *confidently* into the world of opera" (Sutherland, 1997: ix; my italics). The cover blurb of *Opera for Dummies* promises: "Attend a live opera in style with tips for sitting in the right place, wearing the right clothes, and more!" The authors acknowledge that opera can be "intimidating" and can make people feel "insecure" (Pogue and Speck, 1997: 7). To illustrate the point, they offer the following scenario: "You're at the opera house. You open the program book, or you're listening to opera snobs talk – foreign words are flying like bullets. Quick, what do they mean?" *Opera for Dummies* will help secure the reader against such intimidation. But more than this, the book challenges the reader to refuse to be excluded: "In fact, plenty of opera snobs are perfectly *happy* that you don't understand. They'd love opera to be an exclusive club, an elite corps, a sacred order. They're *glad* that opera strikes many as the world's most obscure art form" (ibid: 1). They know that opera has not always been the exclusive preserve of high culture. But they insist that it is not opera which changed but how people used opera socially: "Opera is just as entertaining as it ever was. But these days, it has become much less *familiar*. That's all. After you become familiar with this art form, you'll be amazed at how entertaining it becomes" (ibid: 9). The cover blurb of *Getting Opera: A Guide for the Cultured but Confused* also speaks of potential consumers of opera being "a little intimidated." To overcome this the book promises that it "brings the elusive concepts down to earth, making it accessible to [enable] . . . the opera-shy reader . . . to embark on a thoroughly delightful and *instructive* operatic journey" (my italics). Inside the author elaborates:

My point is, essentially, screw the whole struggle between high and low. And certainly don't be afraid of opera because some force has foolishly built it up as the ultimate in refinement. Opera has historically been a popular art form that aimed to entertain ordinary people. Don't let that bother you, and don't let some uptight classical geek tell you any different. (Dobkin, 2000: 17)

Some of the books also offer advice on recorded opera.[9] In the *Collins Opera & Operetta* each entry includes a recommended recording. *Opera: The Rough Guide* is aware that looking through a CD catalogue of recorded opera can be very "perplexing." It therefore presents itself as "the essential guide through this mass of music," offering "definitive surveys of the recordings" (Boyden, 1999: ix). Similarly, *Teach Yourself Opera* also provides recommended recordings. The cover blurb of *Opera for Dummies* promises to help you "build a great collection of opera recordings." The cover blurb on *Getting Opera: A Guide for the Cultured but Confused* also promises information on "where to begin your CD collection."

There are also currently available a number of CD collections explicitly aimed at the newcomer to opera.[10] Their titles, and how they are advertised, on television and on billboards, are indistinguishable from the marketing techniques used to sell pop music. Similarly, opera singers are increasingly marketed in much the same way as pop stars. Luciano Pavarotti is only the most obvious example.[11]

Resistance to Opera as Popular Culture

The reemergence of opera as popular entertainment has certainly not gone unresisted. There are those, like tenor Jon Vickers, who claim that opera is "being invaded by those techniques that are corrupting our society – big PR, the personality cult, techniques which create hysteria but do not elevate man. They degrade our art. . . . We cannot compromise. . . . We mustn't smear the line between art and entertainment. . . . You cannot bring art to the masses. . . . You never will" (quoted in Levine, 1988: 255).

Other "resisters" focus on particular examples. For instance, the widespread introduction of "surtitles" (equivalent to subtitles) into opera houses in the late 1980s and early 1990s to make opera more accessible, was quickly dismissed by those for whom access is always a problem because it usually means access for "other" people. Although the main line of attack was aesthetic (surtitles are "theatrical condoms"; "a catastrophic gooseberry in the vital act of theatrical intercourse"), it was mostly argued that they were being introduced for mainly three reasons: (1) to accommodate tourists ("celluloid messages for tourists"); (2) to justify higher government subsidies (part of the aim of which is to broaden the class base of the audience); and (3) to attract corporate sponsorship (as such they are a device "to keep uncommitted flippant audiences quiet" – "the growing army of tax-relieved super-rich") (see Evans, 1999: 53, 66, 67).[12]

In 1990 Pavarotti's recording of "Nessun Dorma" (from Puccini's *Turandot*) became a number one hit in the British music charts.[13] Such commercial success on any "quantitative" analysis would make the composer, the performer, and the song, popular culture.[14] In fact, one student I know actually complained about the way in which the aria had supposedly been devalued by its commercial success. He claimed that he now found it embarrassing to play it for fear that someone should think his musical taste was determined by the fact that the aria had been used as "The Official BBC Grandstand World Cup Theme."

Something similar, telling much the same story, happened four years later at Glyndebourne.[15] According to Kate Saunders, writing in the *Sunday Times*,

> Last Sunday [July 10, 1994], when Deborah Warner took her bow as director at Glyndebourne on the first night of her provocative new production of Mozart's *Don Giovanni*, certain sections of the audience erupted in boos and catcalls. . . . This is not the kind of behaviour one expects at Glyndebourne, the rarefied musical hothouse set in a manicured picnic-park of Sussex downland. . . . Sunday's incident was only the latest manifestation of a feisty new phenomenon, the British opera-lover with attitude. . . . The common thread that unites these incidents is a fear of innovation . . . [expressed by] an element of toffee-nosed, conservative stick-in-the-muds who are terrified that innovation will somehow tarnish the glittery snob value of the Glyndebourne experience. (Saunders, 1994: 4)

It appears that fear of innovation is only the surface expression of a much deeper, more troubling fear. As Saunders explains,

> The explosion of popular interest in opera in the 1980s worried people
> who were attracted by its elitist aura. These are the types who threw
> away their CDs of *Turandot* and complain when they heard the plumber
> whistling "Nessun Dorma." I cannot help suspecting that the booers at
> Glyndebourne were also objecting to the cheap standby seats now avail-
> able in the gleaming new theatre, though the opera's management vig-
> orously denied this. . . . [It is the people in] the most expensive seats
> that cause the trouble. They can moan about daring directors and
> designers, but their real grievance, I suspect, is the increasing democra-
> tization of an art form reserved for the rich. (Ibid: 4, 6)

That much deeper, more troubling fear that cannot quite speak its
name, had found cause for concern three years earlier in London's
Hyde Park. On July 30, 1991, Pavarotti gave a free concert in the park.
Some 250,000 people were expected, but due to heavy rain the
number who actually attended was around 100,000. The obvious
popularity of the event would appear to threaten the class exclusivity
of opera as high culture. It is therefore interesting to note the way in
which the event was reported in the media. All the British tabloids
carried news of the event on their front pages. The *Daily Mirror*, for
instance, had five pages devoted to the concert. What the tabloid coverage reveals is a clear attempt to define the event for popular culture.
The *Sun* quoted a woman who said, "I can't afford to go to posh opera
houses with toffs and fork out £100 a seat." The *Daily Mirror* ran an
editorial in which it claimed that Pavarotti's performance "wasn't for
the rich [it was] for the thousands . . . who could never normally afford
a night with an operatic star." When the event was reported on television news programs the following lunchtime, the tabloid coverage
was included as part of the general meaning of the event. Both the
BBC's "One O'clock News" and ITV's "12.30 News" referred to
the way in which the tabloids had covered the concert, and moreover,
the *extent* to which they had covered it. They also covered the "resistance" to the event – the attempt to introduce the "traditional"[16] cultural certainties: "some critics said that a park is no place for opera"
("One O'clock News"); "some opera enthusiasts might think it all a
bit vulgar" ("12.30 News"). Although such comments invoked the
specter of high-culture exclusivity, they seemed strangely at a loss to
offer any real purchase on the event. The apparently obvious cultural
division between elite and popular culture no longer seemed so
obvious. It suddenly seemed that the cultural had been replaced by the

economic, revealing a division between "the rich" and "the thousands." It was the event's very popularity which forced the television news to confront, and ultimately to find wanting, old cultural certainties.

An editorial in the UK magazine *Opera* (October 1991) wondered out loud: "Is Pavarotti the greatest known ambassador for opera, bringing untold thousands to its heady delights, or is he just a slightly unconventional but decidedly cuddly pop star?" This uncertainty was not shared by a reader's letter published in the same issue of the magazine:

> I had the misfortune to attend Pavarotti's concert in Hyde Park. . . . I moved to various spots searching for a place from which he could be heard to best advantage. In every place the majority reaction of the audience was the same – they talked, joked and laughed and occasionally jumped up and down to see if they could see Pavarotti on the stage, pausing only to produce thunderous applause at the end of each aria. It became clear from all this that a Pavarotti event has very little to do with opera as such, but everything to do with Pavarotti as a phenomenon. Through continuous hype, he has now become so famous that it is imperative to see him when he appears, much as one visits Madame Tussaud's on coming to London, or goes to see the three handed man at the fairground. . . . The argument that Pavarotti is a man of the people bringing opera to the masses is a load of tosh, since the masses at Hyde Park showed little interest in listening. At the end he was vociferously applauded. Clearly the audience loved him; whether they like opera is something else again. (Quoted in Evans, 1999: 355)

Situating Pavarotti in the company of waxwork figures and unusual fairground exhibits is to threaten to undo what was done so successfully in the late nineteenth century and the early part of the twentieth century – the institutionalization of opera as high culture. The very thought that an audience might have talked, joked, and laughed and occasionally jumped up and down at the performance of one of the great tenors of all time would be enough to make the elite of Boston and elsewhere turn despairingly in their graves.

Learning From History

Sociologist David Evans makes an interesting distinction "between opera (commodified cultural artefact in performance) and 'opera' (commodified entertainment fragments outside the opera house)" (ibid: 236). In this way, Evans seeks to indicate a difference between opera in the opera house and opera as experienced in television commercials, film soundtracks, sporting events, CD compilations, celebrity concerts by opera "superstars," opera holidays, etc.[17] Although I think this is an interesting distinction, it seems to me to carry with it a certain essentialism – an uncritical residual distinction between art and entertainment. I am not convinced that it is really possible to sustain such a distinction.[18] Perhaps a more productive way to understand what is happening to opera is not to see it in terms of commodities but in terms of social practices of consumption.[19] In other words, it is how and by whom opera is consumed which determines whether it is art or entertainment. This is because the difference between what counts as elite and popular culture is never simply a question of the material qualities of particular commodities. As we have already noted, what counts as popular culture in one historical period can become elite culture in another (and vice versa). What really matters are "the forces and relations which sustain the distinction, the difference . . . the relations of power which are constantly punctuating and dividing the domain of culture into . . . dominant and subordinate formations" (Hall, 1998: 448–9).[20]

Opera has become once again what it was for most of the nineteenth century – a cultural practice that is understood as both art and entertainment – an integral part of a shared public culture, but one which can be articulated to different pleasures and for different social purposes. In the nineteenth century, whether it was art or entertainment depended on who was consuming it and in what context. As Levine perceptively observes, "opera was an art form that was *simultaneously* popular and elite. That is, it was attended both by large numbers of people who derived pleasure from it in the context of their normal everyday culture, and by smaller socially *and* economically elite groups who derived both pleasure and social confirmation from it" (Levine, 1988: 86). To see opera as a cultural form (consisting of many different texts and practices) that is simultaneously popular and elite, it seems to me, is an accurate description of contemporary articulations of opera.

What I think is happening with regard to the popularity of opera is therefore *almost* like a return to the cultural relations of nineteenth-century Europe and the USA. However, there is one crucial difference between then and now. In the nineteenth century, despite the fact that opera could be consumed by different social groups in different contexts and as part of different cultural practices, there was, nevertheless, a very real sense in which those who consumed opera consumed in effect the same opera. Although most of what now counts as opera – and it is a much broader range of texts and practices than existed in the nineteenth century – is an integral part of a shared public culture, there is one key part which is still as socially exclusive as it was intended to be when opera was first institutionalized as high culture: opera in the opera house.

Since 1946, when opera in the UK first received government support (via Arts Council subsidies), opera houses have talked about reducing seat prices in order to make opera more accessible to a broader social mix.[21] In 1983 the then Chairman of the Royal Opera House, Covent Garden, Sir Charles Moser, claimed that "we are desperately trying to widen access" (Moser, 1983: 191); and "if we get more money [government/Arts Council funding], we will reduce seat prices. That's our top priority at the moment, and to widen access" (ibid: 200). In 1995 Sir Angus Stirling, Chairman of the Royal Opera House, repeated the aim to make opera more accessible, claiming "we are doing everything we can to bring seat prices down" (quoted in Evans, 1999: 140). Five years later the *Guardian* (January 22, 2000) quoted a UK government source who said that senior management at the Royal Opera House had been told to "get a better social mix, particularly in the stalls, so it doesn't feel so snooty. . . . They [senior management at the Royal Opera House] must do something to demonstrate they are committed to access." A letter published in the *Guardian* a month earlier made much the same point, if in a somewhat more robust fashion. The letter is a challenge to the current chief executive of the Royal Opera House, Michael Kaiser:

> All this talk of access is bullshit. Access doesn't just mean opening foyers to the public, the odd free concert, the cheap seats that you wouldn't dream of suffering (if you want to prove me wrong on that, sit in the cheapest seats for the next five performances you attend). It means enabling people of modest means who love opera to attend performances in the house their taxes pay for. The reality is that it's easier than ever to buy your way into Covent Garden.

Moreover, as a correspondent to the magazine *Opera* (December 1990) observed: "[In 1962] as an articled clerk on £17 a week, I could afford, and sat regularly in the balcony stall sides [in the Royal Opera House, Covent Garden] at 10/6d [about 52p]. Today at £48, such a seat would require a gross salary of £80,820. Some articled clerk!" (quoted in Evans, 1999: 139).[22]

In the UK, opera houses have seen a huge increase in box office income massively disproportionate to the small increase in attendance. Opera attendance in the UK increased from 1.475 million in 1981 to 1.515 million in 1990. During the same period, however, box office receipts rose from £8.3 million to £22.3 million.[23] It is not surprising, then, that in a survey, carried out in 1990 by the British Market Research Bureau, in which people were asked to rank their consumption of opera in order of frequency of mode of access, attending an opera in an opera house is only placed fourth.[24] Moreover, data produced by the UK Office for National Statistics (1990) shows that in 1986 only 5 percent of the UK population aged 15 and over attended the opera (within this figure professionals, employers, and managers outnumber semi-skilled and unskilled manual by almost 5 to 1).[25]

Although it is true that there is an increasingly shared public culture of opera, which includes opera on CD, on video and DVD, on television, in advertising, in films, on radio, and in books, together with other forms of popular culture with which there is considerable overlap (opera stars performing with pop stars; opera stars hosting variety shows; opera stars performing at the opening of major sporting events), significantly – and running counter to all this – there is little sign of growth in the audience for opera as it is experienced in the opera houses in most of Europe and the USA.[26] Therefore, to return to the question with which I began this chapter: it seems to me that to describe opera as popular culture is to identify only part of what has been happening to it in recent years. I think to see the whole picture is to see that opera is now, as it was for most of the nineteenth century, available for consumption as both elite and popular culture.

Notes

1   The increasing availability of opera is illustrated by the fairly extensive use of opera in advertising and on film soundtracks. Opera used in advertising includes:

Bellini: *Norma*	Ford Mondeo
Delibes: *Lakmé*	British Airways
Delibes: *Lakmé*	Kleenex tissues
Delibes: *Lakmé*	Basmati rice
Delibes: *Lakmé*	Ryvita
Delibes: *Lakmé*	IBM Computers
Gluck: *Orfeo ed Euridice*	Comfort Fabric Softener
Handel: *Serse*	Rover
Mascagni: *Cavalleria Rusticana*	Kleenex tissues
Mascagni: *Cavalleria Rusticana*	Stella Artois
Mascagni: *Cavalleria Rusticana*	Baci Chocolates
Mozart: *The Marriage of Figaro*	Citroen ZX
Mozart: *Così fan tutte*	Mercedes Benz
Offenbach: *Orpheus in the Underworld*	Bio Speed Weed
Offenbach: *Tales of Hoffman*	Bailey's Irish Cream
Puccini: *Madame Butterfly*	Twinings tea
Puccini: *Madame Butterfly*	Del Monte orange juice
Puccini: *Gianni Schicchi*	Phillips DCC
Puccini: *La Bohème*	Sony Walkman
Puccini: *Tosca*	FreeServe
Rossini: *The Barber of Seville*	Ragu Pasta Sauce
Rossini: *The Barber of Seville*	Fiat Strada
Rossini: *The Barber of Seville*	Braun cordless shavers
Verdi: *Aïda*	Diet Pepsi
Verdi: *Aïda*	Michelob
Verdi: *Aïda*	Egypt
Verdi: *Nabucco*	British Airways
Verdi: *Il trovatore*	Ragu Pasta Sauce
Verdi: *Rigoletto*	Ragu Pasta Sauce
Verdi: *Rigoletto*	Little Caesar's Pizza
Verdi: *The Force of Destiny*	Stella Artois

Opera used in film soundtracks includes:

Bizet: *The Pearlfishers*	*Gallipoli*
Bizet: *Carmen*	*Trainspotting*
Catalani: *La Wally*	*Diva*
Delibes: *Lakmé*	*True Romance*
Delibes: *Lakmé*	*The Hunger*
Donizetti: *Lucia di Lammermoor*	*The Fifth Element*
Donizetti: *L'Elsir d'amore*	*Prizzi's Honour*

Dvorak: *Russalka*	*Driving Miss Daisy*
Giordano: *André Chénier*	*Philadelphia*
Handel: *Serse*	*Dangerous Liaisons*
Korngold: *Die tote Stadt*	*The Big Lebowski*
Leoncavallo: *I Pagliacci*	*The Untouchables*
Leoncavallo: *I Pagliacci*	*Moonraker*
Mascagni: *Cavalleria Rusticana*	*Jean de Florette*
Mascagni: *Cavalleria Rusticana*	*The Godfather III*
Mozart: *The Magic Flute*	*Amadeus*
Mozart: *Così fan tutte*	*Sunday, Bloody Sunday*
Mozart: *Così fan tutte*	*My Left Foot*
Ponchielli: *La Gioconda*	*Fantasia*
Puccini: *La Bohème*	*Moonstruck*
Puccini: *La Rondine*	*A Room with a View*
Puccini: *Madame Butterfly*	*Fatal Attraction*
Puccini: *Gianni Schicchi*	*A Room with a View*
Puccini: *Turandot*	*The Witches of Eastwick*
Puccini: *Turandot*	*The Killing Fields*
Rossini: *The Barber of Seville*	*Mrs Doubtfire*
Verdi: *Il trovatore*	*A Night at the Opera*
Verdi: *La Traviata*	*Pretty Woman*
Wagner: *Die Walküre*	*Apocalypse Now*
Wagner: *Tristan and Isolde*	*Excalibur*

2   The Camerata were a group of Florentine intellectuals. The key members (as named by McClary) were Jacopo Peri (1561–1633), composer of the first opera, *Dafne* (1597), and Giulio Caccini (1551–1610). Other leading figures included Vincenzo Galilei (1520–91) and Giovanni Bardi (1534–1612).

3   If our historical starting point is the classical repertoire performed in the vast majority of contemporary opera houses, it could be argued that opera begins with Mozart in 1780 and ends with Puccini in 1926. It is this way of seeing the history of opera which leads to the accusation that it is in effect a "museum culture." Interestingly, the dates fit quite nicely with the idea that opera was invented by the class who reaped the principal share of the rewards of nineteenth-century industrialization. Opera gave them both pleasure and social identity – a sense of being a "class for themselves" (Marx, 1963: 195).

4   The integration of opera into popular entertainment can be demonstrated in a number of ways. For example, one can point to the way in which it was common practice for a night's entertainment at the theater to include stage melodrama, farce, and opera (see Levine, 1988: 90). In this way, the promiscuous mixing of forms of entertainment on the nineteenth-century stage is very similar to what we have come to expect from contemporary television.

  Significantly, it was the circus entrepreneur P. T. Barnum who in 1852 organized and successfully promoted the first major concert tour across the US by the soprano – the so-called "Swedish Nightingale" – Jenny Lind (perhaps opera's first superstar). The *New York Home Journal* referred to "the quiet ease with which the music of the exclusives – Italian music – has passed into the hands of the people.

. . . Now it is as much theirs as anybody's! . . . Opera music has . . . become a popular taste" (quoted in Levine, 1988: 97). The following year *Putnam's Magazine* suggested that P. T. Barnum should become manager of the New York Opera. The terms of their argument point to a popular attitude towards opera: "He understands what the public wants, and how to gratify that want. . . . He comprehends that, with us [the American public], the opera need not necessarily be the luxury of the few, but the recreation of the many" (ibid: 100–1).

5   On the Metropolitan Opera's opening night on October 22, 1883 a contemporary newspaper estimated that the boxes were occupied by people whose wealth was in the region of $540,000,000 (Kolodin, 1936: 5). The following evening the *New York Evening Post* commented: "From an artistic and musical point of view, the large boxes in the Metropolitan are a decided mistake. But as the house was avowedly built for social purposes rather than artistic, it is useless to complain about this" (quoted in Kolodin, 1936: 12).

6   In 1916 the *Atlantic Monthly* carried an article which claimed that "Opera is controlled by a few rich men. . . . It does not exist for the good of the whole city, but rather for those with plethoric purses. . . . [Opera houses] surround themselves with an exotic atmosphere in which the normal person finds difficulty in breathing . . . they are too little related to the community" (quoted in Levine, 1988: 101).

7   In 1914 the *Atlantic Review* published an article in which it was hoped that the increasing popularity of cinema might bring about a situation in which "the art of the stage may escape from the proletariat, and *again* truly belong to those who in a larger, finer sense are 'the great ones of the earth'" (quoted in Levine, 1988: 207; my italics).

8   The following are examples of books which seek to introduce opera to a new audience.

1990	*How to be Tremendously Tuned into Opera*
1991	*An Invitation to Opera*
1993	*Get Into Opera: A Beginner's Guide*
	A Beginner's Guide to Opera
1994	*Opera 101: A Complete Guide to Learning and Loving Opera*
1995	*The Penguin Opera Guide*
	Who's Afraid of Opera? A Highly Opinionated, Informative and Entertaining Guide
1997	*The Good Opera Guide*
	Opera for Dummies
	Teach Yourself Opera
	Collins Opera & Operetta
1998	*Opera (Crash Course Series)*
	Opera: A Crash Course
1999	*Opera: The Rough Guide*
2000	*Getting Opera: A Guide for the Cultured but Confused*

9   There are also a number of books which introduce the newcomer to recorded opera available on compact disc:

1993   *The Metropolitan Opera House Guide to Recorded Opera*
1996   *Classic CDs: Opera Greats*
1997   *Gramophone Opera Good CD Guide*
1999   *Opera: 100 Essential CDs, The Rough Guide*

10   The following are some examples of CD compilations which aim to introduce opera to a new audience:

The Only Opera Album You'll Ever Need
The Best Opera Album in the World . . . Ever!
Opera Hits
Opera Favourites
The Ultimate Opera Collection
The Ultimate Opera Collection 2
Simply the Best Night at the Opera
50 Great Moments in Opera
The Reader's Digest Magical World of Opera
The Greatest Opera Show on Earth
Essential Opera
Opera Spectacular 1
Opera Spectacular 2

11   The following are some examples of the "pop marketing" of opera composers and performers:

The Greatest Tenors of the 20th Century
Great Tenors of the Century
The Essential Pavarotti 1
The Essential Pavarotti 2
The Greatest Pavarotti Album Ever!
The Greatest Puccini Album Ever!
The Three Tenors in Concert 1990
The Three Tenors in Concert 1994
The Three Tenors in Concert 1998
The Three Original Tenors [Enrico Caruso, Beniamino Gigli, and Jussi
   Bjorling]
A Soprano in Red [Lesley Garrett]
Baroque Opera Highlights
Best of Kiri Te Kanawa
The Verdi Centenary Album [Jose Cura]

12   The third motive is illustrative of the division in the dominant class between those rich in "cultural" as opposed to "economic" capital (Bourdieu, 1984). As David Evans observes, "Throughout the opera world there is the assumption that opera knowledge is distributed in inverse proportion to wealth, that the second of these two status group formations is physically as well as materially to be found in the upper reaches and in standing room where they make their presence and status

as 'knowledgeable' felt through loud bar chat, cheers, boos, catcalls and flung flowers, fruit and vegetables" (Evans, 1999: 96–7). Similarly, an editorial in the UK magazine *Opera* described the audience at the Royal Opera House, Covent Garden as "Rich audiences, sponsor's audiences, audiences whose interest in opera may be marginal . . . champagne louts" (quoted in Evans, 1999: 139).

13   Two of Pavarotti's albums (Essential Pavarotti I and Essential Pavarotti 2) achieved the same feat in the British album charts.

14   For different definitions of popular culture, including the "quantitative," see Storey (2000).

15   As Evans observes, the opera festival at Glyndebourne "exists for one of the most elitist audiences in the world" (Evans, 1999: 416).

16   As Stuart Hall points out:

> Tradition is a vital element in culture; but it has little to do with the mere persist-
> ence of old forms. It is much more to do with the way elements have been linked
> together or articulated. . . . Not only can the elements of "tradition" be rearranged,
> so that they articulate with different practices and positions, and take on a new
> meaning and relevance. It is also often the case that cultural struggle arises in its
> sharpest form just at the point where different, opposed traditions meet, intersect.
> They seek to detach a cultural form from its implantation in one tradition, and to
> give it a new cultural resonance or accent (Hall, 1998: 450)

17   At the more unusual end of opera as popular culture, in November 1999 I attended an evening of eating fish and chips and listening to members of Opera North performing excerpts from famous operas (plate 1.1).

18   Although opera does not exist outside the realm of commercial culture, it is not entirely incorporated into it. What I mean is this: opera, like much of "high culture," is artificially protected from the full force of having to make its way in the marketplace by various financial sources – grants, sponsorship, individual and corporate donations.

19   On different social practices of, and different theoretical approaches to, con-sumption, see Storey (1999).

20   Pierre Bourdieu argues that cultural distinctions are used in this way to support class distinctions. Taste is a deeply ideological category: it functions as a marker of "class" (using the term in a double sense to mean both a social economic cat-egory and the claim for a particular level of quality). For Bourdieu, the con-sumption of culture is "predisposed, consciously and deliberately or not, to fulfil a social function of legitimating social differences" (Bourdieu, 1984: 5). He describes opera as "the occasion or pretext for social ceremonies enabling a select audience to demonstrate and experience its membership of high society in obedi-ence to the integrating and distinguishing rhythms of the 'society' calendar" (ibid: 272).

21   An example of how little has changed at the core of opera in the UK can be gathered by considering the Board of Directors of the Royal Opera House, Covent Garden (1992–3): it consists of eight Sirs, a Lord, and a Baroness. Simi-larly, the Board of Directors of English National Opera contains five Sirs, one Earl, and five Lords (Evans, 1999: 150–1).

Harry Ramsden's

FATAL ATTRACTION

♥

AN OPERA AND CHIPS
PRODUCTION
PERFORMED BY OPERA NORTH

♥

An evening of opera excerpts with a theme of
LOVE, JEALOUSY AND DEATH

Including numbers by Verdi, Puccini et al

Friday 19th November 1999

All-inclusive Opera Menu
£16.50 inc. VAT

OPERA NIGHT BOOKINGS:
Tel: 0191 460 2625

Harry Ramsden's Gateshead, Metro Park West, By the Metro Centre,
Gibside Way, Gateshead, Tyne & Wear NE11 9XS

PERFORMANCE IN HARRY'S PRIVATE FUNCTION ROOM
RESTAURANT REMAINS OPEN TO PUBLIC

22 Evans notes that "In 1984 a centre front stalls seat averaged £37, by 1994 £104, a 75 percent rise taking inflation into account" (Evans, 1999: 139).

23 Figures quoted in the *Guardian*, December 11, 1990.

24 Survey results (quoted in Evans, 1999: 403):

1 Opera on CD and audio cassette
2 Opera on radio
3 Opera on TV and video
4 Opera at the opera house
5 Opera at the opera house while on holiday
6 Books on opera

25 For most of the 1990s opera attendance stood at 6 percent of the UK population aged 15 and over. In 1996–7 it rose to 7 percent. Opera attendance in the UK, 1986–98 (based on *Social Trends*, 1990, 1998, 1999, 2000):

1986–7 5%
1991–2 6%
1995–6 6%
1996–7 6%
1997–8 7%

26 There have been false dawns before. In 1936, in the foreword to Irving Kolodin's history of the first 52 years of the Metropolitan Opera, W. J. Henderson refers to "the present efforts to democratize the institution [of opera] in order to keep it alive" (Kolodin, 1936: xii). Following the first television broadcast of a complete opera performance (the Metropolitan Opera's production of Verdi's *Otello* on November 29, 1948), the *New York Times* wondered "What the acquisition of a mass following may mean for opera almost exceeds the bounds of the imagination in its challenging and provocative implications" (quoted in Graf, 1951: 222). Writing in 1951, Herbert Graf argued that opera in the cinema and on television has "social and economic implications of tremendous import. The privileges of wealth and education, formerly preponderant in the world of opera, are being negated by the new inventions" (ibid: 207). Instead of a performance reaching 3,000 it can now reach an audience of millions. Sir Claus Moser, former chairman of the Royal Opera House, described opera in Britain in the 1920s and 1930s as "very much an upper-class activity, the icing on the cake of glamorous living" (Moser, 1983: 187). He then claimed that after World War II "the scene was totally transformed" (ibid). More recently (the 1980s) there has taken place "a fantastic cultural transformation in this country, which has come from a gradual spreading of love for . . . opera throughout the population. . . . The great operatic stars have become pop names . . . they are seen and heard by millions" (ibid: 188).

References

Bourdieu, P. (1984). *Distinction: A Critique of the Judgement of Taste*. Cambridge, MA: Harvard University Press.

Bourdieu, P. (1993). *The Field of Cultural Production*. Cambridge: Polity Press.

Boyden, M. (1999). *Opera: The Rough Guide*. Harmondsworth: Penguin Books.

DiMaggio, P. (1992). "Cultural Boundaries and Structural Change: The Extension of the High Culture Model to Theater, Opera, and the Dance, 1900–1940." In Michele Lamont and Marcel Fournier, eds., *Cultivating Differences: Symbolic Boundaries and the Making of Inequality*, Chicago: University of Chicago Press.

DiMaggio, P. (1998). "Cultural Entrepreneurship in Nineteenth-Century Boston: The Creation of an Organizational Base for High Culture in America." In John Storey, ed., *Cultural Theory and Popular Culture: A Reader*, 2nd edn, Hemel Hempstead: Prentice-Hall.

Dobkin, M. (2000). *Getting Opera: A Guide for the Cultured but Confused*. New York: Pocket Books.

Evans, D. T. (1999). *Phantasmagoria: A Sociology of Opera*. Aldershot: Ashgate.

Graf, H. (1951). *Opera for the People*. Minneapolis: University of Minnesota Press.

Hall, S. (1998). "Notes on Deconstructing 'the Popular.'" In John Storey, ed., *Cultural Theory and Popular Culture: A Reader*, 2nd edn, Hemel Hempstead: Prentice-Hall.

Henderson, W. J. (1936). "Foreword." In Irving Kolodin, *The Metropolitan Opera 1883–1935*. New York: Oxford University Press.

Kolodin, I. (1936). *The Metropolitan Opera 1883–1935*. New York: Oxford University Press.

Levine, L. W. (1988). *Highbrow/Lowbrow: The Emergence of Cultural Hierarchy in America*. Cambridge, MA: Harvard University Press.

McClary, S. (1985). "Afterword: The Politics of Silence and Sound." In Jacques Attali, *Noise: The Political Economy of Music*, Manchester: Manchester University Press.

McConachie, B. A. (1988). "New York Operagoing, 1825–50: Creating an Elite Social Ritual." In *American Music*, vol. 6, Urbana: University of Illinois Press.

Marx, K. (1963). *Selected Writings in Sociology and Social Philosophy*, ed. T. B. Bottomore and Maximilien Rubel. Harmondsworth: Penguin Books.

Moser, Sir C. (1983). "The Appeal and Cost of Opera," *Universities Quarterly*, vol. 37, no. 3.

Office for National Statistics, 1990. *Social Trends*. London: The Stationery Office.

Office for National Statistics, 1998. *Social Trends*. London: The Stationery Office.

Office for National Statistics, 1999. *Social Trends*. London: The Stationery Office.

Office for National Statistics, 2000. *Social Trends*. London: The Stationery Office.

Pettitt, S. (1998). *Opera: A Crash Course*. London: Simon & Schuster.

Pogue D. and Speck, S. (1997). *Opera for Dummies*. Foster City, CA: IDG Books.

Raynor, H. (1972). *A Social History of Music: From the Middle Ages to Beethoven*. London: Barrie & Jenkins.

Saunders, K. (1994). "Opera lovers with attitude call the tune," *Sunday Times*, July 17.

Storey, J. (1999). *Cultural Consumption and Everyday Life*. London: Edward Arnold.

Storey, J. (2000). *Cultural Theory and Popular Culture: An Introduction*, 3rd edn, London: Pearson.

Sutherland, S. (1997). *Teach Yourself Opera*. London: Hodder & Stoughton.

Tambling, J. (1987). *Opera, Ideology and Film*. Manchester: Manchester University Press.

Wolff, J. (1989). "The Ideology of Autonomous Art." In Richard Leppert and Susan McClary, eds., *Music and Society: The Politics of Composition, Performance and Reception*, Cambridge: Cambridge University Press.

Zelochow, B. (1993). "The Opera: The Meeting of Popular and Elite Culture in the Nineteenth Century," *History of European Ideas*, vol. 16, nos. 1–3.

2

Signature and Brand
John Frow

My black T-shirt from the Art Institute of Chicago carries the signatures of 69 dead Masters, from Rembrandt through a full squad of Impressionists to Chagall and Magritte. The format is that of the football or bat signed by the team, and this is part of the joke: this is the Institute's team, and these are the team's "real" signatures, in the sense that they faithfully reproduce the form of the holographs on the canvases that the Institute holds; the signatures bear witness, like a list of names on a testimonial, to the value of the collection. But since they are facsimiles, and since they have been first radically decontextualized and then reassembled in unlikely juxtaposition, they are mentions rather than uses, stripped of their function and performative force. They refer not to the person of the artist who made the work which they authenticate, but to the *system* of signatures which organizes both the aesthetic and the monetary value of works of art. In this chapter I examine some of the features of this system and contrast it with another, that of the brand name, by which it has to a certain extent been displaced; my argument is that there is now something of a convergence between, on the one hand, the commercial branding of aesthetic goods and, on the other, the aesthetic valorization of commercial goods. In order to analyze these overlapping and contrasting systems, however, I need to make a prior argument about the nature of information and the property rights which have come to subsist in it.

Information differs from material goods in two ways: it is not inherently scarce, and it is not consumed by use. Rather, it is inexhaustibly reproducible: if I tell you something I still "possess" it myself, and so on indefinitely. Indeed, the value of information is in most cases enhanced by being shared: it grows, and it finds new uses (Davis and Stack, 1992). Its value is social, but it is inherently difficult to create economic value from it. This difficulty has been increased by the series of inventions of technologies of proliferation, from the printing press to the computer, which make possible, in principle, the infinite replication and dispersal, within an open system, of writing, of images, and of sounds.

The logic of capital accumulation, however, requires that information be transformed into a commodity which can be bought and sold for profit; its openness and indeterminacy must be contained by a private appropriation which will endow it with scarcity and restrict access. This can be effected in one of two ways: by making it secret, or by releasing it in a controlled way by means of the price mechanism. Secrecy is a political form of restriction of access, resting on the power to keep information hidden and counterproductive in its inability to put secret information to use. The price mechanism, by contrast, allows information to circulate, but it requires a complex legal assemblage to make possible the exaction of rent by containing the tendency of information to proliferate freely. This legal assemblage, which restricts access to and use of information without necessarily restricting authorized possession of it, is made up primarily of copyright, patent, and trademark law and works through the creation of a limited property right imputed to private or corporate persons; in the case of "cultural" texts its central category is that of the author, understood as the sole origin of the work and the point of limitation of unauthorized uses. Authorship constrains the potentially infinite iterability of writing, image, and sound, and regulates the power of all their technological multipliers.

Authors are persons exercising a certificatory function within a system of legal and cultural recognition of their rights and powers. In the author system that has prevailed in the West for about the last two centuries, the signature is the mode of expression of the author's contractual will. The social form expressed by the contract is that of a pact between strangers. If the Western juridical subject is defined as the one who has (always already) the right to sign their name in this way, this subject is at the same time constituted and empowered in the act of signature, the writing of the proper name. In non-reciprocal forms of signature (like the signing of a check) the contractual mutuality is reduced to a unilateral action (which is nevertheless still latently two-sided). Here the signature functions as a guarantee, a declaration that I originate and authorize the document I have signed. It functions, that is to say, as a metonym for my person: the signature or the mark, uniquely mine like my fingerprints or my face, commit me in my entirety to legal liability, the extreme form of which would be the pledge of my life or my freedom in the vicarious form of this mark on paper.

Within the institutions of painting and the book, the signature is a guarantee of authenticity and its converse, the repudiation of forgery. In its most fully developed form in Abstract Expressionism (and perhaps also in performance art, where the body itself is on the line) the whole painting (which may be "unsigned") functions as a signature insofar as the brushstrokes or the drip marks are to be taken as fully expressive indices of the artist's personality; or the performance writes in pain the authenticity of the experience.

The signature as written trace of the artist's name appears as recently as the late Middle Ages, although the form "x pinxit" or "x pingebat" did occasionally occur earlier. Since that time it has fulfilled a variety of functions involving diverse forms of compositional specificity. Some of these have been codified by Claude Gandelman (1985): he talks of iconic signatures like the small winged dragon, the *Drachen*, that stands for Lucas Cranach in his *Allegory of Salvation*, and of various forms of rebus, like Holbein's picture of a *hohl Bein*, a hollow bone (an anamorphic skull) in *The Ambassadors*, or Klee's play with the French *clef* in the late painting *Zerbrochene Schlüssel* (cf. Lebensztejn, 1974: 55–6); he talks of various ways in which the signature can be a compositionally functional element, bearing color or line; and he discusses internal mimicry of the painting by the signature, or of the signature by the painting.

What I want to take from his work, however, is the notion of the signature, ambivalently placed within a pictorial space to which it does not fully belong, as a *shifter*, a *débrayeur* setting up a tension between the planes of representation and the represented (Gandelman, 1985: 105). I adapt this argument here to stress the disjunction that the signature introduces between the planes of drawing and writing, of image and verbal text. This disjunction is the index of an act of framing by which the signature leads out of the painting into a context which is

at once intertextual (that is, aesthetic) and institutional: a context of
names and values which I designate, in shorthand, the art system.

Much of twentieth-century art has been taken up with the struggle to displace or contest the power of this system: to contest the aesthetics of the signature. Its exemplary moments, like Duchamp's signing
of a defaced Mona Lisa or his attaching of a false signature ("R. Mutt,
1917") to the *objet trouvé*, the famous *pissotière*, but also the moments
of automatic writing, of Pop, or of performance art involve a radical
renunciation of originality. When Sherrie Levine photographs and
exhibits as her own work well-known photographs by Walker Evans
or Edward Weston she is at once reframing them so that they take on
quite different meanings (like Pierre Menard's rewriting in the twentieth century of *Don Quixote*, not as an imitation but as a new work)
and thereby challenging the notion that the creative originality of the
artist will result in a unique and unreproducible work. This appropriation is a kind of signature.

But is this signature a forgery, or not? Were Levine literally to sign
these photographs, the mark she made would be, presumably, her "real"
signature inscribing her "real" name, and it would correspond to a real
claim of attribution based in real labor exercised in the production of
the image: she has indeed taken and developed this photograph. It is,
however, a rephotographing of an existing photograph or painting:
copyright law might well see it as a simple repetition without any addition of personality or work that would deposit the trace of an original self. But were she to sign the photograph there would in fact be
such a trace, the signature itself (and this signature need not be physically inscribed); the signature, this supplement, this mere gesture of certification, would make the creative difference.

What then is being parodied or challenged here? The act of attribution exercised by way of the signature? But such an act of attribution continues to operate here, both as parody and as a real defense
against prosecution for breach of copyright, since Levine's act of parody
is perfectly defensible in law as an original creative act. Alternatively,
we could say that what is being parodied in the case of the photographs
is the very act of signing a photograph (or, less literally, of claiming it
as a work of art). Photographs are normally unsigned (or they are
signed on the *reverse* of the image), because, as well as designating a
naming right, the signature designates the contention that the work has

been executed with the artist's own hands: the signature is a *writing* of a word, a holograph, whereas a photograph is mechanically executed. Levine's act of appropriation thus invokes and provokes a whole history of rivalry between the photograph and the painting, and a whole history in which the photograph has had to prove its entitlement to creative recognition (cf. Edelman, 1979); but again we must add that Levine's act is as much complicit in maintaining the dichotomy between the handcrafted and singular work of art and the mechanical and infinitely reproducible photograph as it is effective in undermining it.

In all of these cases, and whether or not the act of signature is literal or implicit, we must recognize that we continue to have to do with signed forms, which posit an intentionality, a willed aesthetic integrity that guarantees even the authenticity of the inauthentic; the myth of singularity retains its power even in its renunciation.

The counter-movement against the aesthetics of the signature as well as its historical failure are bound up with the fact that the signature has become intrinsic both to aesthetic and to market value. As a metonym for the self-possessed, self-possessing person, it is the foundation for all intellectual property rights. Peter Jaszi speaks of two overlapping modes of legally controlling the proliferation of meaning. One of them, copyright, is commercial, giving the author the right to control copying of the work for a limited period of time. The other, that of moral rights, is non-commercial, protecting the author's control of the circumstances of release of her work to the public, the right to withdraw the work from circulation, the right to claim attribution ("paternity right"), and the right to object to distortion or mutilation of the work ("integrity right"). The doctrine of moral rights is based in "the idea that the work of art is an extension of the artist's personality, an expression of his innermost being. To mistreat the work of art is to mistreat the artist, to invade his area of privacy, to impair his personality" (Merryman and Elsen, 1987, cited in Jaszi, 1991: 497). Both copyright and moral rights, however, protect the source of market value: the artist's unique personality, which establishes the singularity of the work of art *vis-à-vis* any series it might generate. As Lury (1993: 23) summarizes the movement of intellectual property law: "It was in terms derived from the functioning of the author in aesthetic discourse that individual works and movements entered the market as 'property'; in short, it was through the author-function that cultural value became a thing, a product and a possession caught in a circuit of property values."

It is this problematic of authorization that determines the crucial role of the signature in the art market as emblem and medium of authentication, the guarantee of a value that isn't simply aesthetic, and that entails unthinkable financial consequences when the signature of a "Master" is called into question (cf. Watson, 1992). The signature constitutes the rarity that is the source of market value. Note that what is rare is, in principle, the abstract form of the work: the "model" (Baudrillard, 1988) or "blueprint" or "mold" (Attali, 1985) or (in legal usage) the "work"; in the case of painting or sculpture, with their roots in craft production, the value of this model is entirely fused with that of its singular performance on canvas or in shaped matter; in the case of a musical score or a literary text the realization of the model more usually takes the form of a serial replication ("copies") with only a derived value (books, printed scores), although there may be forms of singular performance (a manuscript, a first edition, the performance of a play or musical work) which acquire value in their own right.

The value-forming role of the signature (and other associated markers of originality) can perhaps most clearly be seen in the history of multiples, where a labor of singularization constructs aesthetic value from serial forms. Melot (1986) gives the example of the collection of engravings: although from the time of the earliest major collectors in seventeenth-century France a distinction had been made between original engravings and reproductions, engravers in both fields were recognized as fully creative artists. From about 1860 this recognition altered with the revalorization of the difference between "original" and "copy." As prints entered the art galleries, the names of engravers, printers, and other intermediaries began to disappear from the margins in a *politique des auteurs* directly parallel to the cinematic auteurism of the 1950s. At the same time, engravers began to fight for authorial status in their own right: from 1850 they began to sign the different proof stages, and from 1880 to number them, producing a hierarchy of variation and value. One of the central strategies of rarefaction was the adoption of old artisanal techniques which, once abandoned by industry, guaranteed a limited production distinct from seriality. In taking up such obsolete techniques as lithography, engravers were disavowing the continuity between the domain of rare or unique artistic creation and that of the industrial production of images. A century later, as photographic prints began to enter the art market proper, similar techniques (hand-processing and the signing and numbering of prints) were adopted as a means of producing the distinctive variation that signifies authenticity. In this context, Melot writes, it becomes possible to understand that such things as readymades and found objects, far from radically challenging the art system, in fact reinforce it in their use of the signature as a strategy for producing scarcity from abundant repetition. The rarefying work of the signature can be seen in an equally clear form in the case of limited edition prints, which fuse a signature-effect with a restricted serial production to produce an object that is at once authentic and multiple; and the same paradox operates in the limitation of Rodin castings to twelve casts of any plaster in order to maintain the authenticity of this limited set. Krauss (1988: 156) speaks of this as the deliberate construction (in this case by an act of parliament) of a "culture of originals."

The post-Romantic aesthetics of the signature owes something of its intensity to its opposition to the aesthetics of repetition against which it defines itself: on the one hand the aesthetics of craft production, in which the model tends to work either by strict conformity to an ideal type or by a pattern of slight variations on a familiar schema (and where the model tends to be fused with a singular performance); on the other, that of mass cultural production, where the indeterminacy of uptake and the high cost of initial production in relation to the relatively low costs of replication require the generation of "a constant stream of unique (if often similar) products with severely limited life spans" (DiMaggio, 1987: 446), strict control of a formulaic product, and constant monitoring and regulation of demand. In the context of mass cultural production the authorial signature becomes less important as a creator of value than the construction of the author's or artist's or actor's or performer's name as the object of a brand recognition – a process closer to the trade mark than to copyright, and one in which the artist is effectively corporatized. Gandelman indeed argues that this process is a function of the art system itself. His argument follows from the difference between the indexical form of the signature (that is, its designation of the presence of the artist: not just "I did this" but "I was here") and the taxonomic function of the proper name: far from being a pure singularity, as much semiotic theory has argued, the "Name," when one abstracts it from the signature which indicates it and "contains" it, loses its "index" character and becomes a "trade mark." Indeed, like the trade mark, the name is of a symbolic order. Thus the name "Degas" abstracted from its index the signature is something like "Ford" or "Cadillac." It does not mean that the artist, Mr Degas, was *there* any more than the name Ford means that Mr Ford has taken part in the fabricating of the car which bears his name. What the signature freed name Degas means is that what we have here is a *a Degas* in a symbolic system opposing Degas to Monet or Bouguereau (just as *a Ford* is meaningful within a context or system which opposes Ford to Dodge or Cadillac). (Gandelman, 1985: 76)

What I want to go on to argue is that there is now, in the words of Lash and Urry (1994: 123, 138), a growing tendency towards a symmetrical articulation between the systems of brand and signature. In this convergence, they write, "ordinary manufacturing industry is becoming more and more like the production of culture," and, conversely, "what all the culture industries produce becomes increasingly, not like commodities but advertisements" – for example, through the process by which a cultural text "advertises" and sells itself as a product within a brand-name structure of cultural marketing. The simplest way to start thinking about the difference between these two systems (in a first approximation which I shall later modify) is to say that the brand is a corporate rather than a personal signature: it is a *quasi-signature*, attached not to a singular object (as in the case of the signature appended to specialized designer one-offs that the French call a *griffe*) but to a product range distinguished from other product ranges. Brands are typically *managed* to ensure that products are consistent with brand image and that competitors do not encroach on it, and typically supported by controlled advertising campaigns which seek to construct and maintain the coherence and integrity of that image. Thus when a reviewer recently wrote of Michael Ondaatje's *Anil's Ghost* that its similarities to *The English Patient* "suggest some degree of brand management" (Tait, 2000: 39), he was indicating a tension between an aesthetic imperative to inventiveness and originality (the aesthetics of the signature) and a commercial imperative to product uniformity across a series (the aesthetics of the brand).

Originating in medieval guild practices of quality assurance and regulation of liability (sixteenth-century whisky producers, for example, shipped their product in barrels branded with their name), the brand evolved towards the end of the nineteenth century into a corporate asset with a central role in the marketing of mass-produced packaged commodities (Aaker, 1991; Wilkins, 1994). Extended distribution chains in these new markets increased the distance between manufacturers and retailers, while economies of scale and scope generated the instabilities of high-volume output without control of sales. The new marketing and advertising cultures of the period were designed to regulate demand by means of the promotion of differentiated products of standardized quality in an extension of corporate planning through the sales process. More generally however, as Ohmann argues, advertisers and marketers were looking for "a nexus between high-speed, continuous-flow manufacturing and the reshaping of people's habits and lives" (Ohmann, 1996: 91). The brand reshapes not only patterns of shopping but ways of using the household (as a center of leisure and consumption rather than of production) and the form and intensity of identification with manufactured goods.

The brand is thus something like a set of meanings and values attached to a standardized product and generating desire – perhaps a historically quite new kind of desire, extending the love of luxury objects to the world of serially produced goods. But to think of the brand as being "attached" to products is misleading: the brand is in principle reducible neither to a product nor to a corporation. Although at a certain stage in its life the brand name may function as a "strict form of designation," it is only when it loses this function that it becomes a brand "in the full sense of the word" (Kapferer, 1992: 115). Starting as a descriptor or a nonsense word, the brand acquires a semantic autonomy and a force of memory which transform it into a self-signifying proper name: the word "Kleenex" loses its reference to cleanness and becomes "a personal name, denoting nothing specific but charged with associations" (ibid: 72–3); the nonsense word "Kodak" becomes a semantic matrix, not the name of a range of products but the auratic source of their meaning and identity. At this level of extension "it is now the product which demonstrates the brand, in the sense that it exhibits the exterior signs of an interior imprint": the Swatch mark moves from naming only watches to being able to sign sunglasses "as long as they look 'swatchy'"; and at a final level of abstraction, "similarity of value is the only source of identity for products of a widely differing nature" (ibid: 116–17). The brand thus acquires a phantasmatic life of its own, floating free of the products it subsumes; in Lury's words (Franklin, Lury, and Stacey, 2000), the brand makes

> available for appropriation aspects of the experience of product use *as if they were effects of the brand*. In the creation of a logo, an image, a sign, or an emblem which condenses the memory of a whole history of advertisements, packaging, and promotion, the object is anticipated, brought into focus in relation to the logo; its properties reconstituted as the effects of the brand's repetition.

Grassl is thus wrong to argue for an ontological realism of the brand, by which he means its dependence on the "affordances," the functional properties and possibilities of the products it subsumes (Grassl, 1999: 331); it is precisely the divisibility of brand and product which makes possible the transfer of brand loyalty "from one generation of product to another or from one product category to another," as well as the licensing and franchising of brands (Haigh, 1998: 7–8).

What work does a brand do? The usual answer in the marketing literature is that brands differentiate products and provide an assurance of quality. But an examination of the legal doctrine associated with brands makes it clear that this answer glosses over something much more fundamental.

The key feature of the brand, writes Haigh, is "its clear and simple mark, with concrete and legally defensible attributes"; it is "a specifically defensible piece of legal property to which an incremental revenue stream is attached" by virtue of the "non-rational hold over the buying behavior of the consumer" which it establishes (ibid: 7, 12). As Schmitt and Simonson (1997: 216) revealingly put it, "Brand and corporate identities help companies create barriers to competition. To some degree, a company or brand can obtain a legally sanctioned monopoly over certain aspects of the identity so as to create these barriers." Although the brand itself is no more than "a complex compound of legal rights," including "copyright, design right, registered design right, trade marks, common law rights (passing off) and trading standards legislation" (Haigh, 1998: 14), its central core is the trade mark. Trade mark doctrine has evolved in a simple and transparent way over the last century, moving steadily from the prevention of deceit (the passing off of one product as another) to the protection of an intangible property right in a word or emblem. In the United States, which

sets the pattern for intellectual property doctrine elsewhere by virtue
of its influence over the international regulatory bodies, there has been

> a growing but incomplete judicial acceptance of more expansive trade
> mark rights, a trend characterized by movement away from the tradi-
> tional "confusion" definition of infringement, which forbids only those
> unauthorized uses of a mark that are likely to confuse consumers as to
> a product's origin or sponsorship, toward a broader "dilution" test, which
> precludes all unauthorized uses that would lessen the mark's "distinct-
> iveness." (Shaughnessy, 1987: 264)

The logic of this shift is that the mark or emblem is not just the designation of a valuable product, but is a valuable product in its own
right (Voortman, 1991: 359); when McDonald's attempts to restrict the
prefix "Mc" even in instances not related to food, when George Lucas
attempted to exclude public interest groups from using the phrase "Star
Wars," when the United States Olympic Committee managed to have
a gay-rights group enjoined from using the generic term "Olympics"
(Dreyfuss, 1991), the "value of investment" doctrine encroaches on the
commons in language by undermining the fundamental principle that
"a title or name composed of ordinary words cannot acquire the status
of property" and that "all words of our language are in the public
domain" (*Ball v. United Artists Corporation*, 1961: 224); it also tends to
prohibit virtually all trade mark parody, the purpose of which is precisely to "dilute" the range of meanings of the mark. The trade mark,
the core of any brand, is a semiotic surplus value which is "legally
defensible" and which increasingly shows up in accounting practice as
an asset in its own right.

   The brand, then, is a semiotic assemblage which brings together a
cause and an effect: on the one hand a "non-rational hold" over consumer behavior, on the other the "incremental revenue stream" which
flows from it. But how is that "hold" to be explained, and what kind
of "identity" is it that can help "create barriers to competition"?

   In 1995 the American telecommunications corporation AT&T split
into three companies and began the quest for a new "identity" for its
equipment spin-off. The market-research firm Landor Associates,
anxious to avoid a merely descriptive name, undertook extensive inter-
viewing of managers, staff, and end-users to generate a list of desired
associations for the new company. After evaluating some seven hundred

possible names, they produced a short-list of twelve, which they then reduced to three; at the same time they selected a short-list of entries from a competition to design a company logo. The names and the logo designs were then tested in thirteen different countries and across a range of language groups, and the final choice was made: the company was to be called Lucent Technologies, and the logo to be a rough hand-drawn red circle. The name was said to mean "glowing with light" and "marked by clarity," and to suggest "clear thought, brightness, and energy"; the circle connoted at once "movement and completeness." Name and image were then combined with a slogan – "We make the things that make communications work" – in a $50 million advertising campaign, and the company came into being in the form of its brand (Schmitt and Simonson, 1997: 26–31).

Such a process of generation of names and images around a desired theme has now become the norm in the launching of new brands, or the revitalization of old ones (many of the utilities privatized since the 1980s have undergone a similar reformulation of their brand identity). Typically it involves the use of specialist firms, the computer generation of names, and their screening for connotational problems in different language contexts and for trade mark registrability (Hart, 1998: 38–9; Fogg, 1998: 74, notes that "the trade mark registers are becoming increasingly crowded, making it more and more difficult to find attractive and appropriate trade marks which are legally available"). Either by the choice of "poetic" signifiers ("lucent," "dawn," "mist," "apple") or by that process of semantic autonomization by which the semiotic work of advertising transforms descriptive or nonsense words into connotationally rich and referentially poor proper names, the brand name is so structured as to designate a rich singularity, coherent, simple, and integral, which evokes a world of beauty, harmony, energy, clarity, desire, freedom, precision . . . anything except a world of profit calculations and revenue streams. Brand identity – the complex of name, image, and slogan – forms a semantic matrix which is to a large degree autonomous both of the products it subsumes and of the corporation which owns and controls it. Its "imaginary significance" (Kapferer, 1992: 79) can thus be advertised independently of particular products: Kapferer cites the example of Nashua, whose advertising in Europe makes almost no reference to photocopiers, focusing instead on the imaginary qualities associated with its Native American name and image; banks similarly tend to prefer non-referential brand

campaigns because "as service companies, they have nothing to show.
They can only point to their values and identity in symbolic terms"
(ibid: 81).

Two further aspects of brand identity are relevant here. The first is
that many commentators think of brands as having or forming a "personality." Morgan (1986: 11) writes that in the years between the world
wars "the commercial symbols became the public faces or personalities of the products and companies they represented"; for Casson (1994:
50), "the most important motivation for branding . . . is that it imbues
products with cultural characteristics. Giving the product a name makes
it possible to think of a 'personality' that goes with that name"; and
for Haigh (1998: 8), "brands have personalities in their own right,
whereas commodities do not." This personalization of the brand may
be reinforced by the use of brand "characters" (Johnny Walker, Ronald
McDonald) or by celebrity endorsement. The second aspect is that
brands and brand advertising seek, by means of the specular circular-
ity of applied market research, to invoke a *recognition*-effect in consumers: in Kapferer's words (1992: 2), whereas "a product's price
measures its monetary value . . . its brand identifies the product and
reveals the facets of its differences: functional value, pleasure value, and
symbolic value *as a reflection of the buyer's self-image*" (my italics). This
matrix of values thus forms an Imaginary, in the sense that it projects
an identity which, reflecting neither the product nor the parent corporation, is modeled on the effect of unity of a person, and provokes
a mirroring identification with the brand on the part of the consumers
of the brand image. Michael Jordan and Tiger Woods wear the Nike
insignia in an act of embodied identification with the brand; kids
throughout the world wear the insignia in an identification with that
embodied identification. In Laplanche and Pontalis's (1973: 210) precise
definition, the brand Imaginary "is characterized by the prevalence of
the relation to the image of the counterpart (*le semblable*)"; it is that
process of imaginary identification which is the source of the brand's
"non-rational hold over the buying behavior of the consumer."

If Tiger Woods and Michael Jordan are components of the Nike
brand, however, they are also brands in their own right: image properties which are carefully managed to control the consistency and
integrity of the mark which they have become. This process of branding is constitutive both of the living and of the dead celebrity: image
and emblematics are typically managed by an agent or marketing

corporation and by licensing and franchising agreements, and the integrity of the mark is defended by legal action and by evolving legal doctrines such as the right of publicity which in the United States protects the marketable persona of the public celebrity (Gaines, 1991). One of the most powerful dead-celebrity brands, the "Diana, Princess of Wales" brand, despite being refused trade mark registration has developed brand extensions and distribution outlets (supermarkets for Flora margarine, the Post Office for stamps and lottery scratch cards) with greater reach than the memorabilia shops which are the usual outlets for such brands, making it imperative, as White and Lomax (1999) write, to defend the brand against the ever-present risk of contamination or dilution.

The star and celebrity systems set a pattern (one that ultimately derives, however, from the signature system) for the culture industry as a whole, increasingly organized, as Lury (1993: 62) argues, "in terms of a regime of rights characterized by branding, in which the manipulation of innovation as novelty is subsumed within the more general phenomenon of the simulation of innovation." The process analyzed by Gaines (1991: 143–74) in which Hollywood stars began in the postwar period to take control of the marketing and exploitation of their own image is now widely practiced by the celebrity figures of high culture. In the world of publishing this process of personal corporatization is marked in particular by the enhanced power of the literary agent in brokering multiple-book contracts which specify such features as length and target audience, as well as in negotiating secondary rights for film adaptation, translation, and so on. Books by the small number of established or emergent celebrity authors are the subject of intensive advertising and promotional campaigns which centrally involve the marketing of the persona of the author in chat and talkback shows, book-signings, festival appearances, and literary lunches; their effect in creating "barriers to competition" is manifested in the ability of branded authors to gain prominent bookshop display space and space in the extended apparatus of literary publicity which now, as in the star system, stretches the author's name across different media (which may be owned by the same conglomerate; cf. Moran, 2000: 38–9). The phenomenon of branding is particularly evident in the case of dead canonical authors, where the integration of received texts into the aesthetic horizon of the present transforms them, as Jauss (1982: 25–6) observes, into kitsch: that is, into precisely the state of continuous

quality assurance that defines the successful brand. Similarly in the art
world, the gallery and auction systems by which reputations are fostered, managed, and marketed have helped develop that "taxonomic"
status of the proper name that transforms it from a certification of
originality into a guarantee of the consistency, quality, and market value
of an *oeuvre* and a distinctive "style." The fact of reproducibility now
comes to function, not as a threat to the auratic value of the singular
work of art, but precisely as its guarantee: the museum or gallery shop,
with its posters, postcards, T-shirts, scarves, and facsimiles testifies in repetition to the power of the solitary masterpiece.

At the same time, as I suggested earlier, there has been a convergence in recent years between the mass-marketing of high-cultural
rarity and the aestheticization (rarefication) of certain forms of popular
or commercial culture. The signature is now an established part of the
fashion industry and of many areas of industrial design – of cars, of
perfumes and cosmetics, of sporting equipment, even of food. Car
designers work within the "styling canons" of the marque (I found this
term on the Alfa Romeo website); Ralph Lauren "signs" both his
upmarket Polo range and his downmarket Chaps range. The designer's
name moves in a continuous flow between the one-off *griffe* and the
signature brand: Yves Saint Laurent, says Kapferer (1992: 30), "is a *griffe*
when he signs his *haute couture* dresses; his name becomes a brand when
applied to lipstick, ready-to-wear clothing, or perfume." Marks &
Spencer's design shop, selling clothing in strictly limited production runs, was called Autograph, but the "autograph" was that of the
design shop itself: a signature without a person attached to it, the *idea*
of signature rather than its actuality. Celebrity chefs, released from
the kitchen to the television program, the celebrity endorsement, the
cooking school, have become artists displaying a "dedication to the
integrity of their art" and producing "signature recipes" (Zahler, 1996:
xi). And advertising has come to think of itself as an avant-garde, its
"creatives" empowered by an aesthetic of "disruption" of conventions
and norms (Dru, 1996).

What does this convergence between the signature and the brand
mean, and what can it tell us about the nature of contemporary cultural production? Both the aesthetics of the signature and the aesthetics of the brand are ideologies; they are regimes of marketing and
authorization which draw in rather similar ways on an imaginary of
the unique person or of personality; brands have a "personality" because

they make use of strategies of personalization (the use of characters, celebrities, direct address) to create something like a signature-effect; signatures stand as metonyms of an originating author or artist, even though the making of any work of art involves an extended number of participants (editors, publishers, proofreaders, printers, paintmakers, curators . . .) and a complex commercial apparatus. Where the brand most significantly differs from the signature is in its more intensive management of the integrity of the brand, and in its use of the intensive semiotic work of advertising and publicity to regulate market demand. This is to say that branding represents a more advanced stage of the rationalized vertical organization of the culture industry, attempting to subject every aspect of production and distribution to calculation and quality control. The deployment of a signature-effect for commercial goods represents a qualification or an addition to the strategy of market saturation which has typically characterized the distribution of mass-produced commodities; post-Fordist marketing concentrates on the development of niche markets, and the use of signature-effects is no more than a way of targeting those niche consumers whose wealth is already indexed in their consumption of "high" art. At the same time – and this is the point of convergence – high art has become entirely a component of large-scale industrial production; no longer a craft, it finds its place as a niche market amongst others in the world of mass production (for a more extended discussion, cf. Frow, 1995). To say this is not to say anything one way or the other about the quality or value of work produced at this point of convergence; it is only to say that it is no longer possible in good faith to oppose an "authentic" aesthetics of the signature to a "commercialized" aesthetics of the brand.

Signature and brand name are shifters, markers of the edge between the aesthetic space of an image or text and the institutional space of a regime of value which frames and organizes aesthetic space. Both are structured by the paradox that Derrida (1988) defines as the iterability of the mark: signature and proper name at once designate a singularity (the uniqueness of the writing of my name, the difference of the brand and its products from all others in the field) and yet can function, can be recognized, only insofar as they can be repeated; seriality is the condition of existence of the singular mark. These two disjunct planes – of aesthetic and institutional space, and of singularity and iteration – converge in a further paradox elaborated in intellectual property law: that "the romantic idea of originality and singularity is the very foothold for the concept of property" (Gaines, 1991: 222). The dual economies of value that underpin all cultural production (Smith, 1988) may exist in tension, and their disjunction is the rationale for the privileged status of "high" art in its self-understanding as a disinterested culture unaffected by market pressure. But the historical logic of the brand was always already implicit in the aesthetics of the signature.

Note

I have drawn here in part, and with permission, on an earlier essay, "The Signature: Three Arguments About the Commodity Form," in Grace (1996: 151–200).

References

Aaker, D. A. (1991). *Managing Brand Equity: Capitalizing on the Value of a Brand Name.* New York: Free Press.

Attali, J. (1985). *Noise: The Political Economy of Music*, trans. B. Massumi. Minneapolis: University of Minnesota Press.

Ball v. United Artists Corporation (1961). 214 N.Y.S. 2d, 219–29.

Baudrillard, J. (1988). "Model and Series." *Art Monthly*, January, 4–7.

Casson, M. (1994). "Economic Ideology and Consumer Society." In G. Jones and N. J. Morgan, eds., *Adding Value: Brands and Marketing in Food and Drink*, London: Routledge, 41–58.

Davis, J. and Stack, M. (1992). "Knowledge in Production," *Race and Class*, 34, 1–13.

Derrida, J. (1988). *Limited Inc.* Evanston, IL: Northwestern University Press.

DiMaggio, P. (1987). "Classification in Art," *American Sociological Review*, 52, 440–55.

Dreyfuss, R. C. (1991). "Expressive Genericity: Trademarks as Language in the Pepsi Generation," *Intellectual Property Law Review*, 297–324.

Dru, J.-M. (1996). *Disruption: Overturning Conventions and Shaking Up the Marketplace.* New York: John Wiley.

Edelman, B. (1979). *Ownership of the Image: Elements for a Marxist Theory of Law*, trans. E. Kingdom. London: Routledge and Kegan Paul.

Fogg, J. (1998). "Brands as Intellectual Property." In S. Hart and J. Murphy, eds., *Brands: The New Wealth Creators*, London: Macmillan, 72–81.

Franklin, S., Lury, C., and Stacey, J. (2000). *Global Nature, Global Culture*. London: Sage.

Frow, J. (1995). *Cultural Studies and Cultural Value*. Oxford: Clarendon Press.

Gaines, J. (1991). *Contested Culture: The Image, the Voice, and the Law*. Chapel Hill: University of North Carolina Press.

Gandelman, C. (1985). "The Semiotics of Signatures in Painting: A Peircian Analysis," *American Journal of Semiotics*, 3, 73–108.

Grace, H. (ed.) (1996). *Aesthesia and the Economy of the Senses*. Nepean: University of Western Sydney.

Grassl, W. (1999). "The Reality of Brands: Towards an Ontology of Marketing," *American Journal of Economics and Sociology*, 58, 313–59.

Haigh, D. (1998). *Brand Valuation: Understanding, Exploiting and Communicating Brand Values*. London: Financial Times Retail and Consumer.

Hart, S. (1998). "Developing New Brand Names." In S. Hart and J. Murphy, eds., *Brands: The New Wealth Creators*, London: Macmillan, 34–45.

Jaszi, P. (1991). "Toward a Theory of Copyright: The Metamorphoses of 'Authorship,'" *Duke Law Journal*, 455–502.

Jauss, H. R. (1982). *Toward an Aesthetic of Reception*, trans. T. Bahti. Minneapolis: University of Minnesota Press.

Kapferer, J.-N. (1992). *Strategic Brand Management: New Approaches to Creating and Evaluating Brand Equity*, trans. P. Gibbs. New York: Free Press.

Krauss, R. (1988). *The Originality of the Avant-garde and Other Modernist Myths*. Cambridge, MA: MIT Press.

Laplanche, J. and Pontalis, J.-B. (1973). *The Language of Psycho-analysis*, trans. D. Nicholson-Smith. London: Hogarth Press.

Lash, S. and Urry, J. (1994). *Economies of Signs and Space*. London: Sage.

Lebensztejn, J.-C. (1974). "Esquisse d'une typologie," *La Revue de l'art*, 26, 48–56.

Lury, C. (1993). *Cultural Rights: Technology, Legality and Personality*. London: Routledge.

Melot, Michel (1986). "La notion d'originalité et son importance dans la définition des objets d'art." In R. Moulin, ed., *Sociologies de l'art*, Paris: La Documentation Française.

Merryman, J. H. and Elsen, A. (1987). *Law, Ethics, and the Visual Arts*. Philadelphia: University of Pennsylvania Press.

Moran, Joe (2000). *Star Authors: Literary Celebrity in America*. London: Pluto Press.

Morgan, H. (1986). *Symbols of America*. New York: Penguin Books.

Ohmann, R. (1996). *Selling Culture: Magazines, Markets, and Class at the Turn of the Century*. London: Verso.

Schmitt, B. and Simonson, A. (1997). *Marketing Aesthetics: The Strategic Management of Brands, Identity, and Image*. New York: Free Press.

Shaughnessy, R. J. (1987). "Trademark Parody: A Fair Use and First Amendment Analysis," *Intellectual Property Law Review*, 263–301.

Smith, B. H. (1988). *Contingencies of Value: Alternative Perspectives for Critical Theory*. Cambridge, MA: Harvard University Press.

Tait, T. (2000). Review of M. Ondaatje, *Anil's Ghost*, *London Review of Books*, July 20, 39–40.

Voortman, J. J. (1991). "Trademark Licensing of Names, Insignia, Characters and Designs: The Current Status of the *Boston Pro Hockey* per se Infringement Rule," *Intellectual Property Law Review*, 357–91.

Watson, P. (1992). *From Manet to Manhattan: The Rise of the Modern Art Market*. New York: Vintage.

John Frow

White, A. and Lomax, W. (1999). *The Boundaries of the Diana Brand: Consumers' Evaluations of Potential Extensions*. Kingston Business School Occasional Papers Series 37. Kingston: Kingston University.

Wilkins, M. (1994). "When and Why Brand Names in Food and Drink." In G. Jones and N. J. Morgan, eds., *Adding Value: Brands and Marketing in Food and Drink*, London: Routledge, 15–40.

Zahler, K. G. (1996). *Superchefs: Signature Recipes from America's New Royalty*. New York: John Wiley.

3

From Brahmin Julia to Working-Class Emeril: The Evolution of Television Cooking

Toby Miller

In the early 1960s, National Educational Television (NET) initially rejected a Boston-based culinary program hosted by a woman named Julia Child. The rationale was that the cooking show was an outdated format from the 1950s. Child was picked up by a regional outfit called the Eastern Educational Network, which was her eventual platform for international fame and fortune. (Ledbetter, 1998: 89)

In her voice — "to-mah-toe," "herbs" with a hard "h" — you hear the patrician New England ancestry, the Smith education, the dozen years spent living abroad. In her manner, you see at heart a California girl, raised in Pasadena, supremely unselfconscious. Drop a fish in your kitchen, and "Whoooo is going to know?" (Cyr, 2000: 40)

People lined up at 6 a.m. to get seats — on a Saturday morning, no less. Inside, the 2,000-person crowd jumped to its feet, cheering and clapping in unison as the music keyed up and an announcer shouted, Let's get ready to rumble. . . . [W]hooping fans were assembled for the taping of a show by Emeril Legasse, a gourmet master chef with blue-collar appeal who has turned the Food Network into Must See TV. Once a 24-hour outlet for Julia Child reruns, the cable channel has become eye-candy for food voyeurs who watch more for entertainment than cooking advice. (Brown, 1999: n.p.)

Yearning for ancient Greece, Michel Foucault once regretfully remarked that the measure of people had shifted since that time from how they managed food to how they managed sex (Foucault, 1997: 253, 259). But assumptions about peoples' subjectivity based on the food they consume continue to be extreme and common. Research on public opinion in the US shows vegetarians are thought to eat broccoli, quiche, brown rice, bean sprouts, and avocado sandwiches; assume anti-war and pro-drugs positions; and drive imported cars (the equivalent nineteenth-century belief was that vegetarianism quelled masturbation). Gourmets, by contrast, are expected to favor caviar, oysters, and French-roast coffee and are regarded as liberal, drug-taking sophisticates. Fast- or synthetic-food eaters are found to be religious, conservative, and liable to wear polyester (Fine and Leopold, 1993: 169, 187; Falk, 1994: 68–70). Now *you* know, too.

There are clear hierarchies implicit in these categorizations. They map a self-styling of cultural politics and personal display onto diet. In each case, the implication is that particular class fractions signify powerfully through what they put in their mouths. Put simply, food's "you are what you eat" tag is a quick, if fallible, classificatory system. When added to television, another device that is used to categorize hierarchically, the combination is powerful. It is also subject to change.

Pierre Bourdieu lists two "paradoxes of the taste of necessity" that captured food's traditional high–low dynamic:

> Some simply sweep it aside, making practice a direct product of economic necessity (workers eat beans because they cannot afford anything else), failing to realize that necessity can only be fulfilled . . . because the agents are inclined to fulfil it. . . . Others turn it into a taste of freedom, forgetting the conditionings of which it is the product. . . . Taste is *amor fati*, the choice of destiny, but a forced choice. (Bourdieu, 1994: 178)

The clear class distinction between an apparently functional diet and a more aesthetic one may be not as neat today as when Bourdieu studied quotidian French tastes three decades ago. Since that time, cooking has become a daily part of television fare, nowadays with its own networks. Being on television brings democratization as surely as it brings commodification – the lifeworld may be compromised, but its pleasures are spread around a little, too. Raymond Oliver made this point three decades ago in his celebration of modern transportation and technology as articulators of cuisine across classes (Oliver, 1969: 7) – he might have added commodification to the list.

We can see the impact of these changes across the media, as per Robert Hanke's examination of the shifting discourse on food in the *Philadelphia Inquirer* and the *Philadelphia Magazine*. In the early 1960s the *Inquirer* ran recipe columns and advertisements related to home dining, with women as the exclusive targets. Functional aesthetics articulated with home economics: simplicity and thrift were called for, other than on special occasions. In the 1970s a special section appeared in the Sunday *Magazine* on places to go, dramatically displacing "Food and Family." The restaurant was now described as a public, commercial, and cultural site of urban sophistication, even attracting the ultimate 1970s fetish: investigative reporting. By the 1980s the Sunday food section included a wine guide, and food writers were dubbed "critics." They offered instruction on enjoyment rather than production (knowledge about, not knowledge of how). Aesthetics had displaced functionality. Taste was not taken for granted, but schooled. Equivalent networks of gossip emerged, along with guides on obtaining the best service in a restaurant. Approximately 25 percent of US newspapers added "Style" pages between 1979 and 1983, 38 percent of those with circulations of more than 100,000. Fairly rigorous distinctions are now drawn in such quarters between *dining* out (costly, occasioned, planned, and dressed for) and *eating* out (easy, standardized, and requiring minimal presentational effort): both are to do with styles of life as much as food consumption, and they are truly big business – grocery purchase and restaurant dining in the US amounts to US$709 billion a year (Hanke, 1989: 221–33; Finkelstein, 1989: 38; Fine and Leopold, 1993: 167; Comcast, 2000).

This chapter addresses the role of television in popularizing "sophisticated" international cuisine through case studies of Julia Child, who appeared on US public television from the 1960s, and the two main food television networks of the 1990s and the new century: the US Food Network and the UK Carlton Food Network. We shall see Anglo-speaking countries' cosmic ambivalence about French culture, an oscillation between contempt and admiration that has found televisual form in popularization and diversification. In the 1960s this means a scion of the US gentry rolling up her jolly-hockey-mistress sleeves and being ordinary on non-profit television. In the 1990s it means multicultural chefs blending world cuisines on a money-hungry, quasi-infotainment cable system. In the process, French food is demystified and rendered one amongst many forms of fine eating.

The trend towards media coverage of cuisine is accelerating away now. The year 1993 brought the TV Food Network to US cable as the idea of CNN's creator (The Week, 1993). Later in the decade we were treated to Carlton's satellite food network on British television. One of its globally exported game shows addresses women audiences (the commercials are mainly for women's health and beauty culture), stressing that the presentational norms promoted apply equally to professional chefs, hosts entertaining, or the solitary but discriminating home cook. The common theme was that food could be fun. (The common *requirement* for programs to be included on the channel was that they be paid for in full by food companies.) By the late 1990s this premium on fun saw the US Food Network featuring Al Roker and other mainstream television personalities, thanks to an annual programming budget of over US$40 million (Food Network Switches, 1999; Food Network Gets, 1999).

This legacy of proving that preparing food can be pleasurable has two antecedents. The first, and most important, is a sexual division of labor that has required women to undertake unpaid domestic tasks on behalf of others. The second is the unattainability of perfectly prepared fine food, the sense that one can never get it right, but that the search is an asymptotic, autotelic pleasure of its own. Distinctions between ordinary fare and fine cuisine are central to this second antecedent.

Buried within that issue lies the popularization of international cooking. Has this led to a democratization, whereby anyone can make, for instance, a "good" French meal, with all its trappings of Eurocentric "quality" discourse? Or has this popularization seen even more cultural capital invested in French food? Of course, there is a powerful egalitarian lineage to French food as well as an elitist one: restaurants were first named as such in France in 1825 and rapidly became sites for democratizing knowledge of different foodstuffs and preparations, as well as spreading notions of correct conduct across societies, beyond the ruling classes (Finkelstein, 1989: 34–6, 46). Could television be the latest technology to share the joy?

Perhaps, but at the same time the spread of television food across the world also indicates the ambiguous place of the US and the UK in global popular culture. The English language offers a version of modernity that many people want, but sometimes at the cost of what makes them a people. In 1999 the new Philippines Lifestyle Network began on cable, with four hours of programming each day coming from the US Food Network (Scripps, 1999), and the old colonial empires stand ready to send out "correct" forms of cuisine to the very areas they had come to govern a century ago, at the same time attaining "alternative" coverage in *Rolling Stone* magazine (Bozza, 1999).

More and more countries over the late 1980s and 1990s imported cuisines from around the globe. Needless to say, customers are not told of the complex economics and politics behind their purchase, as the food is radically disaffiliated from its conditions of production and circulation. Instead, consumers are given a spice of difference to do with the geographic origin of items on the menu, an enchanting quality to what is on offer: tourism in a bowl, as per the Beefeater chain adding South Asian, Mexican, Cajun, and Thai food to its traditional fare under the slogan "Discover the world and eat it" (Fine and Leopold, 1993: 151–2; Cook and Crang, 1996: 132, 144).

In this sense, television food replicates the structure of dominance that characterizes the global political economy of food. Large multinational corporations increasingly control agricultural industries, and farm incomes and working conditions have been subordinated in public discourse to health issues and specialist consumer niches (Friedmann, 1995: 512). One area where activism has been strong and populist – but so has consumption – is that model of dietetic madness and worker exploitation, fast food. The first such franchises began in the US in the 1950s, in response to rising labor costs. The industry decided that reducing the workforce to a strict roster of required hours, transferring labor to the customer, introducing plastic and paper products, and dismissing supermarket purchasing in favor of institutionalized pre-preparation (processed, sliced cheese and individual packages of ketchup) were surefire means of reducing expenditure (Reiter, 1996: 43). In short, the industry was born from, and is sustained by, casual labor and environmental degradation. It is a service-industry model of exploited workers and despoliated space.

But something else is signified on a superstructural level that cloaks these conditions of existence. Sensational expectations were engendered amongst Russian and Chinese shoppers in the 1990s when the first McDonald's opened there: within a quarter of an hour, Moscow teenagers offered to break through the lines to buy hamburgers, and on opening day in Beijing, 40,000 customers were served. A little sad, when you consider the hamburger was invented in the Baltic states, taken up by German sailors on return to Hamburg, and then

popularized in the US by mid-Western migrants as a European deli-
cacy. Today, its international popularity is a symbolic connection to the
US, modernity, and efficiency as much as it is to do with global domination, especially for those used to state socialism: McDonald's used
to offer customers a game where players were given a multiple-choice
test about the composition and size of, for example, the Berlin Wall.
For the French, a globalizing food culture has worked both ways. Fast
food is still new there. Comprising about 5 percent of the restaurant
business, it has been growing rapidly since the late 1980s. The advent
of McDonald's has witnessed a series of transformations. In the 1970s
eating at a chain was considered *chic*: the intelligentsia frequented the
few outlets, and fashion shows associated themselves with hamburger
stands. But by 1989 this otherness had become ordinary fare. French
fast-food chains had started, naming themselves France-Quick, Free-
Time, Magic Burger, B'burger, Manhattan Burger, Katy's Burger, Love
Burger, and Kiss Burger. Half the industry sounded American, and the
very national language seemed under threat. The government re-
sponded by creating a National Council of Culinary Art within the
Ministry of Culture, dedicated to "protecting the culinary patrimony"
from fast food and other stresses (Ritzer, 1993: 2–3; Fantasia, 1995: 230,
202–3, 213, 224, 205–7; Rensi, 1995: xii; Stephenson, 1989: 230). This
fast-food complex is both promoted on, and designed for, a television
world.

Beginnings

Television and food had a totally functional start: frozen dinners were
first marketed in the US in 1953 as a meal to be had in front of the
television or in an emergency. Preparation of food was minimized at
times of leisure and crisis (Beardsworth and Keil, 1990: 142; Mintz,
1993: 51). But this changed a decade later via Julia Child.

    Child brokered French cuisine to the North American WASP pop-
ulation. The A&E Cable network's video *Biography*, entitled *An Appetite
for Life*, describes her as "a national icon" and her *French Chef* series as
"a new French Revolution . . . televised." Before the start of public
television across the country, her show was syndicated by Boston's
WGBH in 1963 through NET (it started at almost the same moment
as Raymond Oliver's recipe program began in France). From the first,

Child was also central to public television's commodification – noted San Francisco station KQED sold her cooking knives that year as its first membership gifts. The series itself was underwritten by Polaroid. Like her book *Mastering the Art of French Cooking*, which was also on sale, Child's avowed intent was to illustrate that "cooking was not a chore but an art." Commercialism lay at the heart of this – her first appearance was an attempt to promote sales of the book, and producers then decided she was the person to build a program around. Starting in 1962 with pilots, she made 119 episodes of *The French Chef*. With national distribution in 1964, the coming of (putatively) non-commercial television to the American scene was signaled by Julia Child as much as anyone else. In recognition of the fact, she won a Peabody Award in 1965 and made the cover of *Time* the following year. *Newsweek* said she was "helping to turn Boston, the home of the bean and the cod, into the home of the brie and the coq." By the mid-1960s KQED was receiving 20,000 letters a week about the show. It was produced in color from 1970, when PBS also began national distribution. Other series followed across the next three decades: *Julia Child and Company, Julia Child and More Company, Dinner at Julia's, Cooking with Master Chefs, In Julia's Kitchen with Master Chefs, Baking with Julia, Cooking in Concert* pledge-drive specials, and *Julia Child & Jacques Pépin: Cooking at Home* (Stewart, 1999: 42, 61, 130–1, 133, 138–9). Child remains part of PBS branding today, a key signifier of the network and its alleged superiority to and separateness from commercial television (Baker and Dessart, 1998: 243).

The ontology of immediacy that live television can offer was clearly in evidence on the first shows. At that time, programs were rehearsed then shot in a single take onto kinescopes. Editing was virtually impossible. Child's manifold errors on camera, such as flipping an omelet or pancake onto the stove then putting it back in the pan, or slapping her hip to identify the loin for Steak Diane *aficionados*, served to make a virtue of low production values, adding a dollop of authenticity and approachability to television. "Mistakes" and eccentricities hid the fact that she spent 19 hours preparing for each program and relied on a large team of unpaid workers behind the scenes, just as the wine bottles on display, though generally filled with non-alcoholic beverages, testified to her jolly attitude, courtesy of their imagined contents (Stewart, 1999: 131; Cooper, 2000). The image stood in some contrast to the Puritanism of much US society and became a winning point with many viewers, reinforcing a casual air that mystified the Tayloristic managerial devices underpinning her performances. She offered tips on hosting a party as well as preparing food, so that viewers could become accomplished hostesses. The context was a widespread American loathing of supposed Gallic indolence blended with a paradoxical admiration for that lifestyle, and a hatred of big government mixed with inferiority alongside national cultural institutions. This was apparent in the fetishized attitude to French food. Something odd, foreign, but somehow better, needed an introduction from a Child-like figure, suitably ensconced in the allegedly Anglo-Celtic Boston, to be acceptable. French food was brokered into ordinariness by the white ruling class – so ordinary that Child qualified for parody on *Saturday Night Live*.

She fitted the bill of what ethnomethodologists refer to as the "personalized stranger," a figure known through media coverage of the details of his or her private life rather than through direct human interaction, but taken by the public to be someone they know at a quite intimate level – not in terms of secrets, but someone with whom diurnal interaction is taken for granted (Watson, 1973: 16, 19, n. 19). In Child's case, this humanized her, clouding the financial imperatives underpinning the program – book sales and commercial underwriting.

This critique does not deny the importance to many viewers of her symbolism. Consider this, from one of my informants:

> There were times, as a desperate young mother living in a provincial town, when I felt that all that stood between me and insanity was hearty Julia Child – cooing at that pink pig in her arms – ready for roasting, demonstrating the art of cooking with dry Vermouth, assuring me that there were places fragrant with herbs and full of deep and pleasurable knowledge, and that anyone who wanted to could participate. Me – at the ironing board at 10.00 pm – imagining myself in those better places (I guess she was like a bedtime story!).

This is evocative prose indeed. It speaks to the paucity of credibly real women on television at the time (the 1960s), the medium's minimal address of women's concerns, and the sense of access that Child offered. This was an access to secular transcendence, and it predated the advent of second-wave feminisms.

The PBS archives hold her recipes from those days, plainly typed lists and instructions that were mailed out on demand. Her braised salmon offering from program number 302 promises that this is "not nearly the *tour de force* that it sounds." The sentence ends with French-language *bravura*, a high note of achievement. But it begins with a careful Anglo adverbial qualifier, a sensible prefix to Gallic style. In the famous program number 261 – The Omelet Show – she avows that viewers require "a devil-may-care attitude for those that may fall on the stove or onto the floor."

In Britain, the key 1970s television chef, Delia Smith, customized French dishes, renationing them for her audience by substituting ingredients to make the food more accessible to Anglo viewers. This was also a speciality of Graham Kerr, a queer-acting but avowedly straight ex-New Zealand air-force officer (originally from the UK) whose fey and seemingly drunk rushes around the set were famous in the US, Australia, and Britain from the early 1970s. Many of my informants recalled him as the first flamboyant man they saw live on television, a sort of culinary Paul Lynd. This queer component to the genre was highlighted when Montréal's main celebrity television chef, Daniel Pinard, came out as gay on New Year's Eve 2000 – regarded by many as a key moment in mainstreaming because of his cultural stature between convention and innovation (Brooke, 2000).

Another key figure was Paul Bocuse, whose French cuisine went onto Australia's multicultural station SBS in the 1980s and into the Federal Republic of Germany alongside Max Enzinger's *Trimm Dich* (*Get Fit*), which introduced nouvelle cuisine there.

Of course, discounts often apply to such cultural exchanges. An ambiguity in the British reaction to French food is nicely exemplified in two television anecdotes. On a 1990 episode of the British talk show *That's Life*, the studio audience was fed some snails, unaware of what they were eating. Once told, their faces distorted into English versions of barnyard animals and they sought to vomit up the remains. Consider also this 1989 commercial for pre-cooked sausages ready for microwave preparation: a yuppie white man is taking advantage of his health-conscious wife's temporary absence to eat some "bangers." His conspiratorial gaze at the viewer concludes with a satisfied "Now that's what I call nouvelle cuisine" (Fiddes, 1991: 33, 97). In the mid-1990s there was some controversy on British television over white presenters Keith Floyd and Robert Carrier fronting the travelogue-tour-series *Floyd on Africa* and *Carrier's Caribbean*, programs that touched on Francophone and Anglophone colonial traditions insensitively. *Far Flung*

Floyd took him to the "Far East" and offering the following to reporters: "We'll have wonderful fun, you know. There are wonderful curries and rice dishes. We can go fishing, we can go into the jungle, we can even eat coconut milk" (Beattie, Khan, and Philo, 1999: 153; Floyd quoted in Strange, 1998: 305).

This blend of the high and low promised a meeting, of course, at a place called midcult. Which is where we greet the new media technologies and deregulatory policies of the last two decades. Their conditions of possibility and operation both draw on the existence of midcult and problematize it. Their niche audiences are also and equally cross-class and cross-racial in their composition. Food television normalizes the exotic for suburbia and exoticizes the normal for a hip *elite*, middle-class homeworkers, and late-night revelers.

Cable and Satellite

Child's equivalent and collaborator in the 1990s is Jacques Pépin, but the notion of the television chef as a role model for women is *passé*. Pépin, French himself, uses his daughter, a Franco-American, as a naive inquirer, the viewer brought onto the set for participant observation. As their book for PBS puts it: "Claudine sees her role as that of the voice of the people." His terpsichories and flights are domesticated by her asking "Can I freeze it?" The book concludes with a paean to the "generous corporate citizens" that underwrite the show. Or rather it doesn't quite end there: on the reverse page there are color advertisements for the products vended by these "citizens" (Pépin, 1996: xviii, 267–8). Pépin is also a United Airlines "Celebrity Chef," complete with the corporation's ringing endorsement of him as a "classically trained native of France" fit to design meals (for First and Business Class – those in steerage must duel with unauthored dross) (Porterfield, 1999). United colors its front-of-house flight menus with quotations from Virginia Woolf and claims that its food comes from "a lifetime of discipline," as per "the collected works of say, O'Keeffe, Bach or Dickinson."

On the avowedly commercial Food Network, Pépin's rough-and-ready Fall River equivalent is Emeril Lagasse, complete with his doctorate from the Johnson and Wales University culinary program (specializing in French food). Lagasse can be heard on television recommending what he calls "Hallapeenose [jalapeños]," featuring grotesque celebrities *manqués* like Sammy Hagar, and doing network promos at the Super Bowl (*Emeril's Tailgating Jam*). His line of cooking technology is called Emerilware (New, 1999; Food Network, 1999; Cooper, 2000). Crass working-class credentialism displaces a blue-blood's slapdash shamateur excellence.

Lagasse provides the Food Network's top ratings. When it offered free tickets to a live taping in the fall of 1997, 50,000 people telephoned in 22 minutes (Brown, 1999; Brooker, 1998). As of late 1999, the Network was available in 43 million US households (up from 30 million in 1998) and due to reach 50 million by 2001, as well as being on-air in Japan, Canada, and Australia. Despite some multiculturalism and increasingly broad programming, French cuisine is one of its default settings (Scripps Networks, 1999; Scripps October, 1999). US audience growth has been steady. From the 1997–8 to 1998–9 seasons, numbers increased from 170,000 to 230,000 among 18–34 year-olds and from 450,000 to 670,000 among 18–49 year-olds. Spectators were mostly working women, with an average age of 44 and household income of US$53,900, the third largest for audiences to basic cable. The overall numbers were up 50 percent and advertising revenue had grown by 80 percent to $36 million, while regional websites across the US were planned. Foodtv.com promoted itself to advertisers as "today's leading food portal," describing its audience as "upscale and connected." The corollary numbers in Britain for Carlton TV suggest predominantly female viewers, aged 35–54 (Univision, 1999; Food Network Gets, 1999; Comcast, 2000; Cable's 1997). Popularization was underway, far beyond the crypto-commodified, quasi-bake-drive-funded, kindness-of-strangers ghetto of PBS.

With the establishment of Britain's Carlton Food Network on cable and digital satellite (the only such service in Europe) and its 1999 expansion to 300,000 multi-choice cable homes in sub-Saharan Africa, this cross-cultural component became all the more significant. Unlike earlier broadcast television in Britain, which had privileged French and some South Asian cuisine, the new genre network had to be all-encompassing. French recipes are far from dominant in the programming philosophy of the station, although Bruno Loubet hosts *Chez Bruno* and *Antony's Morocco* features Francophone foods (Carlton).

Channel Four offers *TV Dinners*, including tales of a 12-year-old Irish scout troop leader who prepares French sauces for her colleagues, all cooked outdoors.

Clearly, food television has taken a globalizing, commercial turn that mines the past even as it invents the present. A multicultural, but very French-inflected US Food Network show recently emerged – Ming Tsai's *East Meets West with Ming Tsai*. Looking "like a self-improvement infomercial, or maybe a Visa ad," it quickly won a daytime Emmy (Schillinger, 1999, p. 60). The network's high-rating Japanese import, *The Iron Chef* (*Ryori no Tetsujin*, literally *Cooking Iron Man*), featured one of Robert De Niro's restaurant employees in regular contests with other celebrities to produce the best Chinese, French, Japanese, and Italian meals. Shot "as if it were a sporting event [with] chefs as gladiators, doing battle before a rich and demonic lord," in the words of production executives at Fuji Television, it began in Japan in 1993 and now airs in the US via a mix of subtitles, dubbing, and the original language – not to mention the theme music from *The Hunt for Red October* (Struck, 1999; executives quoted in *Iron*, 2000). Audiences of displaced hipsters, lost in nameless mid-Western graduate schools, would lay down their Latour long enough to hold cook-offs each Sunday night in emulation of this feral television show, whose protagonist refused to be dubbed into English.

At the same time, vintner Robert Mondavi's American Center for Wine, Food and the Arts in the Napa Valley was announcing "Julia's Kitchen" as a cornerstone, and viewers of Carlton can use its interactive advertising platform to click on banners during cooking shows and gain brand information, recipes, not to mention the chance to fly for free to Morocco – while the Food Network proudly announces signing Wolfgang Puck for his first television series (Exhibition, 2000; Brech, 2000). The Brahmin and her corporate underwriters had been memorialized and displaced (onto off-peak reruns at any rate) by multicultural, commodified hosts. Julia Child, farewell.

Acknowledgments

Thanks for their aid to Barbara Abrash, Manuel Alvarado, Rebecca Barden, Sarah Berry, William Boddy, Elizabeth Botta, Edward Buscombe, Jim Collins, Robyn Donahue, Liz Ferrier, Sara Gwenllian-

Jones, John Hartley, Heather Hendershot, Mariana Johnson, Marie Leger, Eric Kit-Wai Ma, Anna McCarthy, Alec McHoul, Rick Maxwell, Silke Morgenroth, Laurie Ouellette, Dana Polan, Christie Slade, Marita Sturken, Allen Weiss, George Yúdice, Barbie Zelizer, and Vera Zolberg, informants and friendly critics. Thanks also to the audience at a May 2000 session of Consoling Passions.

References

Cable's Food Network to Launch Regional Web Sites (1997). *Media Daily*, 4, no. 5: n. p.

Exhibition Kitchen to be Named for Julia Child (2000). *Times Union Albany*, April 5.

Food Network Switches Menu (1999). *Chicago Sun-Times*, March 31: section 2 5XS.

Food Network Gets its Show on the Road (1999). *Electronic Media*, April 5: 4.

New York – Food Network's (1999). *Multichannel News*, July 12: 66.

Scripps Networks Programming to Air in Philippines (1999). *Business Wire*, July 21.

Scripps October Revenues Increase 8.7 Percent (1999). *PR Newswire*, November 8.

Univision Announces Record 1998–1999 Season and May Sweeps (1999). *Business Wire*, July 21.

The Week United States: Are We at 500 Channels Yet? (1993). *Time International*, May 17: 15.

Baker, William F. and Dessart, George (1998). *Down the Tube: An Inside Account of the Failure of American Television*. New York: Basic Books.

Beardsworth, Alan and Keil, Teresa (1990). "Putting the Menu on the Agenda," *Sociology*, 24: 1, 139–51.

Beattie, Liza, Khan, Furzana, and Philo, Greg (1999). "Race, Advertising and the Public Face of Television." In Greg Philo, ed., *Message Received: Glasgow Media Group Research 1993–1998*, Harlow: Longman, 149–70.

Bourdieu, Pierre (1994). *Distinction: A Social Critique of the Judgement of Taste*, trans. Richard Nice. Cambridge, MA: Harvard University Press.

Bozza, Anthony (1999). "The TV Program Pressure Cooker on the Food Network," *Rolling Stone*, February 18: 67.

Brech, Poppy (2000). "P&G Among the First to Use Carlton Interactive Service," ⟨*http://www.marketing.haynet.com/news/n000511/P&G_amon.html*⟩, May 10.

Brooke, James (2000). "Peppery Plea for Tolerance from a Chef in Montreal," *New York Times*, August 6: K9.

Brooker, Katrina (1998). "On the Food Network: Lust, Weirdos, Saturated Fat," *Fortune*, July 6: 34.

Brown, Jennifer (1999). "Food Network Audience Increases," *Associated Press Online*, March 26: n. p.

Carlton Food Network. ⟨*http://www.cfn.co.uk*⟩.

Carlton Food Network. TV to Tempt Your Tastebuds. ⟨*http://www.ntl.co.uk/adsales/channels/carltonfood.asp*⟩.

Comcast. ⟨http://www.comcastnow.com/networks/foodnetwork.htm⟩.

Cook, Ian and Crang, Philip (1996). "The World on a Plate: Culinary Culture, Displacement and Geographical Knowledge," *Journal of Material Culture*, 1: 2, 131–53.

Cooper, Gael Fashingbauer (2000). "In the Beginning, There was Julia," *Minneapolis Star Tribune*, October 5: 1T.

Cyr, Diane (2000). "A Matter of Good Taste," *US Airways Attaché*, May: 40, 42, 45.

Falk, Pasi (1994). *The Consuming Body*. London: Sage.

Fantasia, Rick (1995). "Fast Food in France," *Theory and Society*, 24: 2, 201–43.

Fiddes, Nick (1991). *Meat: A Natural Symbol*. London: Routledge.

Fine, Ben and Leopold, Ellen (1993). *The World of Consumption*. London: Routledge.

Finkelstein, Joanne (1989). *Dining Out: A Sociology of Modern Manners*. New York: New York University Press.

Food Network. ⟨http://www.foodtv.com⟩.

Foucault, Michel (1997). *Ethics: Subjectivity and Truth: The Essential Works of Foucault 1954–1984, Volume 1*, ed. Paul Rabinow, trans. Robert Hurley and others. New York: Free Press.

Friedmann, Harriet (1995). "The International Political Economy of Food: A Global Crisis," *International Journal of Health Services*, 25: 3, 511–38.

Hanke, Robert (1989). "Mass Media and Lifestyle Differentiation: An Analysis of the Public Discourse About Food," *Communication*, 11: 3, 221–38.

Iron Chef Compendium (2000). ⟨http:www.ironchef.com/about_show.shtml⟩.

Ledbetter, James (1998). *Made Possible By . . . : The Death of Public Broadcasting in the United States*. London: Verso.

Mintz, Sidney W. (1993). "Feeding, Eating, and Grazing: Some Speculations on Modern Food Habits," *Journal of Gastronomy*, 7: 1, 46–57.

Oliver, Raymond (1969). *La Cuisine: Secrets of Modern French Cooking*, trans. and ed. Nika Standen Hazelton with Jack van Bibber. New York: Tudor.

Pépin, Jacques (1996). *Jacques Pépin's Kitchen: Cooking with Claudine*. San Francisco: KQED Books & Tapes.

Porterfield, Jim (1999). "Pépin's Hands-On Cuisine," *Hemispheres*, October: 149.

Reiter, Ester (1996). *Making Fast Food: From the Frying Pan into the Fryer*, 2nd edn. Montréal: McGill-Queen's University Press.

Rensi, Edward H. (1995). Foreword. In Marjorie Eberts, Margaret Gisler, and Linda Brothers, eds., *Opportunities in Fast Food Careers*, Lincolnwood: VGM Career Horizons, xi–xiii.

Ritzer, George (1993). *The McDondaldization of Society: An Investigation into the Changing Character of Contemporary Social Life*. Thousand Oaks, CA: Pine Forge Press.

Schillinger, Liesl (1999). "Ming's Thing: How to Become a Celebrity Chef," *New Yorker*, November 15: 60–7.

Stephenson, Peter H. (1989). "Going to McDonald's in Leiden: Reflections on the Concept of Self and Society in the Netherlands," *Ethos*, 17: 2, 226–47.

Stewart, David (1999). *The PBS Companion: A History of Public Television*. New York: TV Books.

Strange, Niki (1998). "Perform, Educate, Entertain: Ingredients of the Cookery Programme Genre." In Christine Geraghty and David Lusted, eds., *The Television Studies Book*, London: Edward Arnold, 301–12.

Struck, Doug (1999). "Kamikaze Cook-Off," *TV Guide*, November 13: 32–3.

Watson, Rod (1973). "The Public Announcement of Fatality," *Working Papers in Cultural Studies*, 4: 5–20.

Further Reading

"Food: Nature and Culture" (1998). *Social Research*, 66: 1.

Beardsworth, Alan and Keil, Teresa (1997). *Sociology on the Menu: An Invitation to the Study of Food and Society*. London: Routledge.

Bell, David and Valentine, Gill (1997). *Consuming Geographies: We Are What We Eat*. London: Routledge.

Miller, Toby and McHoul, Alec (1998). *Popular Culture and Everyday Life*. London: Sage.

Mintz, Sidney W. (1996). *Tasting Food, Tasting Freedom*. Boston: Beacon Press.

4

"Tan"talizing Others: Multicultural Anxiety and the New Orientalism
Kim Middleton Meyer

As an archetype of contemporary ethnic literature, Amy Tan's *The Joy Luck Club* provides a model of success that spans previously isolated fields. In terms both critical and popular, in the academic as well as the mass market, the arrival of *The Joy Luck Club* marked the inception of a phenomenon in which fiction rich with details of a non-Western culture is perceived as a "good read" – on one level, worthy of inclusion in the canon of multicultural literature, and on another, an engaging tale that articulates the inner workings of a culture for the outsider. However, to explain the popularity of Tan's novel and the ethnic novels that follow in its wake as strictly bilateral elides the possibility of an emergent set of readers who are neither fully separate from, nor fully affiliated with an academic or mass culture. For this group, *The Joy Luck Club* is a good read not for its canon-potential nor for its narrative acrobatics, but rather for the kinds of information about Chinese culture that it offers, and for the value of this information in day-to-day interactions with others.

The immediate and massive popularity of *The Joy Luck Club* pointed to the existence of a previously undiscovered community that had yet to be mined for market share.[1] Since Tan's success, however, a highly efficient mechanism has developed in order to satisfy these readers anxious to acquire knowledge about non-Western cultures. To describe the workings of this mechanism requires a theoretical apparatus that takes into account more than just the textual underpinnings of a particular narrative world: here, Tony Bennett's notion of a "reading formation" expands the boundaries that constitute the novel's context:

> By a reading formation, I mean a set of discursive and intertextual deter-
> minations that organize and animate the practice of reading, connect-
> ing texts and readers in specific relations to one another by constituting
> readers as reading subjects of particular types and texts as objects-to-be-
> read in particular ways. (Bennett, 1985: 7)

With this understanding, novels are not the sole creators of their
context; on the contrary, these novels in a sense "create" the readers
who in turn value particular parts of the narratives – in turn recreat-
ing them. In the case of novels that follow the example of *The Joy Luck
Club*, however, this two-sided reading formation itself must be
expanded to include a third term: the contextual work done by the
publisher and the concurrent construction and conditioning of the
reading group.

The search for an arche in reading group culture produces only
vertigo; does the book create the publisher's marketing which in turn
conditions readers? Or does the publisher look for a certain kind of
novel that has proven to attract readers and hence markets these texts
toward them? A chicken and egg phenomenon, to be sure. Regardless
of origin, reading groups, who, we will see, pride themselves on their
special relationship with texts that are neither academic nor have a
mass affinity, have adopted Anglo American-produced fiction about
Asian ethnicity as a primary term in their milieu. Theorizing systems
of value like the reading group, John Frow describes the production of
"evaluative regularities" (Frow, 1995: 144) for different formations – in
this case, the "insider view" of Asian/Asian American culture dominates the uppermost echelon in the regularities constructed within this
"high pop" domain. Examining the significance afforded to Asian
ethnic fiction by this group, then, discloses two concerns: first, as a
phenomenon in and of itself, in what ways does reading group culture
register within a spectrum of readerships? Through what means are
their ideological needs met, regulated, and further contoured in order
to emphasize their independence from other markets? Second, how and
why does Asian ethnicity attain a position of privilege within this
reading formation? How is the desire for this particular object of value
conditioned and fulfilled?

For the most part, I shall contend, the explosion of popular fiction
rife with non-European cultural markers denotes a sincere desire in
reading groups to learn about the unfamiliar Other. The danger,

however, is the mechanism through which this unfamiliarity is represented and consequently digested by the reading public. Ethnic fiction that utilizes Asian cultural semiosis creates a particular double bind: on the one hand, an educated reading public aware of the value of multicultural "enlightenment" is eager to learn concrete details about cultures that have made and continue to make a tremendous impact on American popular culture and politics; on the other hand, the market value of these cultures is significantly enhanced by an over-valuation of certain stereotypical characteristics that have been historically ingrained in American myth. More succinctly, the search for "authentic" knowledge of Asian cultures is both hampered and spurred on by the desire to know the mystical, inscrutable East. In short, members of reading group culture prize their multicultural awareness and their understanding of difference, which, enhanced by these novels, provides the very information they depend upon to set them apart; the form of multiculturalism that they practice, however, is simply a more subtle kind of the behavior that they purport to disdain.

Only this unique amalgamation of sincerity and exoticization, the market value of difference, can account for the recent phenomenon of Asian/Asian American themed novels. The enormous critical and popular trade novel success of David Guterson's *Snow Falling On Cedars* and Arthur Golden's *Memoirs of a Geisha* designate them as the best and most recent examples of what I would like to call a "New Orientalism." Inheriting Tan's place in this particular register of public domain, Guterson and Golden in fact supersede her oft-cited "meteoric" success, in large part by offering the same kind of privileged information about difference that multiculturalism requires from the "educated" person. In what follows, I will map out a theory of the anxiety of cultural ignorance and the corresponding drive for knowledge that multicultural discourse created. I will then discuss the ways in which these two texts were marketed to the high-pop audience of reading group culture with the promise of typologies of Asian and Asian American difference, as well as how the novels themselves approach their tasks of delivering this information to the reader. Finally, I will examine the reception of these texts, turning to readers' own understanding – as revealed in online bulletin boards – of the "knowledge" gleaned from the novels. Outlining these three components will serve to map the complex interactions that condition the New

Orientalism, as well as those that converge within reading group culture to produce the desire for it.

Multiculturalism and the Anxiety of Ignorance

The struggle for widespread acceptance of minorities and minority literatures on college campuses and in university canons was neither short nor simple; nonetheless, by 1995, "the battles for the inclusion of ethnic literature in the curriculum of American literary studies have been fought, and in many cases, won" (Palumbo-Liu, 1995: 1). David Palumbo-Liu goes on to state that "multiculturalism as a general program of representing the cultures and histories of diverse minorities also has been widely inscribed" (ibid: 1–2). All the more necessary, then, become the concerns about the ways in which the tenets of multiculturalism are introduced, and implicitly, how they are received. In the editor's introduction to *The Ethnic Canon*, Palumbo-Liu sketches in detail the dangers of an uncritical approach to the inclusion of multiple ethnicities in the canon. Most specifically, Palumbo-Liu cites the dangers of both teachers and students understanding "ethnic" or "minority" literatures as an outright, unmediated window into that cultural experience (ibid: 11). Substituting narrative experience for personal interaction, *The Joy Luck Club* (to return to the origins of this essay) becomes a kind of handbook, the digestion of which assures the reader that she has "understood" Chinese American culture. In Palumbo-Liu's astute phrasing, this is "the deployment of ethnic texts as proxies for ethnic peoples" (Palumbo-Liu, 1995: 13).

The desire to "understand" another culture through literature, however, is hardly limited to academe, although the impulse may very well be conditioned by it. The knowledge of the existence of foreign "Others" doubtless produces a kind of anxiety; anthropologists and deconstructionists alike have schematized the functions of difference in the definition and redefinition of the self.[2] At the same time, the mainstream diffusion of the necessity for a multicultural awareness also and perhaps more strongly gives rise to an anxiety of ignorance: a fear of unfamiliarity with cultures that are daily becoming more and more a part of the American landscape. To operate correctly then in an increasingly diverse population with a more global perspective, a certain

amount of knowledge about non-European cultures becomes necessary. Even the famously conservative E. D. Hirsch in his introduction
to the revised edition of *The Dictionary of Cultural Literacy* indicates that
updating his tome required accounting for "the growing consensus over
multiculturalism" (Hirsch, 1993: vii). In the same introduction he cites
the increase in entries related to African American culture, stating that
"it will be obvious from these examples that the entries belong to
American (not just African-American) cultural literacy" (ibid). No
longer, then, are ethnic minorities and the knowledge of their cultures
considered merely ancillary to a dominant body of information;
instead, familiarity with a variety of non-Western cultures is required
to claim fluency with the scope of American culture as a whole. In
addition, Hirsch asserts that this brand of literacy enables communication; in fact he defines literacy as "the ability to communicate with
strangers" (ibid: xv).[3] One might ask who exactly these "strangers" are,
as Hirsch's examples of obviously tendentious communication involve,
among others, "whites with blacks, Asians with Hispanics, and Repub-
licans with Democrats" (ibid). Regardless, possessing concrete knowledge about a variety of cultures is perceived as necessary both for
personal fulfillment (I am culturally literate, hence educated and
American) and for communication (I can talk to you – a "stranger" –
because I know and understand your cultural heritage). Active on both
personal and societal levels, the anxiety of cultural ignorance in large
part results from a broad acceptance of multicultural priority and insti-
tutes a hierarchy for an emergent regime of value. Born out of multiculturalism, the anxiety of ignorance certainly plays a significant role
in the unilateral embrace of novels that purport to reveal the heretofore occluded semiosis of an ethnic minority.

The New Orientalism

In the wake of this multicultural imperative, then, arises a body of
readers much more attuned to the tendencies of traditional Orientalism. For them, the "Orient" and the "Oriental" have become problematic terms. In Edward Said's seminal work, he defines "Orientalism
[as] a style of thought based upon an ontological and epistemological
distinction made between 'the Orient' and (most of the time) 'the
Occident'" (Said, 1994: 2). In this system, the West represents the East

out of a sense of both cultural superiority and fear, the latter empha-
sized by geopolitics during the Cold War. The most recent turn of the
Orientalist screw, however, appears to be motivated less by these feelings of radical separation than by the recognition of proximity – less
a general European phenomenon than a particularly American one.[4]
In Said's study the Europeans created an image of the Orient that in
turn served as an antithesis for the Occident – a negative of the values
that Europe hoped to hold away from itself and define itself against.
As an ideological system, Orientalism revolved around and depended
upon difference and separation. The contemporary evolution of this
Orientalism in the United States is just as indebted to retaining the
idea of difference; it requires, however, a notion of difference that hopes
to neutralize the threat of inevitable propinquity with knowledge.

While Said's Orientalism is marked by the deep divide that the
Europeans found psychologically necessary for dominance in both
political and economic spheres, the New Orientalism accountable for
the success of *Snow Falling on Cedars* and *Memoirs of a Geisha* is instead
symptomatic of the realization of societal interpenetration – the
inescapable fact that the East is now part and parcel of the West. The
"Asian" is the new "Oriental," a linguistic shift that designates a change
in the tenor of perception. If we can acknowledge some of the labor
that the dissemination of multiculturalism has performed, the subtle
evolution of Orientalism becomes more clear.

The current American *brouhaha* over these texts indicates the extent
to which Asians and perceptions of them have a unique constellation
given the nation's history with both Asian immigrants and citizens.
Since the nineteenth century, in fact, immigrants from China, Japan,
Korea, and more recently Southeast Asia and the Asian subcontinent
have settled in America despite continued attempts to challenge their
entry and naturalization.[5] Persistent, pejorative images grew out of and
played upon the fear and distrust of these new Americans. Robert G.
Lee, for example, charts six: "the pollutant, the coolie, the deviant, the
yellow peril, the model minority, and the gook" (Lee, 1999: 8). As his
study of the Oriental in popular culture from the nineteenth century
to the present shows, each of these images arises from a particular historical moment – for example, he pinpoints the origin of the model
minority stereotype as the post-1950 Cold War era, a time when ethnic
assimilation was held up as a paradigm in contrast to the violence
and social upheaval of race riots and militancy. Recognition of the

historical roots of these caricatures points to their gradual abatement. In large part, the overt and caricatured portrayals of the Oriental no longer are publicly sanctioned: the coolie, the Jap, Charlie Chan – all have been widely recognized, for the most part, as racist stereotypes. To say that Orientalism has shifted its focus from these historically documented images, however, is not to argue that the recent American realization of cultural multiplicity has completely eradicated these Orientalist perceptions.

In her excellent article detailing the enactments of Chinese and Chinese American cultures within Amy Tan's novel and the critical responses to them, for example, Sau-Ling Cynthia Wong historicizes the reception of "ethnic novels" and the strategies that mark them as such. Concluding her analysis, Wong states: "The fortunes of once-popular, now overlooked cultural interpreters in Chinese American literary history . . . suggest that cultural mediation of the Orient for the 'mainstream' readership requires continual repackaging to remain in sync with changing times and resultant shifts in ideological needs" (Wong, 1995: 202). Wong here parallels Lee's work, charting the historiographic progress of the idea of the Orient in American literature, locating Tan as only the most recent in a long line of narrators offering an "inside" view of Asian cultures. Positing a new evolution of Orientalism, then, is to identify the ways in which previously overt racism has been self-consciously suppressed only to reestablish itself in a different form; to wit, the cultivation of knowledge purported to render Asian and Asian American cultures transparent becomes an object of value and a marker of status within a high-pop regime. In the case of *Snow Falling on Cedars* and *Memoirs of a Geisha* the effects of multiculturalism and the anxiety of ignorance designate the ideological needs that propel this New Orientalism.

Selling Ethnicity Best

As the impulse behind Orientalism has shifted significantly from that of the last century, so too must the narratives that satisfy the impulse alter their focus. The rapid change in demographics lends a certain urgency to the need to know about Asian cultures. Currently, Asian immigrants mark the largest-growing population in the United States: 1997 census bureau estimates project a 412.5 percent increase by 2050

(Muller, 1999). Perhaps more than any other ethnicity, educated American readers have to know about Asians. In this context, one must answer Sander Gilman's question: "Is the label 'ethnic' a valuable commodity?" (Gilman, 1998: 23) with a resounding yes.[6] Here, the task is to determine the ways in which ethnicity at large, and Asian ethnicities in particular, are packaged as commodities and likewise made valuable. In the specific case of *Snow Falling on Cedars* and *Memoirs of a Geisha* the commodity to be packaged is Japanese American and Japanese difference – the portrayal of which clearly fulfills a set of ideological needs. Like Amy Tan's novels, these two texts negotiate between the entrenchment of cultural difference and the "insider's" view. Playing upon the anxiety of cultural ignorance, they become figured in a two-step process: first, the marketing of the novel creates a promise that the book will deliver the necessary information, and second, the novel itself must adhere to the balance indicated above, providing insider information that cleaves to a progressive notion of difference made readable. The enormous success signaled by the fulfillment of this particularized desire attests to the two-fold savvy and anxiety of a vast population of readers who pride themselves on their cultural literacy, as well as the intrinsic ability of authors and publishers to intuit and satisfy their needs. The simultaneous agreement of all parties to participate within this regime of value here underscores the close examination the New Orientalism requires.

The distinctive delivery system used to disseminate "insider" information is nothing to scoff at. Both *Cedars* and *Memoirs* are currently published by Vintage Books – a publishing house "oriented" toward the high-pop readership. For example, Vintage publishes solely trade paperbacks, eschewing rack-sized "mass" novels. In addition to republishing "classics" from around the world (Vintage International sells both Murakami and Dinesen, William Styron and Nabokov), Vintage purchases publishing rights in order to print the first edition trade paperbacks of contemporary "high culture" reads – their stable includes many of the recent Booker Prize winners (Carey's *Oscar and Lucinda*, McEwan's *Amsterdam*, etc.). In essence, Vintage projects itself as a resource for educated, globally conscious readers who enjoy "quality" fiction. Accordingly, its website and marketing literature tag Vintage as "the . . . source for booklovers" – as opposed to mere book readers or, presumably, those people who study books, setting both the house and its readers apart from mass and academic communities. The press has established itself, then, as *the* dependable provider of "good reads"; easily recognizable from a distance (Vintage Books "letterbox" the title on the spine of the book), anxious readers can expect fiction well-regarded by experts (i.e., the Booker committee, the PEN/Faulkner committee) to be both intellectually impressive and sound in its transmission of multicultural values. Given this carefully constructed public image, it is no wonder that Vintage rushed to include both *Snow Falling on Cedars* and *Memoirs of a Geisha* into its Vintage Contemporaries line (a line that now houses, with little surprise, Amy Tan's novels as well).

In order to secure its profile, Vintage naturally highlights the cultural value of its novels. A cursory glance at the book jackets of these two novels is enough to note the deployment of two distinct yet complementary strategies indicative of the new Orientalism. To this end, the jacket description of *Snow Falling on Cedars* highlights its revisionist reading of American policies during World War II: "Above all, San Piedro is haunted by the memory of what happened to its Japanese residents during World War II, when an entire community was sent into exile while its neighbors watched" (First Vintage Contemporaries Edition). Foregrounding this multicultural priority, the book jacket promises readers information all-too-often elided from traditional history classes – the internment of Japanese *Americans* (note this designation the book jacket forgets) and the racism that allowed it to happen. Lest readers become too wary of a didactic history lesson, however, it immediately goes on to emphasize the novel's compelling mystery plot: "Gripping, tragic, and densely atmospheric, *Snow Falling on Cedars* is a masterpiece of suspense – but one that leaves us shaken and changed" (First Vintage Contemporaries Edition). Ending on this note, the blurb thus promises two for the price of one: insight into what *really* happened and one hell of a mystery. It is as if reading this novel will enable us to grapple with the fifty years of complex, systemic injustice resulting in the internment of citizens; a life-changing experience, to be sure. Appearing only four years later, the strategy evident on the *Memoirs of a Geisha* jacket dispenses almost entirely with the vagaries of plot, focusing instead on the previous success of the book in hardback (presumably due to quality of the information inside): "A literary sensation and a runaway bestseller, this brilliant debut novel presents with seamless authenticity and exquisite lyricism the true confessions of one of Japan's most celebrated geisha" (Vintage Contemporaries Edition, February 1999). Here the emphasis is on the artistry of the narrative and the relative value of the details. The novel's fictional status is backgrounded to emphasize the authenticity of its portrayals; despite Golden's own acknowledgment that "the character of Sayuri and her story are completely invented" (Golden, 1997: 433), the book jacket goes to extreme lengths to complicate the materiality of the main character (who remains nameless for the extent of the description). Ironically, in this unacknowledged paradox, we are enticed to read the "true confessions" of a fictional character. Regardless, the strategy for marketing "Memoirs" appeals to the need for an imperceptibly mediated novel that will provide the real deal – the incontrovertibly authentic and heretofore secret life of the geisha.

As an indicator of the image that Vintage wishes to project, these examples illustrate the ways that *Snow Falling on Cedars* and *Memoirs of a Geisha* profess to satisfy a reader's desire for literary cultural proxies. The publisher does not cease its appeal to the anxiety of cultural ignorance at the boundary of the book jacket, however. With the rise of the reading group in the 1990s, Vintage began to capitalize on this boom by providing "authentic" information for these culturally sensitive, anxious groups via displays in bookstores as well as online. Their website in fact houses an extensive Reading Group Center, which lists tips on how to start a group, recommendations from other groups about what to read, a chat board so that readers can communicate with each other, and most relevantly, a fine stock of reading group guides to specific texts of which *Snow Falling on Cedars* and *Memoirs of a Geisha* are just two.[7]

A comparison of the *Cedars* and *Geisha* guides once again reveals a distinct difference in the ways that the publisher packages the novels' portrayals of Asian/Asian American culture. Like its book jacket, the on line guide to *Snow Falling on Cedars* foregrounds the history of Japanese American internment as an integral part of the plot. In addition to supplying the plot summary present in all of the guides, the *Cedars* guide includes a cogent and well-balanced two-page historical supplement covering Japanese immigration and the federal laws designed to prevent it, American racism toward the Japanese (characterized as "hostility" and "paranoia"), and finally the restrictions and eventual internment of Japanese American citizens after the attack on Pearl Harbor.[8] The novel itself covers many of these points, but it seems particularly necessary for the publisher to explain or reiterate them to the ostensible group in a kind of "cheat sheet" of historical racism against the Japanese and their descendants in America. In so doing, Vintage's readers' guide accentuates the kind of revision of American history which multiculturalism champions: here informed readers can become familiar with the truth about a piece of US history that has all too often been ignored. The reading group guide provides the history lesson that lends tragedy and suspense to the novel; with this out of the way, the readers presumably can concentrate on the story itself. Consistent with the attention drawn to external influences shaping the text, the guide then provides questions that invite the readers to think carefully about Guterson's artistry in constructing the novel (the initial question, for example, considers the effect of flashbacks and disjunctive time as a narrative device). Overall, the *Snow Falling on Cedars* guide details the particular historical moment in order to emphasize and make alluring its role as a complex and multiculturally informed backdrop for the textual and research skills of the novelist.

The explicit attention paid to external forces in the *Cedars* guide serves to show more dramatically the complete elision of such concerns in the guide for *Memoirs of a Geisha*. In fact, in direct opposition to questions that examine authorial practice, the questions Vintage provides center the discussion of the novel on the assumption of the narrative's transparency. More to the point, the first question sets the tone for the constellation of concerns that implicate the novel as the standard bearer of the New Orientalism:

> Many people in the West think of geisha simply as prostitutes. After reading *Memoirs of a Geisha*, do you see the geisha of Gion as prostitutes? What are the similarities, and what are the differences? What is the difference between being a prostitute and being a "kept woman," as Sayuri puts it?

A leading question of the worst type, this query centers around modes of difference – not just the difference between the West and the East (or the quotidian "simple" prostitute and the much more complex, "kept woman" geisha), but also the instantaneously established difference between the vast bulk of Westerners and the readers of "Memoirs," those privileged with insider knowledge that allows them to differentiate between the West and the East, as opposed to those "ignorant" others. And, in case one of these rogue readers *were* to argue for some similarity between the prostitute and the geisha, question three reinvokes the trope of difference: "The word 'geisha' in fact derives from the Japanese word for art. In what does the geisha's art consist? How many different types of art does she practice?" Worse, however, the questions begin to identify the geisha as the dominant signifier of Eastern difference – the site from which difference radiates in the novel. Question nine almost neglects specificity to the text completely: "How do Japanese ideas about eroticism and sexuality differ from Western ones? Does the Japanese ideal of femininity differ from ours?"; and, leaving the realm of sexuality altogether, the seventh question quotes the geisha and asks how her statement reveals the difference between Eastern and Western ideals of destiny. What is perhaps most indicative of the Orientalist approach extant in this line of questioning is not the fact that it drives home an insistence on radical difference and a hierarchy among those Westerners who recognize it; rather, it is the implicit assumption that the novel is unequivocally a source authorized to inspire and finally answer these questions. Only the final two questions of the guide mention Arthur Golden's name, and at no previous point does it even allude to the structure of the novel or the possibility of authorial practice. Even then, the questions do not challenge his authority on the life of early twentieth-century geisha. If any doubt can be cast on Golden's knowledge at all, it revolves around the artifice of his gender:

> In *Memoirs of a Geisha*, Arthur Golden has done a very daring thing: he, as an American man, has written in the voice of a Japanese woman. How successfully does he disguise his own voice? While reading the novel, did you feel that you were hearing the genuine voice of a woman?

Even while the guide makes a point of problematizing Golden's voice – and actually mentions the disjunction between his nationality and that of his character – the possible crack in his "seamless authenticity" comes from the fact that he is a man speaking for a woman. Despite the ubiquitous insistence on cultural difference throughout the guide, the conclusion is that it can, in fact, be bridged by this text; locating Arthur Golden's "daring" narrative leap in the realm of gender assumption rather than cultural appropriation conceals the previously insurmountable contrast nurtured by this guide beneath the more familiar and "universal" narrative debate over gender.

In essence, the marketing strategies that play a significant role in the meteoric success of *Memoirs of a Geisha* and *Snow Falling on Cedars* represent two complementary positions characteristic of the New Orientalism. Both revolve around the locus of ostensibly recognizing, but in actuality constructing, a semiosis of Asian (more particularly Japanese) difference that foregrounds only particular parts of Asian and Asian American culture. The publishing machine behind Guterson's text targets an audience conversant with the multicultural necessity of revisionist history, offering to these readers a valuable body of knowledge that will provide for the anxiety of ignorance about a less-than-mythic American war moment. Along with this knowledge, however, Vintage promises that *Snow Falling on Cedars* will give readers access to the experience of oppression and racism itself, guaranteed to leave them "shaken and changed." Reading the book, a narrative proxy of experience taken for the real, the audience too will have access to the moral high ground of racism's injustice, and will hence possess the historical facts to speak cogently about the racist *past* of the United States. The description of Guterson's work, then, is a two-fold construction of Orientalist difference. On the one hand, the jacket and guide foreground the necessity of knowing about this tragic moment in American history – an appeal particularly powerful to a reading population nervous about its privileged societal status in an increasingly diverse nation. However, the device promoting the novel displaces the systemic injustice and racism to the bygone era of World War II and its immediate aftermath. Combined with the second arm of Vintage's New Orientalist stance – the consistent failure to distinguish between Japanese nationals and Americans of Japanese descent – the marketing mechanism propelling *Snow Falling on Cedars* maps out a trajectory that instantiates difference and simultaneously holds the racist effects of such a political elision permanently in the past. The irony of such a system, of course, is that the putative appeal of the novel lies in the access it offers to information that supports a multicultural understanding of American history.

Like the mechanism behind *Snow Falling on Cedars*, that of *Memoirs of a Geisha* also invokes the rhetoric of difference; at the same time, it studiously avoids the presence of the author, dwelling on the authentic quality of the knowledge to be gained by reading *Memoirs*. Focusing on the vast differences between Japanese and American culture, the promise of "understanding" such difference is held out as a reward. Reading *Memoirs of a Geisha* affords one access to the "truth" of a secret part of Japanese culture, access that arms readers with knowledge that separates them from the quotidian mass culture of America – the mass culture that believes that geisha are really prostitutes, for example. The "life-changing" experience that the reader can accrue through consumption of *Snow Falling on Cedars*, Vintage would have us believe, lies also at the heart of consuming *Memoirs of a Geisha*: epiphanic knowledge of Eastern difference raises one's position within the economy of multicultural awareness. With this strategy, the important difference between East and West is the status that it affords the initiated.

Asian By the Book

To create a novel that fulfills Vintage's promise of providing an image-enhancing notion of Asian difference requires a subtle and nuanced performance of the New Orientalist strategies. In the case of *Snow Falling on Cedars* Guterson's text provides precisely what the Vintage publishing machine claims to furnish: a historical account of American racism, skillfully rendered compelling, not didactic, by way of a romance and a mystery. A brief synopsis of the plot is as follows: a Japanese American man, Kabuo Miyamoto, is accused of murdering an Anglo-American fisherman, Carl Heine. The motive lies in a generation-old dispute – Kabuo's father was in the process of buying land from Carl's father when the Japanese Americans were interned during World War II, preventing final payment for the land. By the time they were freed, Carl's father had died, and his mother refused to turn over the land. The plot thickens, of course: the local journalist reporting the trial, pithily named Ishmael, was the adolescent lover of Kabuo's wife, Hatsue; during internment she rejected Ishmael and married Kabuo. In the end, Ishmael discovers information that will clear Kabuo's name, and must struggle with himself to forgive Hatsue and exonerate her husband.

The obvious pitfalls of the plot aside – reinforcement of antimiscegenation, the trope of the "good white man" saving the minority – Guterson does create scenarios in which he presents the injustice of Japanese American internment sympathetically and accurately, and he shows the overt racism of some characters to be complicit with the governmental hysteria of the period, which is at once contemporaneously opposed by "good" characters who disagree with the governmental decision. Like the mechanism behind *Memoirs of a Geisha*'s success, then, Guterson's text draws a distinct line between the likeable characters who understand Japanese difference enough not to fear it,[9] and those unlikeable, ignorant characters who associate difference with evil – a clear, if simplistic, representation of two broad sides of the multiculturalist debate. While retaining this opposition and hence a hierarchy of those who comprehend difference in the "right" way, Guterson simultaneously contains the events themselves to a particular understanding of historical circumstance in the eyes of his narrator. For Ishmael Chambers, Kabuo's trial catalyzes his need to reevaluate his desire for and bitterness toward Hatsue. As the novel approaches its climax, Ishmael seeks comfort in the denial of agency: "It occurred to him that her husband was going out of her life in the same way he himself once had. There had been circumstances then and there were circumstances now; there were things beyond anyone's control" (Guterson, 1995: 326). Ishmael later repeats this mantra to assuage a much larger injustice: "Hatsue had been taken from his life by history, because history was whimsical and immune to private yearnings" (ibid: 425). For Ishmael, the protagonist and dominant narrator of the novel, world historical events are far beyond the reach of the individual, a stance that releases him or her from any perceived responsibility toward others. In a novel dependent upon racism toward Japanese Americans and their eventual internment for a plot device, to describe history as "whimsical" endorses at least two kinds of quietism: first, aided by a plot replete with flashbacks, the narrative encapsulates racism both personal and systematic (i.e., fear and loathing of Asians existed only in the aftermath of the bombing of Pearl Harbor – not anymore, however); second, while in retrospect readers may realize that internment was wrong, it was, in the grand scheme of history, an accident, and the fault of no single person or community.

At the heart of *Snow Falling on Cedars*' appeal lies a carefully constructed realization of the New Orientalism. On the surface the novel offers concrete detail and sympathetic portrayals of historic racism toward Asian Americans. Ideologically, however, it diffuses guilt: racism is a thing of the past, history was and is out of our hands. With this evocation of knowledge and simultaneous disavowal of responsibility, Guterson accounts for injustice based on difference without dispelling the notion that difference is eternally insurmountable: in the end, Ishmael mends his bridges with Hatsue, but the Miyamotos return to their kin as Ishmael does to his. The reader closes the book, armed with multiculturally sound knowledge of World War II and the "accident" of racism and internment, and with the assurance that despite his or her proximity to this "foreign" culture, Japanese Americans remain identifiably different and self-segregating.

Unlike the critique of *Snow Falling on Cedars*, a textual analysis of *Memoirs of a Geisha* requires little description of plot. The novel is rife with examples of the attempt to impart privileged, insider knowledge of Japanese culture. Many of these incorporate tag lines to signal the upcoming distinction the text will make between West and East. For example, as Sayuri, the narrator, describes a geisha's makeup toilet, she uses one of these lines:

> I must tell you something about necks in Japan, if you don't know it: namely, that Japanese men, as a rule, feel about a woman's neck and throat the same way that men in the West might feel about a woman's legs . . . I suppose it's like a woman in Paris wearing a short skirt. (Golden, 1997: 63)

With a similar move, Sayuri reinforces her authority as an expert on geisha rituals by referring to her *naïveté* in her early years: "I should explain just what Mameha meant by 'older sister,' even though at the time, I hardly knew much about it myself" (ibid: 128). In each of these instances, and in comparable situations throughout the novel, readers are cued by an announcement of Eastern difference that is closely followed by a detailed description of a custom. Vintage Books promised readers this kind of valuable information, and Golden's novel not only delivers it, but alerts them to its arrival. The first example above, which comes early on in the novel, goes so far as to construct a syllogism for the reader, under the assumption, of course, that an ignorant or uninitiated Westerner may not be able to understand the allure of a woman's neck without making reference to the way that his (it is most definitely a masculine reader here) own culture has constructed a rubric that sexualizes women's legs. The narrative conventions of cueing and syllogism serve complementary purposes: both identify and explain

Japanese cultural customs as opposed to Western tradition, and at the same time use the ostensible "understanding" of this difference as an object of value to be possessed by the multiculturally literate.

While Golden narratively foregrounds the value of the geisha's information, he constructs *Memoirs of a Geisha*, like *Snow Falling on Cedars* before it, in such a way that it diffuses any guilt that may arise as readers accrue this knowledge. For Guterson, this is a historical concern, but for Golden, the issue is more voyeuristic. Lest the reader should feel at sea in the span of the memoirs, or should the reader question the motive behind its candid revelations, Golden contextualizes the document by way of a translator's note. The distinguished "Arnold Rusoff Professor of Japanese History" (Golden, 1997: 4) presents us with the brief tale documenting his contact with Sayuri, and his scholarly opinion of the value of her reflections.[10] More importantly, however, the professor describes his role in the dictation of the memoirs as invaluable: "she was so accustomed to talking face-to-face that she would hardly know how to proceed with no one in the room to listen" (ibid: 2). And later: "I regarded myself as the foundation upon which the enterprise was based and felt that her story would never have been told had I not gained her trust" (ibid: 3). With these necessities built into the supposed transmission of the memoirs, Golden creates a context in which the desire to consume the novel is crucial to its very existence. Sayuri required an audience, and consequently her memoirs, by association, fall under the same exigencies. Readers may thus acquire the insider information that Sayuri's candid memoirs contain without a twinge of guilt for eavesdropping: they are the privileged foundations upon which her tale can be built.

The fictional memoirs that make up the body of *Memoirs of a Geisha* reenact the fundamentals of the New Orientalism: they provide Japanese customs in intimate and incredible detail; they associate the possession of this information with a "smarter" or at least more culturally knowledgeable Westerner; and best of all, they appear to depend on this Westerner as an audience. As with *Snow Falling on Cedars* the matrix composed of information about difference and the simultaneous diffusion of guilt in acquiring this information reestablishes the multiculturally aware at the apex of this particular reading formation. As its reading guide promised, *Memoirs* indeed uses the complex and artful figure of the geisha to indicate the numerous ways that the East is incommensurable with the West. With the geisha as the instantiation of insuperable difference, Golden's novel indeed undertakes a "daring" and wildly successful foray into the market value of the New Orientalism.

Book, Line, and Sinker: Readers' Responses

As the final element in the discussion of the mechanism that forwards the New Orientalism, a brief look at some readers' reactions to the novels serves to emphasize the efficiency of Vintage's marketing strategies and the novels' adherence to the promises that those strategies forward. The Vintage website offers two spaces for readers to log their views on various novels: the first is called a "forum" in which readers can log on, register their views and respond to others who have written in; the other is a link entitled "reader reviews" which, obviously, houses reader reviews for various books. Below, I've chosen a quote from each space. Representative of the overwhelming majority of responses, both quotes indicate the degree to which readers adopt similar metaphoric and thematic – and definitively ideological – points to that of the publisher, in turn demonstrating the ways in which "book lovers" absorb and reactivate this New Orientalist position in their own conversations.

The response to *Snow Falling on Cedars* is a reticent one; despite the apparent popularity of the book (detailed both on Vintage's site and on the *New York Times* bestseller list), readers' responses to the book are few and far between. Of these, however, a December 2, 1999 posting most concisely sums up the few vocal readers' positions:

> I just recently read Snow Falling on Cedars and loved the book very much. It made me very sad to think how people were treated around World War II, and how people felt they needd [sic] to judge someone because of their nationality. (1999)

Here, the reader's reaction is a lock-step reproduction of the issues that Vintage foregrounds for Guterson's text, as well as the representation of historical and *only* historical racism that Guterson himself thematizes in the novel. Sheryl (the reader) not only reproduces the pain of racism and relegates it to the past (evident not only in her mention of World War II but also in her use of the past tense), she replicates the substitution of nationality for ethnicity that Vintage so clearly elides in

its guide. With this terminology, those of Japanese ethnicity are eternally Japanese citizens in the nation of America, and henceforth per-
secuted on the basis of being aliens. Despite the political quietism and
vexed vocabulary, however, Sheryl has, it seems, internalized both the
historical details of Japanese American internment, as well as the injustice involved. We may ask which of these, if not the combination of
both, leaves her "shaken and changed" by the novel.

Reader responses to *Memoirs of a Geisha*, like those lauding *Snow
Falling on Cedars*, mirror the concerns of the reading guide and text
almost to the letter. Of the reviews for the book, the second details
the kind of voyeuristic appeal of the novel with abandon:

> Vintage Books really has a grasp on what readers and book clubs want
> to read. Recently I read *Memoirs of a Geisha*, which kept me hooked.
> . . . It was like I stepped into a world I never knew existed. The author
> not only shows a world very few are familiar with. . . . After reading it,
> you feel as though you have traveled on some great journey, exhausted,
> but filled with a new knowledge. (2000)

With her extended description, Susan M. virtually repeats by rote the
thematic strategies that Vintage set forth for the novel. Here, she
emphasizes and reemphasizes the privileged kind of information that
Golden provides for the reader – not only is the knowledge "new," but
it's the good stuff: that which "few . . . are familiar with." Susan clearly
acknowledges the eminence of such knowledge; however, she may very
well go one better than Vintage here with her use of an extended travel
metaphor to describe the transmission of cultural information. Where
the Vintage book jacket indeed invokes the reader "entering a world"
(Vintage Contemporaries Edition, February 1999), it stops short of
invoking the narrative jet lag that overtakes Susan as she finishes the
book. Regardless of the refinements that she makes to the Vintage
mechanism, Susan's review manifests the reification of New Orientalist perspectives, both those that she simply repeats as well as those that
she works to develop on her own.[11]

Is Multiculturalism Enough?

A special issue of *Women's Studies* published in 1992 dedicates itself
to the question "Is Multiculturalism Enough?" The issue charts what
editor Coiner notes as "relief and optimism" concerning the "changes

that have occurred during the last decade," but also calls for "skepticism" (Coiner, 1992: 209). Her attitude of cautious hope is echoed in
contemporaneous pieces that address the variegated effects of a multicultural perspective. Five years later, however, a book of essays detailing the complexities of consumption focuses particularly on the
developing uses of multicultural perspectives in advertising. In her case
study of the marketing use of Latino culture, Roberta Astroff cogently
explains the danger for all commodifiable ethnic representation:
"Market segmentation attempts to control or manage difference, assign-
ing value to certain differences, making invisible those differences seen
as of little value to the market" (Astroff, 1997: 128). In the case of Asian
and Asian American difference, Vintage targeted reading groups as a
culture apt to value certain markers of "Asian-ness," and moved quickly
to discern the market-vulnerable anxieties that could be quelled by
canny management – cause for skepticism indeed.

The first task of this New Orientalism, then, is to appeal to the
anxiety of ignorance and purport to provide for it through "authentic" knowledge. The second, and more tricky narrative task, deploys this
knowledge in such a way that it depoliticizes Eastern difference, making
it a factor in, rather than an impediment to, idealized multicultural
harmony. Whether through historical encapsulation or the ethnographic validity of fictional memoirs, the New Orientalism seeks to
describe a heretofore "inscrutable" culture for readers desperate for
information that justifies their aspirations to multicultural expertise and
the status that such literacy affords. The immediate and prolonged
success of *Snow Falling on Cedars* and *Memoirs of a Geisha* indicates the
market value of a publishing system that addresses such an anxiety,
the rewards available to the novelist capable of fulfilling the promise of
information, and the ideology that readers are all-too-ready to accept
in narrative form.

As a self-perpetuating reading formation, reading group culture and
its component parts – the publisher, the novels, the readers themselves
– consume wholeheartedly their own brand of multiculturalism, fueled
in large part by New Orientalism and the type of non-threatening,
status-enhancing portrayal of Asian difference that it affords. In his 1994
afterword to *Orientalism* Edward Said reflects on the critical intervention that his original work solicited:

> What I called for in *Orientalism* was a new way of conceiving the sep-
> arations and conflicts that had stimulated generations of hostility, war,

and imperial control. And indeed, one of the most interesting developments in postcolonial studies was a rereading of the canonical cultural
works . . . to investigate some of their assumptions. (Said, 1994: 351)

If a historical critique of Orientalism in part called for a reassessment
of canonical works, then perhaps the New Orientalism must then call
for a reassessment of contemporary texts and their political and ideological import; most importantly, it must gesture toward a theoretical
armature prepared to grapple with the diffuse components that constitute the appeal of these novels, and one that recognizes the social
forces that converge to create new, more particularized audiences. In
short, it must demand that the same acute cultural criticism that has
of late reconsidered historical texts concentrate as well on the contemporary sphere and emergent Orientalist systems of any stripe.

Notes

1   Documenting the "publishing legend" of *The Joy Luck Club*'s success, Sau-
     Ling Cynthia Wong notes not only the markers of its popularity (nine months
     on the *New York Times* bestseller list, hardcover sales of 275,000 copies), but also
     the "frenzied bidding" among publishers for the paperback rights (Wong, 1995:
     174).
2   For a brief description of both positions, see Homi Bhabha's (1998) "On the Irre-
     movable Strangeness of Being Different," produced for a special MLA issue on
     the topic of ethnicity.
3   In this, his original introduction, Hirsch announces his self-proclaimed "educa-
     tional conservatism" as a bulwark against "multicultural anti-elitism" that he per-
     ceives as threatening to the ideal of universal communication his cultural literacy
     seeks to provide. The extent to which the tone of the introduction to the revised
     edition mediates the original sentiment indicates the increasing power of the
     anxiety of ignorance that multiculturalism carries with it.
4   Admittedly, this study takes up a particular part of the Orientalism question. Said's
     historical, literary, and anthropological study focuses primarily upon representa-
     tions of the Near East and their political precedents. Here I am examining only
     the intense attention paid to representations of the Far East and Asian Americans
     who are distantly affiliated with such cultures.
5   For a detailed and thorough account of the multiple waves of Asian immigration
     and their accompanying legislation, see Takaki's *Strangers from a Different Shore*
     (1998).
6   In his article "Consuming Social Change: The 'United Colors of Benetton'"
     Henry Giroux details the use of ethnicities as very successful commodities. For

example, his description of the conflation of politics and capital describes the tricky project of articulating difference: "Ideas that hold the promise of producing social criticism are insinuated into products in an attempt to subordinate the dynamics of social struggle to the production of new lifestyles" (Giroux, 1994: 15).

7   Vintage's Recommendations page (2000) charts the top 50 books recommended by "hundreds of groups across the country" (bestbooks.html). Tellingly, *Memoirs of a Geisha* tops the list, and *Snow Falling on Cedars* ranks number five. Both significantly outpace *The God of Small Things* by Arundati Roy and *Beloved* by Toni Morrison (18 and 21, respectively), both of which could be considered "ethnic" bestsellers operating under a non- or at least different Orientalist rubric.

8   Notable in this history lesson is the slippage between "Japanese" and "Japanese American," a term never used in the guide. A particularly disturbing elision considering that "the Japanese surprise attack on Pearl Harbor" is used only a paragraph prior to the statement "Japanese homes were searched for contraband." Not until the final sentence of the historical background does the guide become somewhat clearer about its terms: "In 1988, the US government formally apologized to Japanese citizens who had been deprived of their civil liberties during World War II." Only upon official federal recognition, then, do the Japanese become "citizens." This slippage is made even more distinct as the guide goes to great lengths to define and repeatedly use the Japanese words for first and second generation – issei and nisei.

9   Much is made in the novel of Hatsue's training in traditional Japanese arts (Golden, 1997: 82), which marks her characteristic grace throughout her life, as well as the assumed ubiquity of Japanese and Japanese American boys training in kendo. These are two of several examples where cultural difference is noted either visually or epistemologically in the text.

10   In order to counteract any distaste the reader may feel for dry academic texts, however, the professor is quick to describe his affection for the woman herself, and his note ends with his restrained pathos about her death (Golden, 1997: 4).

11   As both a foil and a further support of the readers' indoctrination into New Orientalism through the Vintage mechanism is the lively debate on the Vintage bulletin board in January 2000. The most intriguing posting reads:

> Our book club just read Memoirs of a Geisha and one would think we discussed something quite different from the book many are raving about in this forum. . . . It bothered many that Sayuri did not reflect more about the circumstances and experiences. A woman writer might have dealt with that more effectively. . . . Though Golden does an excellent job of describing the setting and one does learn a great deal about culture, life in Gion during the 30s and the education of geisha. [*sic*]

While on the one hand this reader (Bonnie White) is actively engaged in critiquing the novel, on the other her point of contention is precisely the Achilles' heel that Vintage itself brings up in the readers guide. While Bonnie questions Golden's ability to write a woman character authentically, she has no problem accepting the verity of Japanese culture that Golden presents.

References

Astroff, Roberta (1997). "Capital's Cultural Study: Marketing Popular Ethnography of US Latino Culture." In Mica Nava, Andrew Blake, Iain MacRury, and Barry Richards, eds., *Buy this Book: Studies in Advertising and Consumption*, London: Routledge, 120–36.

Bennett, Tony (1985). "Texts In History: The Determinations of Readings and Their Texts," *Journal of the Midwest Modern Language Association*, 18: 1, 1–16.

Bhabha, Homi K. (1998). "On the Irremovable Strangeness of Being Different," *PMLA*, 13: 1, 34–9.

Coiner, Constance (1992). "Is Multiculturalism Enough?" *Women's Studies*, 20, 209–16.

Frow, John (1995). *Cultural Studies and Cultural Value*. Oxford: Clarendon Press.

Gilman, Sander (1998). "Introduction: Ethnicity-Ethnicities-Literature-Literatures," *PMLA*, 13: 1, 19–27.

Giroux, Henry (1994). "Consuming Social Change: The 'United Colors of Benetton,'" *Cultural Critique*, 26, 5–32.

Golden, Arthur (1997). *Memoirs of a Geisha*. New York: Vintage Books.

Guterson, David (1995). *Snow Falling on Cedars*. New York: Vintage Books.

Hirsch, E. D. (1993). *The Dictionary of Cultural Literacy*. Boston: Houghton Mifflin.

Lee, Robert G. (1999). *Orientals: Asian Americans in Popular Culture*. Philadelphia: Temple University Press.

Muller, Gilbert H. (1999). *New Strangers in Paradise*. Lexington: University of Kentucky Press.

Palumbo-Liu, David (1995). "Introduction." In David Palumbo-Liu, ed., *The Ethnic Canon: Histories, Institutions, and Interventions*, Minneapolis: University of Minnesota Press, 1–27.

Said, Edward (1994). *Orientalism*. New York: Vintage Books.

Takaki, Ronald (1998). *Strangers from a Different Shore: A History of Asian Americans*. Boston: Little, Brown.

Vintage Books (1999, December 2). Reader forums [responses posted on website *Vintage Reading Group Center*]. Retrieved June 24, 2000 from the World Wide Web: http:www.randomhouse.com/vintage/read/forums

Vintage Books (2000, January 28). Reader forums [responses posted on website *Vintage Reading Group Center*]. Retrieved June 24, 2000 from the World Wide Web: http:www.randomhouse.com/vintage/read/forums

Vintage Books (2000). Reader reviews [excerpts posted on website *Vintage Reading Group Center*]. Retrieved June 24, 2000 from the World Wide Web: http:www.randomhouse.com/vintage/read/readerrevs.html

Vintage Books (2000). Best books for reading groups [list posted on website *Vintage Reading Group Center*]. Retrieved June 24, 2000 from the World Wide Web: http:www.randomhouse.com/vintage/read/bestbooks.html

Vintage Books (2000). Reading group guide for memoirs of a geisha [posted on website *Vintage Reading Group Center*]. Retrieved June 24, 2000 from the World Wide Web: http:www.randomhouse.com/vintage/read/geisha/

Vintage Books (2000). Reading group guide for snow falling on cedars [posted on website *Vintage Reading Group Center*]. Retrieved June 24, 2000 from the World Wide Web: http:www.randomhouse.com/vintage/read/snow/

Wong, Sau-Ling Cynthia (1995). " 'Sugar sisterhood': Situating the Amy Tan Phenomenon." In David Palumbo-Liu, ed., *The Ethnic Canon: Histories, Institutions, and Interventions*, Minneapolis: University of Minnesota Press, 174–210.

5

Class Rites in the Age of the Blockbuster
Alan Wallach

Anyone observing the Sunday crowds at the National Gallery of Art in Washington, DC, or at the Metropolitan Museum of Art in New York might assume, from the casual attire and informal manner of the gallery goers, that visitors to American art museums represent a cross-section of American society. I would argue that the reverse is true: that the art museum in the United States, far from welcoming all visitors, attracts some and repels others, and that it does so on the basis of class; I would also argue that the class biases of these major cultural institutions are inscribed within and reinforced by the space of the museum itself.

What is the character of the contemporary museum audience – an audience that, despite its ever-growing numbers, is so much less democratic than it seems? The work of Pierre Bourdieu provides a useful point of departure for this inquiry, specifically *The Love of Art*, the French sociologist's only extended study of museums and museum goers. Although based "on thin and patchy data," according to one critic,[1] this 1969 book marshals evidence to explain how, in Bourdieu's words, "the sanctification of culture and art, this currency 'of the absolute' which is worshiped by a society enslaved to the absolute of currency, fulfills a vital function by contributing to the consecration of the social order."[2] Through its incisive portrayal of the role of the art museum in European society, *The Love of Art* provoked interest in what might be called "critical museum studies," not least because Bourdieu's findings seemed pertinent to museums and museum audiences throughout the industrialized – and museumified – world.

Plate 5.1   Facade, Metropolitan Museum of Art, New York, July 2000, with banner announcing Chardin exhibition. Author's photograph.

Thirty years after Bourdieu's penetrating portrait of the museums of Europe, the museums of the United States are in the midst of a boom: attendance at American art museums nationwide is skyrocketing.[3] Museums have expanded their appeal by offering experiences that increasingly resemble those associated with popular entertainment and tourism, for instance theme parks like Disneyland and historical recreations such as Colonial Williamsburg. In doing so, they have inevitably – and perhaps intentionally – altered the relationship between the museum's subject – the visitor implied or presupposed by the museum – and the works of art displayed in its galleries. Thus we might ask: does Bourdieu's analysis apply to the American art museum at the start of the twenty-first century? Does the art museum contribute to the maintenance of class hierarchies – or, in Bourdieu's words, "the consecration of the social order"? And if so, how?

Plate 5.2   Facade, National Gallery of Art, Washington, DC, June 2000, with three-part banner for "The Impressionists at Argenteuil." Author's photograph.

A Dimension of the Ethos of Class

In *The Love of Art* Bourdieu provocatively describes the museum in religious terms. He observes that the museum is dedicated to "the religion of art" and this religion involves "an arbitrary distribution of 'gifts'"; that devotees of the religion seek "cultural salvation," or the ability to appreciate works of art; and that such salvation depends upon "the inexplicable vagaries of grace."[4] For Bourdieu,

> It is as if those who speak of culture, for themselves and for others, in other words cultivated people, could not think of cultural salvation in terms other than of the logic of predestination, as if their virtues would be devalued if they had been acquired, and as if all their representation of culture was aimed at authorizing them to convince themselves that,

in the words of one highly cultivated elderly person, "education is innate."[5]

Bourdieu attempts to unravel the socioreligious mystery of "cultural salvation," or what he would later call "distinction," by demonstrating that a love of art is not inborn or inherent. Rather, cultural practice – the likelihood that a given individual will visit an art museum, will stay a specific amount of time, or demonstrate a measurable competence confronting works of art (being able to remember or identify particular works, being able to approach works in a spirit of disinterest) – depends upon various socioeconomic factors, the most important of which is education. Bourdieu bases his argument on data drawn from museum visitor surveys carried out in France in the mid-1960s and in Greece, Holland, Poland, and Spain later in the decade. The *Love of Art* includes elaborate statistical analyses of visitors' age, gender, education, income, and profession. But as Bourdieu observes, "once level of education is determined, knowing the gender or socioeconomic category of visitors generally provides very little additional information."[6] Thus "occupation does not exert a specific influence of its own, as the relationship linking it with visiting is just another expression of the relationship between level of education and visiting." Indeed, "education has a specific and determining influence which cannot simply be made up for by belonging to the highest social classes or by the general influence of peer groups."[7]

Yet Bourdieu believes that formal education, measured in terms of degrees, is not the most basic factor in predicting who will learn a love of art.

> The educational action of the traditional school system can only be fully effective as long as it is exercised on individuals already equipped by their family upbringing with a certain familiarity with the world of art. It follows that the action of schooling, which only reaches children of different social classes very unequally . . . and which only achieves a very unequal success amongst those whom it does reach, tends . . . to strengthen and consecrate initial cultural inequalities by its sanctions.[8]

As is so often the case with Bourdieu, the argument begins to take on the appearance of paradox. While formal education points to the likelihood of ease or discomfort in the presence of artworks, the level of

education a person actually attains is itself dependent upon class position, with its implications for what Bourdieu calls "habitus" – or the
intersection of subjective reality and societal objectivity – and the contents of "family upbringing." In other words, it is class that determines
level and quality of one's education; and class implies inescapable differences in individuals' abilities to appropriate cultural goods. In the
end, as Bourdieu argues, "aesthetics can only be, except in certain
cases, a dimension of the ethics (or, better, the ethos) of class."[9] Hence
the museum functions as a mechanism for differentiating between the
civilized and the barbarous, between members of the upper classes who
possess the "gift," and members of the lower classes who almost
inevitably do not, and for whom it is almost unattainable.

Distinction à l'Américan

The history of American art museums in the twentieth century can be
roughly divided into two phases: the Robber Baron phase, which began
at the turn of the century and lasted until the 1960s, and the Age of
the Blockbuster, which began in the mid-1960s and continues today.
In the era of the robber barons – of those powerful and rapacious
industrialists and financiers who eventually directed part of their
immense fortunes to the founding of museums, libraries, universities,
etc. – the art museum became a site of conspicuous display, much like
the mansions of the robber barons themselves. Grand buildings in the
style of classical Rome proclaimed imperial ambitions. And while the
art museum of the nineteenth century had been focused mainly on
education, with collections typically comprised of copies of sculptures
that remained elsewhere, these new palaces of art featured dazzling
arrays of original works bought in Europe for large and often well-
publicized sums. Museum professionals and aesthetic theorists alike proclaimed a new museological doctrine of "art for art's sake," which made
superfluous earlier efforts to educate masses of immigrant visitors.[10]
Here is Matthew Prichard, assistant director of the Boston Museum of
Fine Arts early in the twentieth century, arguing for the aesthetic value
of the exhibition of original works of art:

> The Museum is for the public and not for any caste or section of it,
> whether student, teacher, artist or artisan, but is dedicated chiefly to

those who come, not to be educated, but to make its treasures their friends for life and their standards of beauty. Joy, not knowledge, is the aim of contemplating a painting by Turner or Dupré's *On the Cliff*, nor need we look at a statue or a coin for aught else than inspiration and the pleasure of exercising our faculties of perception. It is in this sense, furthermore, that they are accepted by those who visit our galleries, in accordance with the teaching of Aristotle, who recognized that the direct aim of art is the pleasure derived from a contemplation of the perfect.[11]

To a large degree this rationale, rooted in the belief that the true purpose of the display of art is the pleasure of the art lover, remains current today.

Of course museums never abandoned entirely the idea that part of their mission was to educate and civilize, but with millionaire trustees firmly in control, places such as the Metropolitan Museum and the Boston Museum of Fine Arts more and more came to resemble elite preserves. Although obliged to open their doors to visitors of whatever stripe or background, these institutions did not believe they were duty-bound to make such visitors feel particularly welcome. Thus the museum became accessible mainly to those who felt no unease or discomfort in the midst of intimidating displays of cultural wealth, who understood what they were looking at (or for) in the ever-growing collections, and who identified with, or aspired to, an upper-class culture or lifestyle that may have been more fiction than fact but which nonetheless set a standard relatively few could attain. In this way the museum became a well-fortified refuge for the art-loving amateur and the gentleman or lady of taste, while for others it was a forbidding or bewildering place.

The Age of the Blockbuster marked the dramatic expansion of the American art museum's audience and at the same time the reorganization and expansion of major art museums along modern corporate lines. The new public that began to appear at art museums in the 1960s was attracted by a new phenomenon that the media eventually called "the blockbuster" exhibition. Not surprisingly, the rise of this new audience coincided with the rapid growth of American higher education that began in the 1950s, and along with it the spread of standardized introductory art history courses. At the same time, corporate wealth began to supplant individual philanthropy, and the corporate influence on museums became pervasive. Not only did corporations take on the role of the museum patron, which brought them dividends in the form of "image" and good will, they also provided models for expansion and reorganization. With boards of trustees increasingly made up of corporate officers, museums began to rationalize and enlarge their operations, offering the public a host of new services and amenities.

As a consequence, the American art museum has become, in the last three decades, user-friendly – to employ a term that reflects the influence of the corporate mentality. Visitors are no longer intimidated by institutional condescension. A lack of specialized art historical knowledge no longer seems to be a barrier to wandering through an exhibition devoted to Olmec sculpture or the canvases of Jan Steen. The museum is, if anything, eager to accommodate untutored visitors with brochures, videos, docent tours, special lectures, computer mini-galleries, touch screens, etc. Most visitors are not embarrassed to rent an acoustiguide at the entrance to the latest ticketed blockbuster or to sign up for a guided tour. Indeed, contemporary museum visitors, like corporate clients, willingly put themselves in the hands of professionals and experts who furnish them with information and insight.

From this we might conclude that American art museums are now far more democratic than they were in the past. Having abandoned most of their elitist pretensions, museums now occupy a more central place in American culture. But does this mean that Bourdieu's analysis no longer applies – that the love of art has become the inalienable right of every American?

The answer to the question is, I believe, a resounding "no." *The Audience for American Art Museums*, the most comprehensive study of American art museum audiences to date, confirms the continuing relevance of Bourdieu's critique to US art museums in their blockbuster phase. Published in 1991 under the sponsorship of the National Endowment for the Arts, *The Audience for American Art Museums* draws upon a "Survey of Public Participation in the Arts," conducted in 1985. Although Mark Davidson Schuster, who analyzes the data, makes no reference to *The Love of Art*, his conclusions about audiences echo those of Bourdieu. Schuster finds virtually no difference between the percentage of Americans who visit art museums (22 percent) and comparable percentages for France (about 21 percent), England (19 percent), and Québec (23 percent).[12] Schuster concludes that "at least in Western countries, [art] museums may well be serving similar segments of their national populations."[13] Thus, with respect to attendance, the United States is not exceptional despite the boom associated with the blockbuster phase of American museum history.

Moreover, like Bourdieu, Schuster maintains that when it comes to the likelihood that someone will visit an art museum, "education [is] the most important predictive variable in [the] list of demographic variables."[14] While 45 percent of those who belong to the highest income group (those who earned $50,000 or more in 1985) visited art museums (as opposed to 16 percent for the lowest income group, those who made $5,000 a year or less), the level of attendance for those who had attended graduate school was fully 55 percent (compared to only 4 percent of those with only an elementary school education).[15] The most educated visitors were also more likely to be repeat visitors. At the time of the survey, those with graduate education comprised only 8 percent of the population but 21 percent of the visitors to art museums, and they made 28 percent of all visits.[16] Schuster even confirms statistically Bourdieu's intuitive argument for the influence of habitus. In 1969 Bourdieu suggested that "individuals already equipped by their family upbringing with a certain familiarity with the world of art" were more likely to visit museums. Schuster shows that those visitors who, as children, had often visited art museums with their parents had a high attendance rate (55 percent), while those who never visited art museums with their parents participated at a low level (14 percent).[17]

Working for the National Endowment for the Arts, Schuster hopes his study will provide art museums with the means for attracting more visitors. But in an uncharacteristic passage, he concedes that "art museums relate more readily to certain individuals than to others and, indeed, are the institutional creation of certain social groups."[18] This is a rare Bourdieuvian insight in a publication that is long on empirical data and desperately short on theory. Moreover, Schuster cannot avoid concluding that "change in audience composition is a slow, resistant process."[19] From this we can infer that American art museums may be able to increase the frequency of their audience's visits by staging blockbusters and other special exhibitions, but the audience itself is unavoidably limited by the demography of class. Schuster's conclusions thus bolster Bourdieu's. Museums remain engines of inclusion and exclusion. As Bourdieu maintained in 1969, this is from a sociological viewpoint their real purpose.[20]

Morphology

Yet it is one thing to maintain, on the basis of statistics, that art museums exclude lower-class audiences, and quite another to argue, as does Bourdieu in the closing paragraphs of *The Love of Art*, that

> if the love of art is the clear mark of the chosen, separating, by an invisible and insuperable barrier, those who are touched by it from those who have not received this grace, it is understandable that in the tiniest details of their morphology and organization, museums betray their true function, which is to reinforce for some the feeling of belonging and for others the feeling of exclusion.[21]

This suggests a critical question. How does what Bourdieu terms "morphology" produce feelings of inclusion and exclusion? What characteristics of the structure and space of the museum attract some and repel others? How, in other words, does the space of the museum acquire its ideological charge?

To begin to answer this question, consider the antecedent institution to the art museum, the princely art gallery of the seventeenth and eighteenth centuries, usually an elaborately decorated space in which a monarch or noble received visitors and staged court ceremonies and dynastic celebrations. Access to the gallery was limited to courtiers and royal guests, which by the eighteenth century might include grand tourists and other art lovers equipped with the necessary letter of introduction. By contrast, the public art museum, an invention of the modern bourgeois state – the Louvre is the prototype – offered unrestricted access. Works of art that had once decorated princely galleries now belonged to all citizens. Yet the new museums also set the terms on which the art within their walls might be enjoyed, and those terms limited entry almost as effectively as the prince's liveried gatekeepers.

The decoration of the princely gallery often featured an iconographic program in which the prince was allegorized as a latter-day Apollo, a bearer of the gifts of peace and the arts of civilization.[22] A visitor paid homage to the prince's virtues and benevolence, if not explicitly then simply by entering and moving through the gallery space. As we shall see, the public art museum also functions as a ceremonial space in which visitors are expected to display obeisance to the presiding deities.

The art museum visitor's immediate experience – and this holds true for all visitors whatever their class or background – depends critically upon the building and its setting, the spaces the building defines, and upon its decorative programs, which include not only permanent embellishments and decorations (e.g., caryatids, moldings, logos, and inscriptions), but also the artworks on display. Every element – building, space, decoration – affects the visitor. A visit to a museum is an ongoing encounter with a variety of symbolic forms with the visitor's response to a large extent predetermined by his or her background and education.

Of course, not all museum buildings are alike; still, most museum buildings conform to one or another recognizable type. There is the universal survey type (the Louvre, the Metropolitan Museum of Art); the Robber Baron mansion (the Frick Collection, the Isabella Stewart Gardner Museum); and the modern art gallery (the Museum of Modern Art, the Guggenheim), to name the most prevalent; and inevitably each type of building contains a particular set of meanings and evokes a certain range of responses.[23] Because it preceded the others and remains the space most associated with the "museum experience," the universal survey type seems the most crucial to examine here.

The exterior of this type of museum – what any visitor first encounters – is likely to recall – indeed to be modeled explicitly upon – the temples and treasuries of ancient Greece and Rome as well as the grand palazzos of Renaissance Europe. The obvious equation between temple form and sacred contents has encouraged the commonplace description of art museums as "temples of art." In addition, the use of a traditional, Greco-Roman architectural vocabulary aligns the museum with the cultural traditions of Western civilization. The temple front recalls the facade of the Parthenon or Pantheon. The building's dome suggests the idea that the museum stands at the center of the tradition of Western culture. Other features reinforce the equation. Thus, for example, Buffalo's Albright-Knox Art Gallery sports no less than two precise replicas of the Erechtheum's Porch of the Maidens. In addition,

the building's marble staircases, columns, pediments, dome, and tri-
umphal arches invoke an architectural rhetoric of state power and a
history of social and political triumph that in France, England,
Germany, and the United States has been associated with the economic
and political triumphs of the bourgeoisie. Finally, decorative elements
on the facade prepare the visitor for the art to be encountered inside.
Busts or statues of artists, or artists' names carved into the building's
facade as, for example, at the Corcoran Gallery in Washington, DC,
connect the idea of art with notions of individual genius.

Approaching the museum thus demands what might be called ideological labor – the receiving and processing of the various symbolic
claims encountered en route to the entrance. Upon entering the
museum, visitors not only confront more instances of triumphalist
architecture – the dome inscribed with American eagles at the National
Gallery, the victory figures flanking the grand staircase at the Metropolitan Museum, and so on – they also find themselves in a space that
belongs to the state or to a quasi-state authority.[24] Proprietorship is a
crucial issue. Visitors may study tablets engraved with the names of
founders and donors or, in the case of the National Gallery tour, a
spectacular Founders Room adjacent to the entrance with portraits of
Mellons, Kresses, Wideners, Rosenwalds, and Dales. But whether or not
visitors interest themselves in the details of philanthropic history, they
are aware on some level that the museum represents an authority that
stands over and above them. Consequently, their comfort or discomfort will depend rather directly upon the extent to which they identify with that very official, if anonymous, authority. Such identification,
however, is not a matter of identifying with bourgeois power per se.
Like the owner of the princely gallery, the authority that presides over
the museum presents itself in the guise of a benevolent promoter of
the arts. Visitors are thus exhorted to identify not with the museum
authority itself, which would be difficult given its tendency towards
anonymity, but with its claims to society's highest values – values associated with art, culture, and civilization.

These claims are not made overtly. Instead, visitors experience them
while engaged in a type of activity that can best be described as ritual.[25]
Not for nothing does the museum building draw its architectural
vocabulary from traditional ritual structures. Although museum architects may think primarily in terms of efficient circulation, the net result
is that art museums are designed primarily for a walk through the

collections. Indeed, what feels most natural in a museum space is the leisurely stroll through the galleries with the visitor pausing, but usually not for long, to consider individual works of art. The museum-goer's activity thus recalls the ceremonies that occur in traditional religious buildings, for instance, the pilgrim's circuit of reliquary chapels in a medieval church. Simply by walking through the galleries of the museum the visitor celebrates and perhaps to some degree internalizes the beliefs and values inscribed in the building's architecture and decorative programs – programs in which a canonical history of art comes to represent the values of culture and civilization, and by implication the virtues of the bourgeois state.[26] For that history to be coherent – for the experience of the museum to be meaningful – the visitor must possess at least a basic knowledge of the history of art. And despite the many and mostly well-intentioned efforts by museum educators, that fundamental knowledge cannot be acquired in the museum itself, but depends upon the visitor's background and education.

Conclusion

At this point our argument appears to have come full circle, returning to Bourdieu's insistence upon the role of education and habitus in determining a love of art. I would, however, observe this difference: feelings of comfort or discomfort, of belonging or not belonging, do not spring from any single experience in the museum but from the totality of the visitors' experience – from the way visitors respond to the ideological claims placed upon them as they move through the museum space. For those unprepared to grapple with those claims, a visit to the museum can be baffling, daunting, overwhelming. If the visitor encounters little with which to identify, how can he or she respond to, let alone resist, the museum's overpowering cultural and social authority? And yet the visitor's sense of inadequacy seems to arise spontaneously – the museum can hardly be called to account. After all, it is not officially exclusionary but open to all. Moreover, the museum space appears to be empty and neutral, a transparent medium for the viewing of works of art. This very transparency, however, suggests that the visitor who fails to appreciate the art on display has only himself or herself to blame; and this inability to appreciate – to find "cultural salvation" – is often experienced as personal weakness or failure. If for certain museum-goers a trip to the galleries reinforces a sense of middle-class identity, of what it means to be a cultured or civilized person, then for others it leads to feelings of inferiority and inadequacy. In capitalist society, cultural institutions are created as if by design to inflict the wounds of class. The art museum, even in our blockbuster age, is no exception.

Notes

An earlier version of this essay appeared in the *Harvard Design Magazine* no. 11 (summer 2000), pp. 48–54. My thanks to Nancy Levinson, co-editor of the magazine, for editorial help; to Paul Mattick for his encouragement and insight; and to Phyllis Rosenzweig for her critical reading of the manuscript.

1 Bridget Fowler, *Pierre Bourdieu and Cultural Theory: Critical Investigations* (London: Sage Publications, 1997), 8.

2 Pierre Bourdieu and Alain Darbel, *The Love of Art: European Art Museums and Their Public*, trans. Caroline Beattie and Nick Merriman (Stanford, CA: Stanford University Press, 1990), 111. *L'Amour de l'art* (Paris: Les Éditions de Minuit) appeared in 1966. Commissioned by the French government, the book confined itself to research carried out in French art museums. A new version published in 1969 incorporated comparative data gathered in Greece, Holland, Poland, and Spain. I will refer to the book as by Bourdieu, since Bourdieu was responsible for the text and was clearly the driving force behind the entire enterprise. Yet while *The Love of Art* embodies Bourdieu's preoccupation with aesthetics, taste, and class, the book was necessarily a collaborative project, with Darbel "formulating the sampling strategy" and Dominique Schnapper working with Bourdieu directing the research which was carried out by teams. See the preface (pp. viiff.) which is wholly devoted to giving credit to Bourdieu's many collaborators.

3 See Judith H. Dobrzynski, "Art Museum Attendance Keeps Rising in the US," *New York Times* (February 1, 1999); Ralph Blumenthal, "My Renoir Beats Your Vermeer," *New York Times* (June 6, 1999); and Judith H. Dobrzynski, "Blockbuster Shows Lure Record Crowds to US Museums," *New York Times* (February 3, 2000).

4 Bourdieu and Darbel, *The Love of Art*, pp. 1–4.

5 Ibid, p. 4.

6 Ibid, p. 17.

7 Ibid, pp. 17ff.

8 Ibid, p. 27.

9 Ibid, p. 47.

10 For a fuller account of this shift, see Alan Wallach, *Exhibiting Contradiction* (Amherst: University of Massachusetts Press, 1998): 38–56.

11 Cited in Walter Muir Whitehill, *Museum of Fine Arts Boston, A Centennial History*, vol. 1 (Cambridge, MA: Harvard University Press, 1970): 201–2.

12   J. Mark Davidson Schuster, *The Audience for American Art Museums*, National Endowment for the Arts, Research Division Report 23 (Washington, DC: Seven Locks Press, 1991): 13. Sweden, where the participation rate was 31 percent, was an exception to the average of about 20 percent.

13   Ibid, p. 18.

14   Ibid, p. 5. See also p. 19, where Schuster describes education "as the key demographic predictor of attendance." See as well the logit curves on pp. 23, 26.

15   Ibid, p. 6.

16   Ibid, p. 39.

17   Ibid, p. 28.

18   Ibid, p. 18.

19   Ibid, p. 10.

20   Bourdieu and Darbel, *The Love of Art*, p. 112. Because museum attendance keeps rising, it might be inferred that Schuster's study, based upon surveys conducted in 1985, is out of date, and that Bourdieu's argument about the relationship between class status and museum attendance no longer obtains. Glenn Lowry, director of the Museum of Modern Art, implies as much when he observes in a 1999 article that "ten years ago . . . the average visitor to the Museum of Modern Art was female, white and 55 years old, with a household income in excess of $70,000 a year. Today that museum visitor is 35, with a household income of less than $50,000 a year." Yet in the same article, Lowry admits that "almost every audience survey I know of still indicates that museums are mainly the preserve of the well educated," thus corroborating Schuster's and Bourdieu's conclusions. Lowry goes on to ask "can museums ever become truly populist institutions, used and enjoyed by all?" In his answer, Lowry asserts that "museums are ultimately about a rarefied experience, the discovery, enjoyment and contemplation of art, an endeavor that is, and should be accessible to all, but whose appeal by definition is limited." In other words, the experience of art must remain restricted to educated − i.e., upper-class − audiences. That the director of the Museum of Modern Art uses the phrase "by definition" to describe art's limited appeal says worlds about the extent to which class bias is a necessary component of the "rarefied" experience of art. See Glenn D. Lowry, "The State of the Art Museum, Ever Changing," *New York Times* (January 10, 1999), section 2.

21   Bourdieu and Darbel, *The Love of Art*, p. 112.

22   For a discussion of the princely collection, see Carol Duncan and Alan Wallach, "The Universal Survey Museum," *Art History* 1: 4 (December 1980): 452−3; Germain Bazin, *The Museum Age*, trans. Jane van Nuis Cahill (New York: Universe Books, 1967): 129−39, 198−9; Neils von Holst, *Creators, Collectors and Connoisseurs*, trans. Brian Battershaw (New York: G. P. Putnam's Son, 1967): 95−139.

23   See Duncan and Wallach, "The Universal Survey Museum," p. 451.

24   In most municipal art museums in the United States, the city owns and maintains the museum building and the board of trustees holds title to the collection.

25   For a fuller discussion of the museum as a ceremonial or ritual structure, see Duncan and Wallach, "The Universal Survey Museum," pp. 449−51.

26   I drastically abbreviate the discussion in Duncan and Wallach (ibid: 460–3), which
     describes how the iconographic program of the princely gallery evolved by stages
     into the commonplace museological program featuring a canonical history of art.

References

Bazin, Germain (1967). *The Museum Age*, trans. Jane van Nuis Cahill. New York:
   Universe Books.
Blumenthal, Ralph (1999). "My Renoir Beats Your Vermeer," *New York Times*, June 6.
Bourdieu, Pierre and Darbel, Alain (1969). *L'Amour de l'art*. Paris: Les Éditions de
   Minuit.
Bourdieu, Pierre and Darbel, Alain (1990). *The Love of Art: European Art Museums and
   Their Public*, trans. Caroline Beattie and Nick Merriman. Stanford, CA: Stanford
   University Press.
Dobrzynski, Judith H. (1999). "Art Museum Attendance Keeps Rising in the US," *New
   York Times*, February 1.
Dobrzynski, Judith H. (2000). "Blockbuster Shows Lure Record Crowds to US
   Museums," *New York Times*, February 3.
Duncan, Carol and Wallach, Alan (1980). "The Universal Survey Museum," *Art History*
   1: 4, 448–69.
Fowler, Bridget (1997). *Pierre Bourdieu and Cultural Theory: Critical Investigations*. London:
   Sage.
Schuster, J. Mark Davidson (1991). *The Audience for American Art Museums*, National
   Endowment for the Arts, Research Division Report 23. Washington, DC: Seven
   Locks Press.
von Holst, Neils (1967). *Creators, Collectors and Connoisseurs*, trans. Brian Battershaw.
   New York: G. P. Putnam's Son.
Wallach, Alan (1998). *Exhibiting Contradiction*. Amherst: University of Massachusetts
   Press.
Whitehill, Walter Muir (1970). *Museum of Fine Arts Boston, A Centennial History*, 2 vols.
   Cambridge, MA: Harvard University Press.

6

Museums and Department Stores: Close Encounters
Carol Duncan

It is no longer possible to take for granted the idea of the art museum as a sanctuary for the silent contemplation of art objects. One can still find quiet art museums in the United States or quiet corners in even the busiest ones. But the idea of the museum as a sanctuary, a place set apart from more mundane concerns, is harder to sustain in big museums like the Metropolitan Museum in New York, the Art Institute in Chicago, or the Los Angeles County Museum of Art. With their crowds of noisy visitors, big advertising budgets, and ever-growing retail departments – not to mention their growing dependence on corporate sponsorship – these institutions look more like a part *of* the business world than a realm apart from it. Museum stores, once small shops or even single counters selling postcards and a few publications, have grown into superstores, complete with franchised outlets and websites that do millions of dollars in sales. When does a special exhibition *not* conclude with a boutique full of ties, teapots, or other merchandise copied from or reminiscent of something in the show?

This is not to say that art museum professionals have stopped producing thoughtful shows; in my view, what museums offer these days is on the whole more enlightening and much better researched than the standard museum fare of a generation ago. What I am saying is that the ever greater and more visible amounts of museum space given over to commerce has had the effect of eroding the museum's special status as a commerce-free zone. Art museums are, after all, nominally public spaces dedicated to the preservation of what are, presumably, collectively held higher values – values that, at least in theory, exist above the special interests of any one section of society. As such, art museums are expected to keep their distance from commercial culture. In a similar way, they are expected to observe the boundary between "high" and "popular" culture, whatever that might mean at any given moment. As categories of cultural analysis, the commercial and the popular can not always be distinguished, but the presence of too much of either in a museum can compromise its integrity and very identity as a museum. It is telling that even art museum shops avoid the popular if it veers too far from the "tasteful." The merchandise they stock normally references "high" art in some way – usually in the form of reproductions or replicas of the museum's collections – and caters to a clientele whose purchases reinforce a middle- (if not always high-) brow taste. Museums, then, steer carefully between their need to maintain the appearance of disinterestedness and their interest in the budget- and attendance-enhancing allures of commerce.

Yet the museum's mandate to keep a distance from and even stand in opposition to the commercial and the popular has not always been observed. Indeed, the belief that art museums of the past maintained a kind of purity but are presently becoming compromised by commercialism is something of a fiction. This chapter will discuss an interesting moment, culminating in the 1920s, but continuing into later decades, when art museums, far from maintaining an aloofness from industry, sought relations with it. According to some observers of the time, museums and department stores were scarcely distinguishable. As one of them asked in 1928, "Now that we have department stores, do we need museums of art?"[1]

As the historian Neil Harris observed, in the nineteenth and early twentieth centuries, art museums – in particular the Victoria and Albert in London (hereafter the V&A) and major American museums like New York's Metropolitan Museum of Art and Boston's Museum of Fine Arts – had a lot in common with world's fairs and department stores.[2] In fact, art museums, especially museums of decorative arts, world's fairs, and department stores are components of a single development that was as much economic as it was cultural. The establishment of the V&A (known as the South Kensington Museum until 1901) was directly inspired by the success of the first world's fair, the Great Exhibition of 1851, held in the Crystal Palace in London.[3] In turn, both fair and museum were responses to an extraordinary growth of industry and commerce and an accompanying culture of consumerism that was already fully underway in both Europe and America. As increasing numbers of manufacturers competed with each other in the international market, new forms of retailing and marketing were required to distribute an unprecedented volume of goods. The department store appeared and flourished as one of the most successful responses to this development. The world's fair, the museum of decorative arts, and the department store were not only linked to each other by economic causes; they also overlapped in their cultural functions. Through their displays of objects, all three promoted the culture of consumerism and stimulated and/or facilitated markets for manufactured goods. Above all, they introduced notions of good taste to a broad, middle-class public, and taught the pleasures of spending rather than saving unused purchasing power.[4]

At this point, it is necessary to distinguish the V&A from other art museums, especially within British museum culture, which usually differentiates between *museums* and *galleries*. There are significant differences between the V&A Museum and a British art gallery, the National Gallery in London being the premier example. The difference bears directly on the question at hand, namely, the presence or absence of commercial interests in museums. Generally speaking, museums are dedicated to educational purposes, galleries to the aesthetic contemplation of art (although the latter could also be construed as educational in a broad sense). The V&A, opened in 1857, was intended to advance the commercial life of the nation and give its manufacturers a competitive edge by making available to English craftsmen beautiful examples of decorative and applied art from the past – objects of glass, silver, iron, marble, and other materials – from which they could learn principles of design. Displays of decorative arts were also thought to have an improving effect on the lower orders of society, since, it was reasoned, objects of practical use are more comprehensible to the uneducated than "higher" art forms. In contrast, the British art or picture gallery was addressed to those more refined sections of the nation with presumably loftier needs. It descends not from industrial fairs but from princely and aristocratic art collections.[5] The gallery's displays of (mostly) oil paintings and (occasionally) sculpture, arranged to reveal the "genius" of past civilizations, was meant to transport visitors to a realm of spirit, well above the mundane pursuits of a commercial and manufacturing economy. But while the art gallery and the museum of decorative arts remained distinct types of collections in Britain,[6] in the

United States the two were brought together as parts of a single museum type. The American elites who founded the nation's major art museums in New York, Boston, and Chicago in the decade of the 1870s, were enthralled by the V&A's much vaunted power to improve and civilize the working classes, but they were also dazzled by the old master collections in the Louvre Museum (where, unlike British models, sculpture was included) and other impressive European art galleries. The omnibus type they invented became the norm for almost all later American art museums.

In effect, then, American museum culture, as it took form in the later nineteenth century and the first three decades of the twentieth, grew out of a fusion of two distinct and (if one bothered to think about it) contradictory museum concepts, the one making (or claiming to make) commerce and manufacturing a central concern of the museum, the other putting it out of bounds. The contradiction, however potentially troublesome, could usually be ignored, since both "fine" and "decorative" art collections can be rationalized as educationally or aesthetically significant, or both, depending on how one defines those terms. Moreover, what most American museums have actually accumulated – old master and modern oil paintings, Renaissance bronzes, eighteenth-century furniture, medieval armor – the mix of "fine" and "decorative" art we see in most museums – these actual museum collections almost always consist of the kinds of things sought after or once owned by the museum's upper-class donors and supporters. This has left American museums open to the charge, especially leveled when populist sentiments run high, that their displays have very little to do with educating anyone, let alone workers and businessmen, but have everything to do with the vanity of millionaires who wish to see their home furnishings celebrated as manifestations of the highest taste and the rarest of treasure. In self-defense, museums could confidently claim that simply by exhibiting beautiful objects of pewter, glass, or silver, they were fulfilling their mandate to educate artisans – confidently, because few doubted the wisdom of the V&A assumption that displays of beautiful objects could improve the products and even the deportment of workers.[7]

Inevitably, people began to compare museum displays of decorative objects to shop windows. The comparison was not usually flattering to museums. In 1881 the English social reformer W. Stanley Jervons argued that the V&A's presentations of decorative arts failed to realize the museum's goal of educating workmen. Jervons did not question the museum's assumption that displays of objects as such could be instructive. What he criticized was the museum's haphazard approach to display – its disorganized and overcrowded cases. Viewers can hardly focus on their contents, he complained, and the idea that anyone could become civilized simply by wandering past them is absurd. Shop windows, he wrote, are more attractive, up–to–date, and instructive, and people prefer them with good reason.[8]

In American cities, too, the activity of gazing into glass cases to scrutinize museum objects suggested window shopping, and window shopping increasingly suggested department-store browsing. By the turn of the century the department store had fully evolved as the summit shopping experience. Indeed, department stores transformed "shopping" into a pleasurable leisure activity that could include browsing, taking refreshments, and even attending a concert. As semi-public, often elegantly scaled spaces, many department stores could fully equal art museums in architectural splendor as well as cultural attractions. They certainly surpassed them in conveniences, offering comfortable, well-appointed waiting rooms, fine restaurants, day-care facilities, and even dentists' offices.[9] Wanamaker's (Philadelphia), Macy's (New York), Marshall Field's (Chicago), and scores of other stores were famous for their sumptuous interiors, amenities, and even (in Wanamaker's especially) exhibitions of fine paintings. Indeed, great merchant princes like Wanamaker, Filine (Boston), and Bamberger (Newark) could represent themselves as entrepreneurs with both civic and cultural missions, merchants in whose establishments the customer could improve her taste and the manufacturer his product.

Among museum professionals, no one gave more thought to the similarities between museums and department stores than John Cotton Dana (1856–1929), the director of the Newark Museum from its founding in 1909 until his death in 1929. A Progressive Era intellectual and pragmatic reformer, Dana's approach to museology grew out of his experience as a library reformer.[10] By the turn of the century – when he came to Newark – he had become a key figure in the movement to modernize American public libraries. He was one of the first librarians to open stacks to the public, established the first children's reading rooms, and, in what was an unconventional move, advertised the library in local newspapers. Departing even more fundamentally from the library culture of his day, he ridiculed the concept of the library as a sanctuary of high-minded classics and stocked all manner of materials not normally found there – magazines, newspapers, directories, popular novels, engravings, photographs, and anything else useful or interesting to users. He also started a collection of Japanese prints, and in the library's unused upper floors, began to mount exhibitions of art. This activity eventually led to the founding of the Newark Museum Association in 1909, which Dana directed until his death twenty years later. The new museum would occupy rooms in the library building for its first sixteen years, until, in 1925, it moved into its own purpose-built structure down the street.

Newark was hardly unique in creating new cultural institutions such as museums and libraries. Since the 1870s American urban elites had been building libraries, museums, and concert halls at a brisk pace. Such institutions were considered necessary ornaments for any city that wanted to be taken seriously as a prosperous and civilized community. Art museums not only conferred upon their benefactors social distinction, they also effectively announced the arrival of a city to national and international business and banking communities. Like other prestigious institutions of high culture, art museums signaled a city's political stability and economic health. Newark had certainly arrived into those conditions. Situated across the Hudson River from New York City and well-connected by rail and water to the whole of the eastern seaboard, the city had been an important manufacturing center since the Civil War. Now, at the beginning of the twentieth century, it was well on its way to becoming one of the nation's major industrial giants.

Yet another factor had much to do with the founding of American institutions of high culture in this era. Especially in the industrial north, urban populations were continually augmented by a stream of immigrant labor from all corners of Europe. For example, Newark's population in 1913 was two-thirds foreign born. In this and other American cities, the growing presence of Italian, Jewish, German, Irish, Greek, Slavic, and other immigrants made the founding of cultural institutions urgent. Fearful of being culturally and politically swamped, "old-stock," Anglo-Saxon Americans built art museums partly as buffers between themselves and the newcomers, and partly in the hope that these cultural institutions would unite the disparate class and ethnic elements of the cities into one community with a single (Northern European) culture.

By the time Dana came to Newark in 1902 there were big new art museums in all of the major American cities and in many of the middle-sized ones as well. These municipal museums almost always began as impressive but largely empty buildings. Americans had learned early that the quick way to get a museum was to first erect a showy building and then wait for status-seeking millionaires to fill it up. Both the Metropolitan Museum of Art in New York and the Art Institute in Chicago, both typical museums of the Gilded Age, were loaded with references to ancient temples, Roman baths, and Renaissance palaces. Both were quickly filled with boat-loads of treasures purchased by millionaire businessmen who combed Europe for what they took to be old master paintings and antique furniture, china, glass, tapestries, stucco ceilings, and anything else they could buy and transport home. When they could not buy or dig up originals, they filled their museums with quantities of plaster casts of ancient and Renaissance sculpture or put modern pastiches of them on their neo-classical buildings (as in Chicago and New Orleans).

Dana was determined to make the Newark Museum as different as possible from the standard model. Indeed, he conceived it as a Progressive alternative to that model. Calling it "a museum of service," it was to be an example for other industrial cities, an experiment that asked the question, What kind of museum best serves the needs of a modern, industrial city? – instead of the usual question, How can our city acquire a Louvre-type museum? Over the length of his museum career, in an endless stream of booklets, pamphlets, newspaper and magazine articles, Dana expounded what was wrong with American art museums and what his Newark Museum was doing instead. Along the way, he also began campaigning for a building that would allow him to realize more fully his Progressive ideas. In all of these writings he never tired of lampooning the pretentiousness, solemnity, and snobbery of the conventional museum model.

Dana grounded his critique of museums in ideas common to many Progressivist theorists of his time. His earlier writings are especially flavored by the ideas of Thorstein Veblen, whose widely read book, *The Theory of the Leisure Class* (1899), Dana called "delightful." In it, Veblen detailed the upper class's insatiable appetites for luxuries, arguing that

its expensive leisure pursuits, over-cultivated manners, sumptuous fashions, immense houses, and stupendous art collections were but different ways of conspicuously consuming and wasting wealth. The value
of such ostentatious waste, Veblen argued, resided largely in its capacity to differentiate class status – to distinguish its users from their social
inferiors, those on whose productive creativity and labor the idle rich
parasitically lived. For Veblen, "taste," or a "sense of the beautiful," does
not exist independently of the economics of social use: if we find cost-
lier things more beautiful than cheap ones, it is not necessarily because
we put more monetary value on the beautiful but because the concepts of beauty that thrive in our culture tend to validate as beautiful
that which is more expensive.[11] Veblen helped Dana to a broad, Pierre
Bourdieu-like theoretical perspective complete with ideas about the
social meaning of aesthetic values. With relish, he applied these ideas
to conventional museums, which he described as

> temples of dead gods, or copies of palaces of an extinct nobility, or costly
> reproductions of ancient temples, or grand and elaborate structures
> which are of service only as evidences of conspicuous waste by the rich
> and as ocular demonstration of the unwise expenditures of public funds.

Dana also shared with Veblen and other Progressives the conviction
that a better future was in the making – a future predicated on the
collapse of the present "leisure class" and one in which a rational and
democratic industrial culture would triumph. Others, too, including the
corporate scientist and socialist politician Charles Steinmetz and the
liberal political analyst Walter Lippmann, believed that the workings
of modern business and the imperatives of large-scale production were
inexorably moving society to a more rational and efficient stage, a
new era of mass-produced plenty to be managed by an elite of highly
trained technocrats. Dana seems to have been convinced that this better, more productive, and more enlightened future would be brought
into being by business, not simply because business seeks profits, but
because in seeking them, it becomes a pragmatic, modernizing force.
"Business runs the world," he wrote.

> The world gets civilized just as fast as men learn to run things on plain
> business principles. A public institution does its best work when it is
> useful to men of business.[12]

Libraries and museums, argued Dana, were instruments that could not only shape the workforce of the future but provide entrepreneurs with the information they needed to develop their businesses and in general help build the culture needed for an industrial future.

With that future in mind, Dana envisioned a new kind of museum, an educational force designed to help bring about and serve a new industrial order. To accomplish its task, this new museum must differ in every respect from the conventional model – from the kinds of objects it displays to the kind of looking and learning it stimulates to the kind of people and community it serves. In his writings Dana contrasted this bright and optimistic museum vision to the "gloom" of the old museum, which he portrayed as a graveyard of leisure-class fashion and wasted wealth. His museum would not be "one more of those useless, wearisome, dead-alive Gazing Collections,"[13] "awesome to a few, tiresome to many and helpful to almost none."[14] It would not be filled with costly and ancient oil paintings, objects Dana thought attracted "undue reverence" and "extreme veneration."[15] Nor would its collections be shaped by the hobbies and enthusiasms of "the memorial-seeking rich."[16]

In many ways, Dana's ideal museum was an American Progressivist reworking and Machine-Age updating of London's Victoria and Albert Museum. As noted above, the V&A was greatly admired in the American museum world of the late nineteenth and early twentieth centuries. Educated opinion firmly believed that displays of decorative arts – textiles, ceramics, ironwork, and the like – had the power to improve the skills, taste, and even the morality of the working classes and generally enhance modern life.[17] So entrenched were these ideas that American museum officials routinely cited their displays of decorative arts as concrete proof of their public-mindedness and accountability as educational institutions. It was even argued that the decorative arts democratized art museums, since uneducated persons could relate more easily to them than to the more intellectually demanding higher arts.[18] However, as Dana knew, the objects acquired by public art museums and exhibited as decorative arts were usually the kind of things collected by American millionaires in search of aristocratic identities – clocks, silver, or china made for European nobility. As he put it,

> The kinds of objects, ancient, costly and imported, that the rich feel they must buy to give themselves a desired distinction, are inevitably the

kinds that they, as patrons and directors of museums, cause those museums to acquire.[19]

Dana understood that his museum would have to show enough predictable museum treasure to satisfy conventional expectations and also keep up competitively with other cities. A few old master paintings near the entrance would suffice, he thought.[20] Whatever paintings the museum acquired after that would be works made by living American artists. Such a policy, he insisted, was the best way for a museum to foster and improve art production and appreciation in its community. In fact, the Newark Museum began collecting American art long before other museums, and built an outstanding collection, including works by some of the best progressive and modernist artists such as John Sloan and Max Weber.

In any case, Dana's model museum was not simply a collection of things, and least of all costly and ancient things. "It is easy for a museum to get objects," he wrote, "it is hard for a museum to get brains." A brainy museum touches, instructs, and entertains common people, makes life "more interesting, joyful and wholesome,"[21] is alive with learning children and adults, and abounds with information, handbooks, and leaflets. Dana's museum would certainly exhibit objects. It would, however, privilege not oil paintings, but things people use – well-designed things that working people can afford, things made in their own city with modern technology, things they might purchase in Newark's stores. As Dana himself recognized, the museum he wanted to create would have much in common with a department store. To be sure, he was not the first to compare window shopping with visiting a museum; in fact, he knew and admired Jervons's book (cited above), in which that comparison is made. But Jervons had focused solely on the aesthetics of display, and concluded that store windows were superior to the V&A's cases mainly because they were less cluttered. Dana, writing in 1913, took the comparison much farther:

A great city department store of the first class is perhaps more like a good museum of art than are any of the museums we have yet established. It is centrally located; it is easily reached; it is open to all at all the hours when patrons care to visit it; it receives all courteously and gives information freely; it displays its most attractive and interesting objects and shows countless others on request; its collections are classified according to the knowledge and needs of its patrons; it is well lighted; it has convenient and inexpensive rest rooms; it supplies guides free of charge; it advertises itself widely and continuously; and it changes its exhibits to meet daily changes in subjects of interest, changes of taste in art, and the progress of invention and discovery.

"A department store is not a good museum," Dana cautioned, "but so far are museums from being the active and influential agencies they might be that they may be compared with department stores, and not altogether to their advantage."[22]

A decade later, comparisons between museums and department stores would become familiar journalistic exercises. The 1920s would also see cooperative efforts between art museums and department stores. In the teens, however, art museums tended to keep more of a distance from the commercial world of retail, and Dana's comparison, aimed as criticism of conventional institutions like the Metropolitan and Boston's Museum of Fine Arts, stung.[23] Dana shared none of this uneasiness about commerce. On the contrary, he developed a remarkable institutional relationship between his museum and Newark's most illustrious department store, L. Bamberger & Company, facilitated by his friendship with its co-owner, Louis Bamberger.[24] In fact, the passage quoted above comparing department stores and art museums may well have been inspired by the store's splendid new eight-story building, which had opened just a few months before (October 15, 1912) and was only blocks from the museum. With its sixteen elevators and escalators, its restaurant, auditorium, and – as one newspaper described it – its "roominess, light, ample ventilation and convenience of arrangement," the new building was a national leader in department store architecture and a state-of-the-art environment for visual displays and public events.[25] Bamberger, its most visible executive, was also a good example of the kind of civic-minded, liberal department-store owner that his generation sometimes produced.[26]

Bamberger had been a founding member of the Newark Museum Association in 1909 and remained an avid supporter of Dana and his struggle to realize his vision of a progressive museum. Indeed, in 1925, when the museum was finally able to move out of the Library and into its own building, it was because Bamberger donated the half million dollars the new building cost. Moreover, the architect for the new structure, Jarvis Hunt, was not the usual beaux-arts designer of American museums, but the man who had just finished (in 1922) the latest addition to the ever-expanding L. Bamberger & Co. But many years before, the generous and philanthropic Bamberger seems to have become something of a Dana disciple – although, in the absence of letters, it's hard to know which way ideas might have flowed. Whichever way they went, Newark's only museum and its premier department store began a collaborative relationship that prefigured things to come elsewhere.

In 1913 Bamberger's staged a spectacular event that so fully realized Dana's ideas it is difficult to believe he did not have something to do with its inception. The entire store was converted into an exposition of industrial arts that lasted ten days. Over fifty booths showed goods manufactured in Newark. Many included demonstrations of how the exhibited products were manufactured from raw materials, the exhibiting manufacturers having installed factory machines in the store for that purpose. There were demonstrations of diamond cutting, a working ribbon loom, the manufacture of corsets, baseball uniforms, men's shirts, glass, bathtubs, sweaters, and much else. On display in the basement was the first incandescent lamp made by Thomas A. Edison in 1880. The occasion was festive. Winona Hoffman and Her Band gave two concerts daily in the new store's auditorium. Over 400,000 visitors attended what was the biggest and most important such show in the city's history. The entire event was repeated in 1914 and again in 1915. In 1914 President Wilson initiated the opening from his desk in Washington, DC. By touching a telegraph key, he triggered a switch in Newark, which lit up a large battery of electric lights in the form of an American flag, at which point an orchestra began playing.[27] Surely, Dana's vision of a "museum with brains," where people of all ages enjoy learning about interesting things that will make their lives better, owed something to these expositions. And just as surely, the original idea of holding an industrial fair in a department store – of celebrating the city's producers and its most successful retail distributor – was Dana's, or if not his alone, the product of a Dana–Bamberger dialogue.

The publicity surrounding the event was also flavored with a museum-like rationale. As the city's press reported, the purpose of the *Made in Newark* exposition was not to make money, but to educate the public about Newark's manufacturers.[28] The mission of the exposition thus came very close to what Dana was beginning to define as the central mission of his museum. It was, in fact, just now – around 1912–13 – that Dana became more ambitious about his museum and more interested in developing it as a museum of decorative arts.[29] In a series of letters, pamphlets, and articles, written and/or published from this time forward, he began defining his vision. He also began campaigning for its support among Newark's wealthy businessmen, arguing that his museum serves the interests and needs of an industrial city like Newark, improves the taste of the population, educates them about the city's industries, and provides businessmen with useful information about the newest technological advances. The museum thus stimulates the city's commerce, instills civic pride in its citizens, and psychologically prepares the population for its role as workers and consumers in the industrial society of the future. Echoing the original mission of the V&A, but with a mass-produced, machine-oriented emphasis, Dana's Progressive era museum would promote and celebrate commerce as the life-blood of the city. As did L. Bamberger & Co. when the entire store became the *Made in Newark* industrial fair. Nor is it surprising, given his friendship with Dana, that Bamberger described his intentions in Dana's museum terms:"The big show is NOT a commercial enterprise in any sense of the word. It is a fair – an exposition – a *civic* function."[30] Of course, it *was* very much a commercial enterprise, and a very successful one, at that, bringing much publicity to the store's civic gesture. In any case, Dana would often realize just this kind of "civic function" in his museum, both in the teens and, after the move to the new building, in a series of exhibitions devoted to New Jersey industries, among them shows about clay products (1915), textiles (1916), and, in the inaugural exhibition of the new building in 1926, leather. Like the Bamberger fair, these exhibitions often included demonstrations of manufacturing processes and machines used in them. But this was not the end of the museum–department store connection.

In the decade of the 1920s, as industry reached unprecedented levels of production – levels that could not be absorbed by consumers – competition between retailers increased.[31] Department stores sought to stimulate sales and attract more customers by developing new strategies. These were especially aimed at winning the public's confidence in a store's ability to offer its customers the most tasteful merchandise and the latest fashions at the lowest prices. In this competitive climate, stores discovered the profitability of "non-profit," good-will cultural presentations that enhanced their image as arbiters of good taste. Accordingly, they democratized, advertised, and merchandised the pleasures and advantages of "good design" and the "fine" arts with great energy. As the journalist Zelda Popkin observed, department stores

> have given themselves over to the teaching of aesthetics, because this is a stimulus to business. . . . Our merchant princes [the department store owners] have gone in for the role of Lorenzo de Medici because they thus create prestige and good will for their establishments. They give concerts, stage art exhibitions, historical pageants, aviation dinners, out of which they derive no cent of profits directly, because these stunts get publicity, stimulate public interest, and make the public regard them as the community institutions which they eventually hope to become.[32]

Displays of art, even when not for sale, could enhance a store's reputation as a source of tasteful and fashionable products.[33] Numerous department stores had art departments. In the twenties, Wanamaker's was showing works by Walter Kuhn, Stuart Davis, Joseph Stella, George Ault, Guy Pène du Bois, and Jules Pascin.[34] Macy's changing exhibitions of talented but affordable artists were regularly reviewed in the *New York Times*, whose critic called the store a "missionary of art," since it exposed its shoppers to things they would not ordinarily see.[35] As Zelda Popkin (among many others) observed, many women who regularly frequented department stores did not attend lectures or hear concerts, and "most of them have seen only the outside of art museums and galleries. . . . In a very literal sense the department store is their university."[36] In her article Popkin surveys the presence of other cultural events in department stores as well, not only in New York, but also in Atlanta, Chicago, Cleveland, Pittsburgh, St. Louis, San Francisco, and elsewhere. According to the *Times* even members of the American Association of Museums agreed "that the Fifth Avenue stores were 'the best museums in the world, because of the large crowds inspecting the window displays and the artistic quality of the displays.' "[37] And, as journalists frequently noted, modern art was much more readily seen in department stores than art museums, for example a 1928 display in Lord and Taylor's which included paintings by Friesz, Laurencin, Utrillo, Vlaminck, Braque, Derain, Dufy, and Picasso.[38]

It was, understandably, to the decorative arts and home furnishings that department stores seemed to devote their most ambitious exhibition efforts. The mid- and later twenties saw a series of "art in trade" or "art in industry" shows, as they were called, and a number of them involved art museum professionals. It should also be noted that, by now, art museums, led by the Metropolitan in New York, were finally joining Newark in promoting and exhibiting the decorative arts.[39] That is, whether approached from the museum side or the commercial side, the divide between the commercial space of the store and the public, institutional space of the art museum seemed less fixed than ever. By the later twenties department store exhibitions not only surpassed museum shows in size and scope, they also seemed bent on usurping their professional staffs. Macy's week-long *Art-in-Trade* exhibition of May, 1927, was one of the first of these very large shows. The well-known set designer Lee Simonson designed the space, and staff from the Metropolitan Museum of Art helped with the installation. Accompanying the show was a four-day symposium, held in an auditorium constructed in Macy's for the event. An advisory committee of distinguished professionals from museums, education, publishing, fashion, architecture, various arts organizations, and the commercial world chose the speakers, among whom were Robert DeForest, President of the Metropolitan, John Finley, President of the Arts Council of New York City, the sculptor Paul Manship, Stanley McCanless, an instructor in stage lighting at Yale University, Mrs. George P. Snow, of *Vogue Magazine*, and many others. The exhibition and symposium received extensive – and approving – daily coverage in the *Times*. A recurrent theme in this coverage was that the combined communities of arts and museum professionals and commercial retailers and designers were helping American manufacturers of decorative arts successfully compete in international markets. Above all, they were educating American consumers aesthetically and providing them with opportunities to enrich their daily surroundings with art.[40] One reviewer, noting the willingness of American artists to design for machine-made, mass-produced objects, concluded:

> The Macy exhibition demonstrated conclusively that a home could be established in this country upon a fairly moderate scale of expenditure with art coming in at every turn. Textiles, pottery, silver and prints go far toward emphasizing the individuality of a house, and in these

fields at least the priceless element of art can be had for only a little price.[41]

In 1928 Macy's held another large exhibition, occupying an entire floor of its new building, and representing decorative arts from six nations. Once again, a committee of professionals from the arts, business, and museums planned and installed the show and organized an accompanying symposium of distinguished artists and educators. The opening was a significant diplomatic event, involving numerous foreign ambassadors, consulates, and attachés, and generating much newspaper copy.

In Newark, where museum culture and department store culture had a long history of cross-fertilization, such shows were perhaps less of a novelty. Nevertheless, in the twenties, they became more like museum events and less like industrial fairs. Thus, in 1929, Bamberger's announced an exhibition entitled *3,000 Years of Art in Modern Rugs and Carpets*, which included objects borrowed from museums in New York, Brooklyn, and Newark, and clearly aspired to the quality and scholarship of a serious museum show. Lee Simonson, the "exhibition architect," gave it a stylish installation, and John Cotton Dana wrote the foreword to the show's catalogue, an elegant and important-looking publication. An accompanying lecture program featured museum professionals, art educators, and design experts, and speeches delivered on the opening day were broadcast on Bamberger's own radio station, WOR.[42] Newark also saw what appear to be joint museum–department store exhibitions. An international show of ceramic art held in the museum in 1929 (plate 6.1) ran simultaneously with special shows of ceramics at Bamberger's and other New Jersey stores (plate 6.2). At one point, Bamberger's literally became an extension of the museum: in 1931 a branch of the Newark Public Library opened on its premises, and since Dana had put branches of the museum into all the library branches, some museum display cases were actually installed in Bamberger's store windows.[43] Meanwhile, the museum, now in its new building, continued to mount "art-in-trade" and "design-in-industry" exhibitions. One such show, a detail of which is reproduced here, included useful objects made of metal – in this detail, a curtain fixture, a hammer, a lantern, and a door knob – all on loan from various retail establishments (plate 6.3).

Finally, Dana, always the educator, thought up an ingenious way of showing visitors to his museum that they could enjoy aesthetically

Plate 6.1   International Exhibition of Ceramic Art, view of English section, Newark Museum, 1929. Collection of the Newark Museum.

pleasing objects in their homes at very little cost. In 1928 he sent members of his staff into nearby stores with instructions to purchase well-designed objects for no more than 10 or 25 cents. Their purchases were then installed in museum cases under a sign that proclaimed, "Beauty has no relation to price, rarity or age." The exercise, repeated in 1929, went as high as 50 cents (plates 6.4, 6.5).

The above account of art in department stores and manufactured goods in museums ends in 1929. With the advent of the Great Depression, sales in department stores dropped dramatically – 49 percent between 1929 and 1933 – and, for a time, stores found it difficult to mount ambitious exhibitions.[44] When the worst of the Depression passed and business picked up, so did the selling and exhibition of art. For example, the American Artists Congress held its Second Annual Membership Exhibition in Wanamaker's store in New York in May, 1938, in a gallery

Plate 6.2 Exhibit of ceramics at Hahnes Department Store, 1929. A placard links the display to the Exhibition of Ceramic Art running concurrently in the Newark Museum. Collection of the Newark Museum.

on the fifth floor. Museum culture also continued to find a place for the recognition of modern design. Which brings me to the Museum of Modern Art in New York, with which I end this account.

Probably no institution took more from the legacy of John Cotton Dana and the Newark Museum than the Museum of Modern Art. Alfred Barr, the MoMA's founding director, fully acknowledged the debt. In 1929, just after Dana died and just before the MoMA opened, Barr wrote an *homage* to Dana and the Newark Museum. In it, he contrasted conventional art museums – those "fabulous dump heaps of the

Plate 6.3 Examples of hardware from the Design in Industry Exhibition, Newark Museum, 1929. Collection of the Newark Museum.

Plate 6.4 Examples of glass and ceramics from the Inexpensive Objects Exhibition, 1929. Also called the 10c Exhibition. Collection of the Newark Museum.

Plate 6.5 Case of glass and black and white textile from the Inexpensive Objects Exhibition, 1929. Collection of the Newark Museum.

sixty or seventy previous centuries" – to the Newark Museum, which "opened its doors to the world of today," to our machine-made, mass-produced civilization, and revealed to us the "order and proportion" in "steam radiators and ten-cent store crockery."

[Dana] had the vision to perceive that art is not a means of escape from life but a stratagem by means of which we conquer life's disorder.[45]

Not incidently, these words prefaced a short article on the soon-to-open MoMA that appeared in *Charm*, a magazine published by L. Bamberger & Co. from 1924 to 1932 and distributed to the store's middle-class charge-card holders (it was also sold). Full of articles about the arts, literature, and modern design, it looked not like promotional literature for the store but a smart, sophisticated periodical devoted to cultural matters. Amidst articles about new trends in fashions and home furnishings were serious pieces by well-known writers and artists – reviews by Malcolm Cowley, an essay on film directing by Herman Mankiewicz, covers reproducing works by Picasso and other modern-ists.[46] The issue with Barr's essay has one of the museum's Van Goghs on the cover. As a cultural artifact, it nicely documents this moment in which the public, presumably disinterested space of the museum and the commercial space of the department store enjoyed the friendliest of relations, cultural and institutional. As Mary Ann Staniszewski has observed, "the great divide that separates high culture from low, the original from the mass-produced, the commercial from the aesthetic was extremely permeable."[47]

From the 1930s through the 1950s the MoMA remained deeply committed to the promotion of modern design and staged numerous exhibitions that unabashedly addressed the museum-goer as a con-sumer. Among these was a MoMA version of Dana's *Inexpensive Objects* exhibitions. The first one, called *Useful Household Objects Under $5* (1938), was a popular traveling show that made stops at department stores; the museum did variants of it up to 1950. It also staged many furniture shows, often in close collaboration with manufacturers and retailers.[48] It is fitting that the MoMA's store, full of modern, well-designed objects, has long figured as an integral part of the museum, a logical extension of its commitment to the cause of good design. In some ways, the MoMA realizes more fully Dana's original hopes for his museum. But then, Dana had addressed his lessons in consumerism to a city of immigrants and industrial workers who had little share in the fabulous profits of the twenties economy and even less to spend in the thirties. In midtown Manhattan, Barr could play to a different class constituency, one for whom a $5 household item could be regarded as inexpensive. In the decades after World War II the divide between "high art" and commercial art would widen, and the distance would come to be seen as natural to museum culture. Eventually, even the memory of looking at art in department stores or shopping in the museum faded. Perhaps it is telling that MoMA's design department, once on a lower floor and closely connected to the painting galleries, now occupies a space more isolated from the rest of the collection, upstairs in the attic-like fourth floor.

Notes

1   John Cotton Dana, "Is the Department Store a Museum?" *The Museum* (published by Newark Museum Association), II (no. 1, July–August, 1928), 1–2.

2   Neil Harris, "Museums, Merchandising and Popular Taste: The Struggle for Influence," in M. G. Quimby, ed., *Material Culture and the Study of American Life* (New York: W. W. Norton, 1978), 140–70.

3   Michael Conforti, "The Idealist Enterprise and the Applied Arts," in Malcolm Baker and Brenda Richardson, eds., *A Grand Design: The Art of the Victoria and Albert Museum* (exhibition catalogue) (London: V&A publications, 1997; New York: Harry N. Abrams; Baltimore: the Baltimore Museum of Art, 1997), 23–47.

4   William Leach's *Land of Desire: Merchants, Power, and the Rise of a New American Culture* (New York: Pantheon Books, 1993) is the outstanding study of museums and department stores and the rise of consumerist culture. Hrant Pasdermadjian's *The Department Store: Its Origins, Evolution, and Economics* (London: Newman Books, 1954), more limited in scope, is also excellent.

5   See my *Civilizing Rituals: Inside Public Art Museums* (London and New York: Routledge, 1995), 32–47.

6   At least in theory. In practice, the V&A also collects oil paintings and has a superb collection of fine sculpture. However, nineteenth-century culture assumed a difference of *purpose* between the V&A's art holdings, and the fine arts collections of galleries. The former were addressed to English craftsmen and artists as producers, while the latter were meant to be contemplated as art.

7   See Conforti, "Idealist Enterprise," p. 37, for the influence of the V&A in the charters of American museums.

8   W. Stanley Jervons, *Methods of Social Reform* (1883) (New York: Reprints of Economic Classics, Augustus M. Kelley Publisher, 1965), 53–78. Michael Conforti notes widespread criticism of the V&A after the 1880s. See "The Idealist Enterprise," p. 23.

9   Perry Duis, "Whose City? Public and Private Places in Nineteenth-Century Chicago," Part 1, *Chicago History*, spring 1982, XII (no. 1), 18–19.

10 He was the first librarian of the Denver Public Library (in the 1880s and 1890s) and also headed the public library in Springfield, Massachusetts, before coming to Newark.

11   Thorstein Veblen, *The Theory of the Leisure Class* (1899), introduction by C. Wright
      Mills (New York: Mentor Books, 1953). See especially pp. 60ff. and 95ff.

12   "The Literature of Business" (1894), reprinted as the introduction to Earnest Elmo
      Calkins, *Business the Civilizer* (Boston: Little, Brown, 1928).

13   *The New Relations of Museums and Industries* (Newark, NJ: Newark Museum Asso-
      ciation, 1919), 13.

14   *The New Museum* (Woodstock, VT: Elm Tree Press, 1917), 12; and *A Plan For A
      New Museum* (Woodstock, VT: Elm Tree Press, 1920), 12.

15   *The Gloom of the Museum* (Woodstock, VT: Elm Tree Press, 1917), 20.

16   *The New Museum*, p. 22.

17   The rationale was fully articulated in 1836, in the Report from the Select Com-
      mittee on Arts, and their Connection with Manufactures (House of Commons,
      Reports, vol. IX.l). The goals of the V&A (originally called the South Kensing-
      ton Museum) were taken directly from the 1836 Report. See also E. P. Alexan-
      der, *Museum Masters: Their Museums and Their Influence* (Nashville, TN: American
      Association for State and Local History, 1983), ch. 6; and J. Minihan, *The Nation-
      alization of Culture* (New York: New York University Press, 1977), 112ff.

18   See, for example, M. G. van Rensselaer, "The Art Museum and the Public,"
      Metropolitan Museum of Art *Bulletin*, 1917, XII: 57–64.

19   *Gloom*, 5–8.

20   "Increasing the Usefulness of Museums," *American Association of Museums*, X
      (1916), 80–7.

21   *Gloom*, 20.

22   *The Gloom of the Museum*, as it first appeared in *The Newarker* (the bulletin of the
      Newark Public Library), II (no. 12, October 1913), 400.

23   In 1913 Dana mocked the conventional art museum for its "absurd fear that it
      will be commercialized and debased if it shows what is being done today in the
      field of applied art . . . and display[s] articles made by machinery for actual daily
      use": *The Gloom . . . ,*," in *The Newarker*, 391–404. Portions of this article had
      already appeared in letters to the *New York Times* in previous months. It was
      reprinted in 1917 (cited above). Apparently, the piece did sting. Benjamin Ives
      Gilman, chief ideologue for the Boston Museum of Fine Arts, wrote Dana a letter
      defending his museum against Dana's charges, as did the museum's director,
      William R. French (Dana papers, Newark Public Library).

24   The store, although it bore Louis B.'s name, was held in partnership with Felix
      Fuld, a third partner having died in 1910.

25   *Newark Evening News*, "Opening of new Bamberger's," October 15, 1912, 8: 2.

26   L. Bamberger & Co., like Wanamaker's in Philadelphia and Filenes's in Boston,
      was a leader in enlightened employee relations. The store gave its workers above-
      average wages, paid vacations, illness benefits, discounts, stock benefits, and pro-
      vided a procedure for grievances. See Philip J. Reilly, *Old Masters of Retailing* (New
      York: Fairchild Publications, 1946), 25–30; and Frank I. Liveright, *One of America's
      Great Stores*, typescript manuscript, dated 1966, New Jersey Reference Division,
      Newark Public Library.

27   *Newark Evening News*, February 24, 1914, 4: 7. For this and other information
      about Bamberger's, see John E. O'Connor and Charles F. Cummings, "Bamberger's

Department Store, *Charm* Magazine, and the Culture of Consumption in New Jersey, 1924–1932," *New Jersey History*, 102, nos 304 (fall/winter, 1984), 1–33.

28   *Newark Evening News*, February 3, 9: 1.

29   Probably as a result of contact with the German Werkbund, whose products Dana exhibited in 1912.

30   *Daily Exposition Recorder* (the official paper of the exposition), published by L. Bamberger & Co., February 3–12, 1913 (italics mine).

31   Pasdermadjian, *The Department Store*, pp. 42–55 and 124–8.

32   Zelda F. Popkin, "Art: Three Aisles Over," *Outlook and Independent*, 156 (no. 13, November 26, 1930), 502–3, 515–16. Another of many such articles on this theme is Miriam Beard, "Business Cultivates the Arts," *New York Times Magazine*, January 31, 1926, 2.

33   John Wanamaker had regularly decorated its store interiors with his collection of paintings. He owned works by Reynolds, Constable, Titian, Hogarth, Manet, and others and installed them without crowding (Leach, *Land of Desire*, p. 136). See also Popkin, "Three Aisles Over," p. 503.

34   *New York Times*, February 10, 1924, VII, 10: 2. According to William Leach (*Land of Desire*, p. 136), after the 1913 Amory Show, the Gimbel brothers also acquired works by Cézanne, Braque, and Picasso and showed them in their stores.

35   *New York Times*, February 8, 1925, VII, 10: 4 and March 21, 1926, VIII, 14: 5.

36   Popkin, "Three Aisles Over," p. 156.

37   Report on the the American Association of Museums Annual Meeting of 1926, *New York Times*, May 19, 1926, 24: 8.

38   The store also organized a debate between two architects concerning the relative value of modern and traditional interiors (*New York Times*, January 23, 1928, 18: 2; February 29, 1928, 10: 4; March 4, 1928, IX, 14: 1; March 7, 1928, 2: 5). This show was featured in several long articles in the *Times*, including Walter Rendell Storey's "France Sends Us Her Decorative Art," *New York Times Magazine*, 1928, V: 14–15.

39   Beginning in 1919, the Metropolitan Museum in New York, for example, held annual shows of batiks, stained glass, and other hand-crafted objects said to have been inspired by the museum's collections. See, for example, the Metropolitan Museum of Art *Bulletin*, 1920, vol. 15, p. 90.

40   *New York Times*, April 28, 1927, 11: 1; April 29, 1927, 20: 4.

41   Elizabeth L. Cary, "Exhibit at Macy's Showed Our Resources and Progress," *New York Times*, May 3, 1917, VII, 9: 1. Cary and other writers often cited the important *International Exposition of Modern Decorative and Industrial Arts* held in Paris in 1925 as the primary impetus for these shows.

42   *Newark Evening News*, February 21, 1929, 8: 2; and *New York Times Magazine*, March 17, 1929, 14–15.

43   Although Dana did not live to see it, he had approved its plan before his death in 1929. According to a library publication, this was not Newark's only example of a library branch in a department store. Kresge's also had a library branch on its seventh floor, near the restaurant and the picture department. The St. Louis Public Library had similar arrangements with local stores ("Branch Libraries in Department Stores: Newark's Successful Experiment," *The Library*, IV (no. 5),

November 1931, 35). The Bamberger branch opened in 1931, after Dana's death, but had been planned since 1928. In fact, Dana had the idea of lending museum exhibits to stores, branch libraries, schools, and factories much earlier (e.g., in "Increasing the Usefulness of Museums," 1916).

44   Pasdermadjian, *The Department Store*, p. 45.
45   Alfred H. Barr, Jr., "Museum," *Charm,* November 1919, 15.
46   O'Connor and Cummings, "Bamberger's . . . ," pp. 5–10.
47   Mary Anne Staniszewski, *The Power of Display: A History of Exhibition Installations at the Museum of Modern Art* (Cambridge, MA: MIT Press, 1998), 174.
48   Staniszewski, *Power of Display*, pp. 160–74.

References

Alexander, E. P. (1983). *Museum Masters: Their Museums and Their Influence.* (Nashville, TN: American Association for State and Local History).

Barr, Jr., A. H. (1919). "Museum," *Charm,* November, 15.

Beard, M. (1926). "Business Cultivates the Arts," *New York Times Magazine,* January 31, 2.

"Branch Libraries in Department Stores: Newark's Successful Experiment," *The Library* (bulletin of the Newark Public Library), IV (no. 5), November 1931, 35.

Cary, E. L. (1917). "Exhibit at Macy's Showed Our Resources and Progress," *New York Times,* May 3, 1917, VII, 9: 1.

Conforti, M. (1997). "The Idealist Enterprise and the Applied Arts," in M. Baker and B. Richardson, eds., *A Grand Design: The Art of the Victoria and Albert Museum* (exhibition catalogue). London: V&A publications; New York: Harry N. Abrams; Baltimore: Baltimore Museum of Art, 23–47.

Dana, J. C. (1894). "The Literature of Business," reprinted as the introduction to E. E. Calkins, *Business the Civilizer,* Boston: Little, Brown, 1928.

Dana, J. C. (1917). *The Gloom of the Museum.* Woodstock, VT: Elm Tree Press. (First appeared in *The Newarker,* the bulletin of the Newark Public Library, II, no. 12, October 1913), 391–404.

Dana, J. C. (1917, 1920). *The New Museum.* Woodstock, VT. Elm Tree Press, 1917, 12; and *A Plan For A New Museum.* Woodstock, VT: Elm Tree Press, 1920, 12.

Dana, J. C. (1919). *The New Relations of Museums and Industries.* Newark, NJ: Newark Museum Association.

Dana, J. C. (1928). "Is the Department Store a Museum?" *The Museum,* published by the Newark Museum Association, II, no. 1, July–August, 1928, 1–2.

Duis, P. (1982). "Whose City? Public and Private Places in Nineteenth-Century Chicago," Part 1, *Chicago History,* spring, XII (no. 1), 2–27.

Duncan, C. (1995). *Civilizing Rituals: Inside Public Art Museums.* London and New York: Routledge.

Harris, N. (1978). "Museums, Merchandising and Popular Taste: The Struggle for Influence," in M. G. Quimby, ed., *Material Culture and the Study of American Life,* New York: W. W. Norton, 140–70.

Jervons, W. S. (1883). *Methods of Social Reform*. New York: Reprints of Economic Classics, Augustus M. Kelley Publisher, 1965.

Leach, W. (1993). *Land of Desire: Merchants, Power, and the Rise of a New American Culture*. New York: Pantheon Books.

Liveright, F. I. *One of America's Great Stores*. Typescript dated 1966, New Jersey Reference Division, Newark Public Library.

Metropolitan Museum of Art (1920). *Bulletin*, vol. 15, p. 90.

Minihan, J. (1977). *The Nationalization of Culture*. New York: New York University Press.

O'Connor J. E. and Cummings, C. F. (1984). "Bamberger's Department Store, *Charm* Magazine, and the Culture of Consumption in New Jersey, 1924–1932," *New Jersey History*, 102, no. 304 (fall/winter), 1–33.

Pasdermadjian, H. (1954). *The Department Store: Its Origins, Evolution, and Economics*. London: Newman Books.

Popkin, Z. F. (1930). "Art: Three Aisles Over," *Outlook and Independent*, 156, no. 13, November 26, 502–3; 515–16.

Reilly, P. J. (1946). *Old Masters of Retailing*. New York: Fairchild Publications.

Rensselaer, M. G. van (1917). "The Art Museum and the Public," Metropolitan Museum of Art *Bulletin*, XII: 57–64.

Report from the Select Committee on Arts, and their Connection with Manufactures (1836). House of Commons, Reports, vol. IX.l.

Staniszewski, M. A. (1998). *The Power of Display: A History of Exhibition Installations at the Museum of Modern Art*. Cambridge, MA: MIT Press.

Storey, W. R. (1928). "France Sends Us Her Decorative Art," *New York Times Magazine*, V: 14–15, February 19.

Veblen, T. (1899). *The Theory of the Leisure Class*, introduction by C. W. Mills. New York: Mentor Books, 1953.

7

Which Shakespeare to Love?
Film, Fidelity, and the
Performance of Literature
Timothy Corrigan

The ferocious defense of literary works is, to a certain extent, aesthetically justified; but we must also be aware that it rests on a rather recent, individualistic conception of the "author" and of the "work," a conception that was far from being ethically rigorous in the seventeenth century and that started to become legally defined only at the end of the eighteenth. . . . All things considered, it is possible to imagine that we are moving toward a reign of adaptation in which the notion of the unity of the work of art, if not the notion of the author himself will be destroyed. (Andre Bazin, "Adaptation, or the Cinema as Digest," 1948)

Miramax Films' *Shakespeare in Love* (1998) is, of course, not about William Shakespeare; it is about authorship and performance. With the original production of *Romeo and Juliet* as the backdrop plot, the film crisscrosses the stumbling physical world of Elizabethan players, plays, and politics with the emotional and lusty passion of Will and Viola, the woman who, in this imagined account, inspired *Romeo and Juliet*. Parallel sequences link Will and Viola's courtship at her balcony with the rehearsal of the famous balcony scene in the play, while a staged rumble between Montagues and Capulets is crosscut with an actual rumble between the actors and an angry gang that confronts them. The triumph of Shakespeare's play and the film itself becomes ultimately, as Queen Elizabeth herself announces *deus ex machina*, to create real emotions through the fictive drama of a stage. Real because, with

Plate 7.1 Joseph Fiennes as *Shakespeare in Love* (Miramax Films, 1998). Museum of Modern Art Film Stills Archive.

a personal and historical source in Shakespeare's life and a cinematic embodiment in a physical Shakespeare, the performance is real.

With a range of plot tricks and linguistic puns more ascribable to Tom Stoppard's literary gymnastics than to William Shakespeare's life, the result is a film more about how dramatic fiction – or more accurately the fiction of personal performance – redeems historical reality than about anything like a lost historical reality. As the complexity of the Shakespearean text and its Elizabethan verse becomes diverted to the physical performance of love, the ghost of Shakespeare materializes here as, quite literally, a contemporary body, resurrected by and for contemporary film culture. An unfaithful player (with a wife in Stratford) rather than a faithful adapter (of another's idea), Shakespeare the high-concept star and his vehicle *Shakespeare in Love* would gross $93 million in the US alone, finally win an Oscar, and in doing so become a remarkably incisive engagement with the central issues in contemporary cinematic adaptations of classical literature: the romance of authorship, the commercial bond of personality and popularity, and the elevation of performance over textuality.

The distributor Miramax is hardly alone here. During the 1990s many studios, American and abroad, have returned to one of film's most consistent and reliable patterns of adapting classic literary authors and texts for the movies. In the last decade alone, a sampling – to choose arbitrarily and only those works in English – would include: *Hamlet* (Franco Zeffirelli, 1990), Sally Potter's *Orlando* (1993), Martin Scorsese's *The Age of Innocence* (1993), Ang Lee's *Sense and Sensibility* (1995), Jane Campion's *Portrait of a Lady* (1996), Trevor Nunn's *Twelfth Night* (1997), Douglas McGrath's *Emma* (1996), Marleen Gorris's *Mrs. Dalloway* (1998), Julie Taymour's *Titus* (1999), and Michael Almereyda's millennium *Hamlet* (2000). One could extend this list considerably and still not include less recognizable or oblique versions of the classics such as Amy Heckerling's valley-girl version of *Emma* retitled *Clueless* (1995), *The Taming of The Shrew* as *Ten Things I Hate about You* (1999), or the 1999 version of *Pride and Prejudice* called *The Bennett Boys*.[1] Yet, however one extends or limits this selection of classic adaptations of the 1990s, there is a significant trend: like *Shakespeare in Love*, these films not only retrieve literary classics for film adaptations but promote them as a version of high-concept blockbusters, those descendants of *Jaws* (1975) and *The Godfather* (1972) able to attract massive audiences with the signpost of a single star, special-effects innovations, or, in this case, the aura of classic literature.

The large number of classic adaptations in the last decade, from canonical literature or other kinds, does not, by itself, indicate some sea change in American or European film culture. Adaptations have always been one of the most popular, reliable, and profitable sources for the movies,[2] and classic literary adaptations have consistently appeared throughout this century and always acted as cultural flash points that illuminate the changing contours of film practice and its negotiations of a place within a larger social history. Film adaptations – especially the canonical kind, I believe – have always told us much about our sense of history, class, language, and more often than not those revelations have described an agenda of legitimation whereby literature in effect attempts to elevate the movies above the popular (and therefore dangerously suspect) culture.

In the 1990s, however, the revelations are different enough to suggest a critical rearrangement of film culture, perhaps as a reflection of

changes in larger cultural borders. What the ways of literary adaptations in the 1990s suggest is not, to use some of the standard models,
the elevation of low culture through the appropriation of high culture
or the popular expansion of all into a general middlebrow culture.
Movies like *Clueless* or *Ten Things I Hate about You* at first glance seem
to follow those old patterns, but adaptation today is not, as most com-
mentaries would have it, primarily about textual integrity versus popularization.[3] More pertinent to my focus here is a dispute in *Clueless*
about the source of a line from *Hamlet*, Polonius's advisory "To thine
own self be true." While the protagonist Cher wins the argument
because her source for the line is Mel Gibson and Zeffirelli's *Hamlet*,
not Shakespeare, the point is not whether this is a mocking triumph
of pop culture over high culture. What counts here is not the line and
its appropriation or misappropriation but rather who performs that
line, and in this case, Cher's personal ability to recall and reactivate it
– significantly as a way of winning the heart of a boy friend she has
yet to acknowledge.[4] As we shall see, the disputed line "To thine own
self be true" could in fact work as a highly charged motto not only
for Cher but for the central dynamic that links classic literature, filmmakers, and their audiences in the last fifteen years.

In this context, some of the projects of cultural studies appear to
have turned back on themselves. To put it very succinctly, cultural
studies has worked in recent decades to pressurize and undermine the
notion of the singularity of texts and their authors by dispersing both
into the field of popular culture or daily culture at large. From this
perspective canonical writers and works have come to represent an illu-
sory and fossilized sense of individuality that can and should be dis-
mantled, while the popular describes a wider social and usually political
circulation of a work and author in a way that dissipates their traditional authority. With the performance of film adaptation on and off
the screen today, however, there has been a reclamation of those very
ghosts of textual singularity and authority that cultural studies has
worked so assiduously to bury.

Preceding and preparing for the drama of *Shakespeare in Love*, two
years earlier Baz Luhrmann's 1996 *William Shakespeare's Romeo + Juliet*
would also boldly highlight the single name traditionally associated
with high or academic culture. It would court and claim a massive
youth market, despite the warning from a companion of teen star

Claire Danes: "Forget Shakespeare! This movie is so cool, you shouldn't even mention him. It'll keep people away." As Timothy Murray describes it in his brilliant study *Drama Trauma*, here "the traumatic antithesis to 'cool' is Shakespeare" (Murray, 1997: 5). The critical provocation, however, is that *William Shakespeare's Romeo + Juliet*, like so many other recent cinematic Shakespeares, has become a scene and name to which both the cool and not-so-cool in today's film culture – those uniquely contemporary "repeat viewers" – flock again and again, seemingly in order to perform and affirm themselves, almost as a matter of faith and often as an anxious and personal faith in the ghosts of literature.

Fidelity and Infidelity

As a dense meditation on the clash of the popular and canonical, the textual and the authorial, one of the most important and intelligent adaptations in the 1990s is Peter Greenaway's *Prospero's Books* (1991). In Greenaway's version of Shakespeare's *The Tempest*, the book in all its material textuality generates an incredibly rich array of other textures and corporeal performances until Prospero ultimately decides to "drown my book"; its rescue by Caliban in the film's conclusion becomes, for many, the wistful surrender of the book's monumentality to the desecration of mass culture. However one evaluates Greenaway's putatively conservative stance and lack of a postcolonial politics here, he is right about what concerns him: under the force of the image, the text and the book may be in the process of disappearing, drowning, or being irrevocably torn apart. As Greenaway indicates, popular culture in itself may be less the culprit than the redundancy of cultures through history and the necessity of materializing that written text in so many imagistic embodiments. Even if we (incorrectly no doubt) limit the problem to this century, texts and authors have been subject to a chain of recuperations and exchanges, and literary texts and authors, like Shakespeare and *The Tempest*, have unavoidably become notorious infidels, forced to be thrown over as lost sources and origins. In this light, is it coincidental that characters and stories of so many other recent classic literary films – Newland Archer in *Age of Innocence*, the Bard in *Shakespeare in Love*, and, in a much tamer sense, so many of those hesitant Austen heroines, to name only a few – act out the temptations of infidelity against the background of rapidly accumulating social texts and textures?

Literary adaptation on film is, as Dudley Andrew (1984) has reminded us, only one kind of adaptation of one kind of source. Our artistic, film, and cultural heritage in the largest sense has been permeated with adaptations of music, paintings, news reports, dances, sporting events, and so on. Film adaptation has a history that is as long as film history itself, involving both classic and popular novels from Sienkiewicz's *Quo Vadis?* (1913) to Tolstoy's *Anna Karenina* (2000) to classic theater like *Medea* and *Oedipus Rex*, as well as vaudevillian sketches, the poetry of Walt Whitman and Tennyson, and especially in recent years, comic books. Literature clearly has a special attraction for the cinema for at least two reasons: its traditional emphasis on character and narrative and its ready-made dialogue. Pragmatically speaking, the appeal of literature through the century has been linear plots ready made for the classical narrative styles of film and a vocal range of linguistic textures (such as dialogue and voice-overs) crucial to film after the introduction of sound in the late 1920s.[5]

Film adaptation has traditionally been about fidelity only in that it is about authority. Fidelity has been a term used to enlist the cultural power of literary texts to validate and champion specific movies, while reminding them and us of who's always in charge – the original text. Fidelity supposedly indicates a quantitative and qualitative measure of accuracy in how, for instance, descriptions of settings, the nuances of dialogue and characters, or the complexity of themes are moved from the page to the screen. Yet that has always been an impossible measure across two radically different media and one that has usually been called upon to judge and humble film culture in relation to classic literature or bestsellers.[6]

This assignment of cultural authority to the literary text – and faith in it – has much to do with the dangerous promiscuity of the image. Literary (or other) texts have never stood a chance against the power of the image, and, since the first days of hermeneutics and exegesis, iconic representations have been the target of containment – needing to reduce the too-free interpretive power of the viewer – to make unregulated choices – before the image.[7] As visible fragments or invisible subtexts, the literary text appears in the film as, in its numerous positions, an interpretive grid to control the instability of images through the designating power of words. Borges's "Pierre Menard" or Michel Tournier's *Friday* pose very little threat to *Don Quixote* or *Robinson Crusoe*. Films do.

Attempting to loosen the grip of fidelity, traditional critical schemes for distinguishing the movement of literature onto film have still, I feel, been haunted by it, including Geoffrey Wagner's (1975) innovative tripartite schema of transposition, commentary, and analogy or Dudley Andrew's (1984) subtle distinctions of borrowing, intersecting, and transforming sources. Like those vaguer notions of appropriation and popularization, these different models continue, in varying degrees, to confirm the priority of the literary text while expanding the possible ways a film may engage it (that "source" which we may not need to be fully faithful to but which we still must begin with in order to comment on it, analogize it, or borrow from it). As Andrew and these others make clear, these different schemes need to be adjusted to the demands and pressures of changing historical contexts, in which an implicit or explicit attitude towards the literary text being adapted measures the cultural standing of the cinema. Yet even Robert Stam's (2000) sophisticated, culturally attuned discussion of adaptation seems to me to bear the marks of textual guilt: carefully mobilizing historical and social contexts to unhinge fidelity from its moral connotations, it remains bound to a larger faith in textuality by rearticulating film adaptation specifically in terms of intertextuality and translation.

Leaving aside other kinds of adaptation (pulp fiction or experimental literature, for instance), classic literature especially has demanded fidelity. As the many recent analyses of Shakespeare on film indicate, this involves more than the narrative realism associated with nineteenth-century novels.[8] However constructed in general and with Shakespeare in particular, classic literature usually provokes the strongest attitudes and strictest expectations for adaptation because of the canonical status of these texts. Whether it's *The Odyssey* or *Ulysses*, the classics imply a transcendent vision of history through which works of the distant past stay meaningful in the present, an enactment of unmediated agency whereby the author and text disappear into each other, and of course a textual singularity according to which the language, form, and structure of a classic is untranslatable and unique. In addition, one of the key issues in adaptation of classic literature is audience: if the texts suggest they transcend the vicissitudes of time as the unique and unmediated expression of genius, literate audiences must certainly know those texts and even illiterate audiences must presumably recognize those texts in order to participate in the values of film adaptation as an act of fidelity or infidelity. This assumption of textual familiarity has been dubious at all points in film history, but it has, for most of that history, been a crucial cornerstone of classic adaptations, since to be faithful to a missing stranger becomes either a meaningless exercise or the most abject of cultural rituals.

Throughout film history, classic film adaptations have testified to the cultural permutations that inform the demands of fidelity as it takes on different guises. Much too schematically, Shakespeare on film can act as a map for some of these changing relationships between the chosen classical text and the positioning of a film audience, all making different claims on how to be faithful to a classic literary partner. During the preclassical and silent era of films (roughly 1900 to 1925) Shakespearean texts and figures acted, for instance, "to reframe culture."[9] From one reelers (like Vitagraph's 1908 *Julius Caesar*) to early features (like Edwin Thanhouser's 1916 *King Lear*), Shakespearean texts work as verbal and visual citations that import particular value to this still clumsy descendant of vaudeville, so that movie-going might locate a cultural consensus rather than an entertaining distraction. With the coming of sound and other technological advances, during the 1930s, classical texts could be recreated with the kind of textual detail that would promote the equation of fidelity with textual accuracy or fullness. Through these advancing powers film could aim to be as creative or "recreative" as its source and thus "to visually aestheticize" literature as part of film art and education. Like the 1935 Technicolor adaptation of *Vanity Fair* as *Becky Sharp*, Max Reinhardt's 1935 *Midsummer Night's Dream* recovers the literary original purporting to match its literary brilliance with film's new technological powers. In the shadow of the Hays Office and other watchdogs of the growing powers of this most popular medium, film adaptations could claim to be adequate aesthetic vehicles that, through these adaptations, would also fulfill their role as art educators and promoters of aesthetic value.

Through the 1940s and 1950s the expanding technological power of film refocuses the artistic or aesthetic capabilities of film "to realize" that literature. As Laurence Olivier's *Henry V* (1944) most famously demonstrates in its flamboyant transition from the props and papers of the Globe Theater to the open fields and graphic battles of France, film now marks how the textual authority of literature begins to give ground to the greater realism of the cinema.[10] The historical and global parameters of adaptation would clearly change in the decades following, and, keeping with our scheme to suggest succinctly the transitive relations of different historical trends, the art cinema of the 1950s could be characterized as an effort "to rewrite" classic literature, while at least one strain of the 1960s and 1970s stresses the powers of film "to spectacularize" literature. If *Throne of Blood* (1957) represents a creative usurpation of Shakespeare's text *Macbeth* in the name of Kurosawa's personal and cultural powers of representation, Franco Zeffirelli's *Romeo and Juliet* (1968) is doubtless the most renowned example, until recently, of Shakespeare's economic power to draw the growing youth market to the spectacle of literature.

All these abbreviations of the historical relationships between film and the classic literature of Shakespeare imply a central connection between those relationships and (1) the developing technological powers of film to create more convincing representations of reality and (2) the social context of an implicitly addressed audience. In those terms, since the 1940s the steady rise of various realisms has continued to push out the claims of textuality as the faithful measure of adaptation, while audiences for adaptations have grown more demarcated or targeted (in the wake of the breakup of the major studios, the globalization of film markets, the emergence of a growing youth audience). Indeed these two shifts have often run counter to each other, and even today spectacles of realism (often as the retrieval of lost literary worlds or exotic settings like the ancient Tuscany of Kenneth Branagh's 1993 *Much Ado About Nothing*) compete with adaptations whose formal complexity (Jean-Luc Godard's 1987 *King Lear*, for instance) addresses largely arthouse audiences. In both cases or when both aims overlap in the same film what is increasingly eroded is the tradition of fidelity to an original text. Set before the force of realism or the particularity of a film's address, the text has certainly not disappeared, but it has conceptually fragmented and dissipated to the point where it lacks the stability needed to be a recognizable partner in whom to invest our faith.

In the wake of this expanding realism and individuation of film audiences, classic adaptations have become much less about textual fidelity and authority – or at least there is now far more anxiety about or repression of both. Instead, film adaptation now concentrates on the film and the audience's ability "to perform" literature. As an enactment in which the dynamics of presentation can subsume the memory of any source material, performance here suggests at least an equivalency between text and presentation that usefully distances it from the usual dependent relations in which a film maintains some kind of subservient or secondary position *vis-à-vis* the text. Choice, random or interpretive, always underpins performance as a testimony to the activity of the performer, an activity and mobility occurring on many registers in contemporary adaptations. On the one hand, contemporary film adaptation is more and more judged not by some attainable or unattainable literary text but by the activity of the individuated performance of actors, filmmakers, or, we shall see, distributors. (Not surprisingly, evidence, although admittedly thin, suggests that films more and more lead viewers back to the text for a first reading that, apparently, they may not find it necessary to even finish.)[11] On the other hand, the variety and redundancy of adaptations that have accumulated through this century implicitly acknowledge and require the critical performance of contemporary spectators on some level as they can now view and enjoy adaptations through the pleasure of their different historical and cultural incarnations.

Note that the cinematic performance of literature is critically different from that of theatrical performance studies in which, for instance, Shakespeare's texts necessarily change with each stage performance.[12] With contemporary film the actual dramatization of the text becomes a permanent performance on film, and so the temporal and historical instability of the performance becomes a temporally recoverable and repeatable encounter on film, videotape, or DVD. The infidelity of film before the literary text thus offers the tentative possibility to recover other rituals of identification and faith as temporary bonds between viewers and film performances. Faith is always performative towards something or someone, and on films that faith can be both personal and selective. We may forget Shakespeare, but we are loyal to Claire Danes and Baz Luhrmann, to John Gielgud and Peter Greenaway.

Being William Shakespeare

If faith in classic literary texts has suffered, authors have thrived. Regardless of the fate of their texts, classical authors have made their way increasingly and prominently into the adapted stories they write and onto movie marquees. Emily Brönte makes a cameo appearance in her film *Emily Bronte's Wuthering Heights* (1992) and in *Sense and Sensibility* (1995) the commentary of Jane Austen merges with that of the protagonist Elinor. When not on the screen, authors still control movie titles today: *Bram Stoker's Dracula* (1992), *Mary Shelley's Frankenstein* (1994), and *William Shakespeare's Romeo + Juliet* (1996) all unmistakably remind us of the author no matter how much they forget the literary text. Even when invisible or missing, authors resurface as *auteurs*: from Gus Van Sant's eccentric and idiosyncratic remake of *Henry IV, Part I* as *My Own Private Idaho* (1991) to more seemingly faithful adaptations of texts like Martin Scorsese's *Age of Innocence* (1993), the vision, style, and signature of the filmmaker as *auteur* supplants the missing literary author as a controlling and defining agency. Classic adaptations may not always be fixated on authors or *auteurs*, but the prominence of authors today indicates a key source of the contemporary fascination with classical literature, the primary agency for the filmic performance of that literature, and, ultimately, a way back to fidelity.

Contemporary film adaptations of classic literary texts are, even the happiest ones, always about loss: loss of texts, loss of history, loss of faith, loss of relevancy, loss of meaning. Classic texts are ghosts, and film images are reminders of worlds that have vanished or that never existed. While this atmosphere of loss fosters the accusations that these classic adaptations smack of nostalgia, more importantly that nostalgia reflects back on its source, on a contemporary environment riddled with social, historical, and subjective fragmentation, dislocations, and hyperrealisms – those cultural conditions so often associated with a postmodernism haunted by the dream, if not the memory, of coherency and clarity. In this logic, nineteenth-century literature's characters and narratives, as well as Shakespearean drama, become compensations for the perceived abandonment of grand or coherent narratives, spatial condensations and expansions, and personal paralysis or unmotivated characters that seem to describe much of contemporary life. The faithful unhappy ending of Scorsese's *Age of Innocence* thus appropriately looks backward and forward through the twentieth century: Newland Archer surrenders to a culture overwhelmed with the fetishized textures of dinner tables, clothing, and convoluted rhetoric; in the final images he stares up at the former lover's apartment he cannot enter, trapped by a historical moment in which he is unable to act.

The contemporary antidote for this fragmented and over-determined social text becomes the possibilities of human agency, of an active and meaningful transformation of those conditions of disori-entation through the public performance of self and self-interest. In the unfaithful happy ending of the 1995 *Scarlet Letter*, the adulteress Hester Prynne frees herself, outrageously, of the cultural paralysis of a Puri-tanical society, and, in our contemporary societies, "identity politics" offer a way to use a shifting and centerless global culture as a stage for self-assertion and individual rights that would overcome traditional oppressions. Indeed, today the most ideal figure of human agency as the active making of meaning may be the author, for if the referent and text are gone, the agency of the author still remains as an active, meaning-making presence. In the twisted adaptation of Patricia Rozema's 1999 *Mansfield Park*, the heroine thus becomes the author whose additions to the novel are an elaborated engagement barely mentioned in Austen's original: at the center of this adaptation, Fanny/Austen confronts her father's despicable and ruthless colonial-ism, and so makes the agency of authorship a powerful tool against colonialism and for the claims of postcolonial identity politics. And, of course, a good marriage.

Authors on or in films are, however, only metaphoric displacements of the real agents of film: sometimes actors but, usually and more effect-ively, *auteurs*. As I suggested about adaptations from Olivier's to Kuro-sawa's, the waning of textual authority in the face of historical and filmic realism in the 1950s opened the way for a different literary authority, the film author as *auteur*.[13] Historically, auteurism is the crit-ical and pragmatic policy most associated with the *Cahiers du cinéma* and the French New Wave of François Truffaut and Jean-Luc Godard and others. Besides the leveling pressure of realism, the original polemic of auteurism included, with some irony, an attack on the supposed dependence of postwar movies on literary adaptation and a demand to release filmmaking from these and other patriarchal oppressions. Of the many other historical factors contributing to the shaping of auteurism, the development of lightweight Arriflex camera equipment would come to the support of Alexandre Astruc's 1948 essay on "the camera-stylo" in which the modern camera would be likened to a pen that would transform the modern filmmaker into a writer. By the 1960s academia would quickly rally round auteurism as a way of bringing European art cinema into colleges and universities through the presence of *auteurs* who resembled existential authors and films that demanded the interactivity of a thinking viewer who reads films like books.[14] Through what I have elsewhere called the "commerce of auteurism" (Corrigan, 1991), auteurism evolved through the 1970s into the 1990s as a transformation of this literary heritage into a more public performance that positioned *auteurs* as commercial points of identification for a fluctuating viewing public. Through *auteurs*, in short, contemporary audiences begin to participate in a hermeneutics of image making balanced between interpretation and self-performance.[15]

As reader-performers, film viewers consequently also come to performative life as an equally assertive agency in the wake of auteurism. From the 1960s through the 1990s we can then identify three literary phases for film audiences following the lead of *auteurs* (non-sequential and often overlapping): viewers as readers, viewers as browsers, viewers as embodiments. Readers of film are that most transparently literary phase whereby viewers engage art films or new wave cinemas as a matter of active interpretation: dramatized in the writer/filmmaker collaborations of, say, Alain Resnais and Robbe-Grillet's 1961 *Last Year in Marienbad* or Renais and Maguerite Duras's 1959 *Hiroshima Mon Amour*, these films require of viewers the attentive formal analysis usually associated with complex literary texts and challenging modernist writers.[16]

The more recent browsers are clearly a product of the proliferation of viewing technology from VCRs in the 1970s through the DVDs of today and Web movies of the future. Through these technologies viewers can now literally control the film as a selection and performative process that allows audiences to browse, for instance, among an array of adaptations. Depending on the whims or aims of distributors, viewers may sample numerous versions of Laclos' *Dangerous Liaisons* from Roger Vadim's 1960 adaptation to Stephen Frears's 1988 film and Milos Forman's retitled *Valmont* (1989). Within the vast library of available classic adaptations (the product of historical accumulation and quite different from the singular *event* of past filmic adaptation), fidelity has become a fully archaic aesthetic measure, except as one can be faithful to one's own self, desires, tastes, imagination, and inclinations (provoked perhaps by a memory of or desire for the ghostly palimpsest of a literary text). In effect, what the activity of technological browsing describes is how viewers have acceded to positions somewhere between that of a critic and a performer who might seek to spot the original text in the film, to compare film versions, or to engage in a variety of other "performative" interactions. Films no longer realize or rewrite texts, viewers select and measure versions of adaptation as participatory agents.

As a byproduct of this technological mobility and in part a reaction to its surplus of choices, contemporary film viewers more and more want and need authors and *auteurs* to embody images, to share and organize those images and texts as expressive positions and performances. If authors like Shakespeare have, for at least two centuries, been the embodiment of texts, *auteurs* have become, for contemporary viewers, the displaced embodiment of authors within today's image culture. Just as human agency can represent a solution to the larger excesses and unmoorings of contemporary culture, viewers today may deal with the burden of a culture of lost texts and massively redundant images through identification and interaction with the various expressive agencies provided by *auteurs*. With *auteurs*, viewers find the signature needed to replace the dead literary author, to guide the selection and comparison of films, to decipher and anchor adaptations with a visible or invisible original text, to reveal the secrets of a text in the performance of personal expression. Most ambitiously, Rainer Werner Fassbinder's adaptation of *Berlin Alexanderplatz* (1980) declares itself – stylistically throughout its 15 hours but explicitly in the final self-referential episode – as Fassbinder's film, not Döblin's novel. As is so common today, the spate of recent Proust adaptations – from Volker Schlöndorff's *Swann in Love* (1984) to Raoul Ruiz's *Time Regained* (2000) and Chantal Akerman's *The Captive* (from *La Prisonniere*) (2000) – attracts and sustains audiences as much more in the name of the filmmaker as that of the novelist. Viewing classic adaptations is thus relayed through the authority and perspective of the *auteur* in whom the viewer rediscovers a faith in the fidelity of individual vision and idiosyncrasies of self-expression.[17] Through the agency of the *auteur*, the viewer is true to "thine own self" in a double sense: true to oneself because loyal to a filmmaker's personal perspective.[18]

Make no mistake, though, this is not a postmodern free-for-all and the promoted illusion of authorial agency should not be confused with liberation. Parodied so well in *Being John Malkovich* (1999), embodied performance is not freedom, and *auteurs* are not radical subjects. Despite their historical and etymological bond, moreover, *auteurs* and audiences are not classic authors; they are personal performers and agents of tastes and intellectual interests. For contemporary film culture, this is big business. The technological and historical activation of mobile and selective viewers has been met and addressed head on precisely by exploiting the memory of a classic text, shredded, dissipated, and endlessly translated, and by redirecting it through the evolving figure of the high-concept *auteur*, offering not original texts or real authors but a different literary figure, the commercial *auteur*, as agent and guide.

In the most recent cinematic *Hamlet* distributed by Miramax, Ethan Hawkes is Hamlet, a vaguely auteurist slacker, constantly viewing himself and his world through a video image, as he wanders through the high-tech millennial world of a corporately postmodern New York. Like all Hamlets, surrounded by real and imagined perfidy and treachery, he struggles to believe in something or someone that would propel him into action. As in all versions, this crisis of faith becomes concentrated on whether or not to believe in the ghost of his father, and in this version, that ghost of the dead father is appropriately Sam Shepard, a celebrated literary and theatrical *auteur*, pursued for the secrets of infidelity he may reveal and the faith he requires. When faith ultimately ignites across Hamlet's student film-within-the-film, the scales are tipped not by the film but by the revealing participation of the audience and specifically the uncle who of course sees only himself in Hamlet's hackneyed art film. In *A Midwinters' Tale* Kenneth Branagh would go looking for his own Hamlet and his own lost Shakespeare. In this tale of a rural theatrical production of *Hamlet* set appropriately in an abandoned church, a passionate director ends up searching less for an authentic Hamlet or Shakespeare than for the mutual faith of the cast members and the confirming faith of a local audience. In this, Branagh would eventually require more visible institutional assistance.

Kenneth Branagh and Miramax Films: The Inner Life of Shakespeare and the Secrets of Faith

British and German Romantics, around 1800, remade Shakespeare's plays through the cult of the author known as Bardolatry; in the 1950s the *Cahiers du cinéma* reinvented John Ford, Fritz Lang, and other filmmakers as postwar *auteurs*. Today, Miramax Films has become one of the most proficient vehicles for matching performative *auteurs* and the adaptation of classic literature, using distribution and promotion strategies to transform that literature into a high-concept attraction significantly different from the quietly respectable niche it previously inhabited on the BBC or Masterpiece Theater. As part of this project, Miramax has recently enlisted Kenneth Branagh, one of the most productive and performative *auteurs* of contemporary cinema who, as blasphemous as it may seem to some, fits nicely with Miramax's less classical *auteur*, Quentin Tarantino. If Tarantino is Miramax's director of pulp texts, Branagh has become their *auteur* of classic texts, and Miramax is shrewd enough to understand that the two can coexist in a contemporary film culture less concerned with texts than with filmic performance. Whereas Miramax has employed Tarantino as the promotional marketing voice for exotic or offbeat films like those of John Woo, Branagh acts as a similar vehicle for classic Shakespeare. In both cases, the filmmaker is the crucial performative agency for recycling the secrets of lost materials and texts.

Miramax Films has worked at the intersection of three histories and strategies for distributing film and locating audiences: as the powerful progeny of classic film divisions, as a specialty film distributor, and, more recently, as a subsidiary/partner of a major studio, Disney. The major studios began to create Classics Divisions in the 1980s as a response to the commercial and artistic force of the new waves that arrived in the 1960s and the audiences they fostered. United Artists Classics originated this movement in 1980 by distributing *The Last Metro* of French New Wave director and early spokesperson for the concept of auteurism, François Truffaut. By 1983 Orion Classics joined this specialized distribution of European films with a marketable cutting edge, including Stephen Frears's *My Beautiful Laundrette* (1986), Wim Wenders's *Wings of Desire* (1988), Pedro Almódovar's *Women on the Verge of a Nervous Breakdown* (1988), and Agnieszka Holland's *Europa, Europa* (1991). In 1992, in the midst of a financial crisis, Orion Classics became Sony Pictures Classics and pursued with equal acumen an art cinema with commercial potential, beginning with two films, one conventional and the other a daring adaptation: Merchant–Ivory's *Howard's End* and Sally Potter's *Orlando*. With classic adaptations such as these, however, classic divisions were never exactly the disciples of a new wave mission to create new film languages, revolting against, in

Truffaut's famous formulation, literary bias that acted as the crutch of old father filmmakers. Rather, these new art films would often use an old literary language to renew classical film forms.[19]

Miramax, another descendant of these classic divisions, has pursued this heritage in its support of a wide variety of alternative films through the 1990s, beginning with a 1981 adaptation of a Gabriel García Márquez work, *Erendira*. Its commercial breakthrough came with Steven Soderbergh's *sex, lies, and videotape* (1989) and continued with Michael Verhoeven's *The Nasty Girl* (1990), Peter Greenaway's *Prospero's Books* (1991), Tarantino's *Reservoir Dogs* (1992), Leslie Harris's *Just Another Girl on the I.R.T.* (1993), Kevin Smith's *Clerks* (1994), and Masayuki Suo's *Shall We Dance?* (1997). Miramax's abilities and achievements have been, however, not only about discovering and developing quality source material.

As it has evolved, Miramax has become an especially savvy and profitable distributor of so-called specialty films, a skill that has been significantly assisted by its 1993 partnership with Disney Studios. First and foremost, what Disney has brought to Miramax is distribution money that far exceeds any of Miramax's competitors. If Disney may find mildly attractive the artistic and classic heritage of this partnership, together with Miramax's ability as a promoter and distributor, they have turned substantial profits from that classic heritage through the creation of what might be called the literary blockbuster film, built on promotion and distribution budgets that skillfully saturate markets with an unusually large number of distribution prints. As an example, the Italian/French production budget for *The Postman* (1994), a film about the bond between an Italian working-class man and Chilean poet Pablo Neruda, was $4 million. With a promotional and distribution budget of nearly twice that cost ($7 million) for its US release, Miramax in effect remade that film by eliciting and fashioning new audiences that set box-office records for a foreign film in the US. Although one of its crowning commercial achievements, *Shakespeare in Love* is thus hardly an anomaly in the strategic creation of blockbuster audiences for specialty films. Besides grand commercial and critical achievements like Roberto Benigni's *Life Is Beautiful* (1998) grossing $53 million, Jane Campion's *The Piano* (1993) making $40 million, and the 1994 *Pulp Fiction* over $100 million, two of their greatest financial successes have been literary adaptations: if successful independent films may return $3 million domestically, in 1992 *The Crying Game* grossed $65 million and in 1996 *The English Patient* $79 million. Michael Almereyda's *Hamlet* (2000) may eventually prove to also fit this list.

Specialty films like these, and Miramax's perhaps more than any other, make an art of developing tactics of solicitation and enlistment of presumably more discriminating and individuated viewers. Specialty films promise personal experiences through films whose textual secrets frequently ask for more interpretive participation whereby audiences actively engage in private jokes, insider information, shared secrets, or cultural games surrounding the film. Specialty films distinguish their audience and that distinction assumes recognition, loyalty – and faith.

For these films, the central distribution strategies are positioning, platforming, and word-of-mouth, all of which work to generate a shared loyalty, trust, and faith between viewers and the film, as social performance of the film.[20] An advertising term, "positioning" is about placing the film in the mind of a potential viewer. The practice of platforming aims to expand that audience by gradually increasing the number of places a film is screened: beginning, for example, with a successful film festival appearance (such as those at Sundance or Berlin), a film may then be distributed to certain major urban centers and later to smaller markets around the US or the world as larger and larger audiences confirm its value. Word-of-mouth promotion develops and underpins platforming through radio interviews, reviews, and free appearances by actors and directors, and as the term suggests, implies the bond of personally shared tastes and knowledge. Perhaps the most celebrated example of this participatory exchange with audiences is Miramax's adaptation of *The Crying Game* to American markets. For both British and American audiences, the film was promoted first on the basis of its artistic novelty and integrity, associated primarily with Jordan's cultural reputation as a serious director of British films (such as the 1986 *Mona Lisa*). After only moderate success when first released in England, however, Miramax acquired the film for distribution. Removed from that British–Irish political context and deflecting the three traditional marketing taboos of race, political violence, and homosexuality, Miramax repackaged the film by promoting it around the romantic and sexual "secret" of the supposed female Dil's hidden masculinity, rapidly drawing record audiences for a British production released in the US.

Marketing and distribution in these instances promote – as is increasingly common today – the participation in secret or personal truths shared, exchanged, and performed between individual viewers.[21] For this, a recognized literary source positions a film for word-of-mouth platforming even before it appears, often in a manner that has little to do with an audience's actual experience of that literary source. Whether that literary work is *The English Patient* or *Hamlet*, readers of the original may return to the movie to measure it against the text, and this traditional rapport immediately offers a special bond to audiences who know the source, who can recognize and differentiate textual moves or casting decisions. Yet the promotional value of classic or recognized literature exceeds such textual relations, since to "recognize" a film can immediately "specialize" that film and identify that audience as participating in that act of literary recognition. The secret of special knowledge, in these instances, is commonly the ghost of the literary text.

As Hamlet feared and Miramax consistently demonstrates, however, literary ghosts often need spokespersons to articulate and perform their lost secrets. And none accomplish this more efficiently today than performative *auteurs*, who, as I've suggested, can mediate and even supersede that actual experience of any original text. Without meaning to sound too cynical or flippant, I believe it is Tarantino who anticipates Branagh in this position, less so than the usually cited precursors Olivier and Welles. While all these directors collapse their presence as directors with their appearance as actors in their films, there are significant historical differences between Branagh and the two other Shakespeareans: as I already indicated, Olivier's film work on Shakespeare's plays can be categorized as "realizations" of the different plays that actualize them through film technology, actor empathy, and historical insight; Welles "rewrites" Shakespeare so that we see perhaps more the creativity of Welles than the truth of Shakespeare. With Branagh, however, Miramax has found an *auteur* like Tarantino who, instead of reauthorizing pulp fiction and blaxploitation films, draws viewers back to Shakespeare's plays by remaking them through a performative personality that marks and absorbs the history of Shakespeare on film as singular performance.

Much of Branagh's performance as an *auteur*/agent lies outside the cinema. From his public consultations with Prince Charles about *Henry V* to his premature 1989 autobiography *Beginning*, it is difficult to find a more consistently public performer of his ideas and self-image. His career spans work as a renowned theatrical director and actor for both stage and screen, including a 1995 adaptation *Mary Shelley's Franken-stein* and a role in the 1999 *Wild Wild West*. But it is Branagh as the filmic reincarnation of Shakespeare for which he is most acclaimed and coveted by Miramax: as director/actor of *Henry V* (1989), *Much Ado About Nothing* (1993), *Othello* (1995), *A Midwinter's Tale* (1995), *Hamlet* (1996), and *Love's Labours Lost* (2000), he has pursued and redefined the heritage of Olivier and Welles. After participating in the produc-tion and distribution of this last film, Miramax Films has increased its stake in the Shakespearean Branagh by signing him to a multi-film deal that would extend into the next century and generate an expanding range and variety of Shakespeare adaptations (including productions of *Macbeth* and *As You Like It*).

What Miramax clearly understands and is betting on is this record of commercial versatility, whereby Branagh will continue not simply to pay homage to Shakespeare's different plays but will involve audi-ences in the evolving revelations of his own performance of those texts. Rather than realize or rewrite these classic texts, Branagh, I'd argue, adapts them to numerous performative poses, attitudes, postures, and affects – all as a kind of agent for the otherwise unknowable textual secrets. Branagh's Shakespeare appears always, like Shakespeare in love, as a performing heart, not a text.

Here the structure of a Branagh adaptation consistently aims at a kind of popularization but one whereby that popularization is ulti-mately about erasing the text to release what he calls an "inner life" that establishes personal bonds with his viewers.[22] His performance of Shakespeare, for instance, continually foregrounds private relationships in a signature fashion: for Branagh, what most reveals Hamlet and Ophelia is an intimate sexual relationship; his King Henry (unlike Olivier's) wrestles ostensibly with self-doubt and private confusion. Each adaptation, moreover, becomes built on a dramatically different context: from the nineteenth-century Scandinavian opulence of *Hamlet* and the rustic and ribald world of Tuscany in his *Much Ado* to the musical stages of the 1930s for *Love's Labours Lost*. The stylistic threads that unite these films are two: a heterogeneous and personal theatri-cality and a predominance of close-ups. Ranging from vaudeville to the Royal Academy of Dramatic Art, mixing actors such as classical theatrical players like Paul Scofield, Emma Thompson, Derek Jacobi and Hollywood stars like Michael Keaton and Alicia Sylverstone, these adaptations insist on singular performative skills and personalities as mediums for a lost text through which, in Branagh's words, an "intimacy" is communicated that is not available on stage. In his *Henry V* the stylistic emphasis on close-ups thus works to draw out "the internal life" and "a level of intimacy" of the characters in a way Olivier's version clearly does not (Crowdus, 1998: 38).

All these tactics then move towards establishing personal experiential bonds relayed between Shakespeare, Branagh, and the viewer as "a good experience with Shakespeare":

> For many people there continues to be a sense that this writer and his work, which has this Masterpiece status, is something to fear and dread, something that will somehow expose their lack of learning and intelligence. My experience has been that when people have had a good experience with Shakespeare, it's beyond perhaps just the snob factor, and feeling rather clever, it's something that can open up a certain part of themselves which, from that point, starts to be much less intimidated by great works of literature.

He continues in an interview appropriately titled "Sharing an Enthusiasm" by describing the paradox that, while Shakespeare may be equal to many other cultural experiences today, Branagh aims at a special "place" where he would be the very personal agent of the spiritual secrets of Shakespeare's invisible text:

> I'm simply *attempting*, as part of what a lot of other people are doing as well, to allow Shakespeare to be seen without prejudice, and without the implicit assumption that I believe it will be good for you or better than any other piece of cultural entertainment you may experience, but that it deserves a place. . . . Shakespeare unlocks that part of us which is currently bereft of that poetry or mystery, something that is expressed in the ongoing obsession with New Age philosophies or philosophical books attempting to exercise that part of us seeking some kind of spiritual fulfillment. I believe these plays, written by a great poet, affect us, in conscious and unconscious ways, spiritually. (Ibid: 34)

The Shakespearean text is a performative pretext for Branagh out of which he creates distinctly individualistic attitudes framed as a commercial *appeal* − in every sense of that word − to viewers seeking, among numerous cultural possibilities, expressive affirmation. Almost always, Branagh's adaptations gesture towards the original text (like the beginning of *Much Ado* when Beatrice reads and the screen prints the song lyrics "Sigh No More, Ladies"). Yet what has distinguished Branagh from his competitors and precursors is a creative submission of those texts to dramatically changing attitudes and postures in which that text becomes usurped by the (assumed) performative singularity of Branagh as personality. The authentic Shakespeare becomes Branagh's *Hamlet*, an exhaustive performance of the First Folio. The patriotic and masculine Shakespeare appears in Branagh's *Henry V* as a combination of Batman and Rambo.[23] The spectacular Shakespeare becomes *Much Ado About Nothing* as a combination of Hollywood western and multicultural blockbuster. And perhaps the most self-conscious of all is, ironically, the generic Branagh of *Love's Labours Lost*, a tongue-in-cheek musical Shakespeare.

That each of these retakes previous historical models of adaptation is, like his regular quotation of past film adaptations (Hamlet's blond hair as a gesture towards Olivier's Hamlet), a way of both confronting the historical burden of adaptation and making it evident where textual authority resides in contemporary film culture. If classic texts suggested historical transcendence, performative *auteurs* can now do so in matters of expressive agency. In Branagh's movement between them – and one only need think of Harold Bloom's recent bestseller book *Shakespeare: The Invention of the Human* and the burgeoning industry to promote Shakespeare, the man and personality, to know Branagh is hardly alone here[24] – he draws attention away from the text and to the performative virtuosity that we, the audience, are invited to participate in as a shared recognition not of the textual Shakespeare, lost to time, but of the performative Branagh as an agent of the dead, overcoming time.

The arguments about how faithful Branagh's and other adaptations are thus seem to me misplaced and misdirected. He is true to himself and his performance. Nor do arguments about popularization or integrating high culture into low seem to be as pertinent as they may have been in 1920 or 1935. His aim is not to be popular but to be personal. What Miramax and Branagh make clear is that authors and agency, not texts, are the cultural issue today. If the canonical text appeared recently dead or dissipated by the social and psychoanalytic suspicions opened by cultural studies, this premature conclusion has been countered by the widespread resurrection of that text in the theatrical body of the film *auteur* (among other bodies). Whether we now in fact read canonized works of literature more or less is not really the point; culturally we have learned to suspect them (both inside and outside academia) to the point that they have become secondary or even irrelevant for many. The problem for cultural studies today may be that the cult of the author and embodied agency have replaced that text with more power than ever, so that what contemporary film culture offers is the experience of authorship as a participatory engagement or performance. The most potent stars of film culture today are now *auteurs* and authors, and *auteurs* who perform as classical authors offer that special and deeply suspect freedom according to which the classical experience regathers history as a personal image and communication. Film is not the only cultural vehicle for this activity, but its personal and temporary permanency (repeatable and durable) and its social mobility (across all sorts of public and private spheres) make it a remarkably efficient, if troubling, replacement for the books and stages.

Perhaps this shift is a marker of what Christopher Clausen has described as our "post-cultural society," in which culture stands for neither singular hegemony nor multiple contending subcultures. It is a culture represented by an unsettling focus on individual freedom, and in this case, that freedom buttressed by the kind of nostalgia embedded in classical authors. If the texts themselves have faded as texts and come into focus as images, classical literature is not any more marginal than ever. As always film adaptations call attention to the complex agency that acts as cultural guide through which we experience that literature now and ever, and today that agency reinscribes our individuality in acts of shared performance of lost secrets. Or, to put this another way: in the vast array of post-culture, the question is not about high or low, text or image; the issue is the activity of performative choice and what that might mean.

The verbal jokes and cultural references within *Shakespeare in Love* continually draw on a modern retrospective knowledge of history – that ranges from specialized information about the plays of John Webster to the more popular knowledge of Sir Walter Raleigh and his famous cloak or the recognition of Romeo and Juliet's now clichéd balcony scene. Many of these references have no real bearing on the narrative or thematics of the film and so act as moments of performative excess, serving mainly to engage and distinguish audiences by what they may know or bring to the film. The film thus becomes not so much a recreation than an ironic reincarnation and engagement with an audience's ability to identify with authors (Shakespeare, Marlowe, Webster, Stoppard) and their play with fragmented texts. In the ending of *Shakespeare in Love*, Will's lost love and lost self finds salvation in authoring a *Twelfth Night* as an imagined/real return with his lost Viola to the shores of a tropical island. Unlike in Greenaway's *Tempest*, this island is not about books and literature, lost or won, but about the power of film and its embodied authors to luxuriate in a blasphemous disregard for literary, historical, textual, or even logical accuracy, about the ability to stage and perform one's inclinations and desires as a way to salvage a romantic fidelity. With typical Stoppard irony, of course, knowing the final literary reference does not make any more historical sense of that ending but only confirms the performative dexterity of viewers who might know or not what Shakespeare wrote.

Notes

1   This sketch of film adaptations also selects only from contemporary adaptations of so-called "classic literature" or canonical literary works, without acknowledging the exponentially larger category that could include popular fiction and best-sellers such as two 1999 releases, *The Talented Mr. Ripley* and *The Cider House Rules* (both products of Miramax Films).
2   See Corrigan (1999).
3   These two consistently used terms only, I believe, state the obvious, not only about film but virtually every other cultural practice. A famous appropriator of other stories and material, Shakespeare was also one of the most successful popularizers in the history of literature.
4   For an alternative reading of Cher's "appropriation" of these lines, see Boose and Burt (1997).
5   See Marie-Claire Ropars-Wuilleumier (1970) on the impact of new sound technology on adaptations in the 1930s.
6   Consider this: How often has that evaluative measure been evoked for theatrical stagings of novels or stories? Why is the issue rarely raised when discussing less weighty stories brought to the screen (say, Hitchcock's decisive reworking of Cornell Woolrich's story for *Rear Window*)?
7   For the complex early history of this relation between text and image, see Hans Belting's *Likeness and Presence* (1994).
8   Some of the many recent studies on adaptation and Shakespeare include Shaughnessy (1999), Desnet and Sawyer (2000), and Boose and Burt (1997). See Giddings, Selby, and Wensley (1990) on the connection between nineteenth-century fiction and narrative realism on film.

9   This phrase come from Roberta Pearson and William Uricchio's *Reframing Culture* (1993).

10 See Bazin's extraordinary essay "Theater and Cinema" in Bazin (1971) for a much more subtle and complex argument for Olivier's efforts to "realize" *Henry V*.

11 See Whelehan (1999), p. 18.

12 Stephen Orgel (1988) has argued that textuality has always been a problematic idea with Renaissance plays. He shifts the focus, in a particularly contemporary turn, from the text to the agency of Shakespeare, claiming that the inability to control an authentic text through the history of its performance was "a situation he understood, expected, and helped to perpetuate" (ibid: 7).

13 I've argued elsewhere (Corrigan, 1999) the ironic paradox that, just when auteurism begins to assert itself, Hollywood, through the force of the HUAC hearings, is dismantling the political and artistic force of the screenwriter/author.

14 Indeed one of the most influential critical interventions in the film/literature debates, most notably articulated by Robert Richardson (1969), paired the two practices through the shared technical strategies of authors and *auteurs* such as D. W. Griffith and Joseph Conrad.

15 See "The Commerce of Auteurism" in *A Cinema without Walls* (Corrigan, 1991).

16 Godard's *Contempt* becomes virtually a meta-film for film adaptations during this period, describing the comically semiotic encounter when Fritz Lang attempts to adapt *The Odyssey* for a Hollywood producer.

17 A recent project is timely in this regard. Michael Colgan, artistic director of Dublin's Gate Theatre, is adapting nineteen Beckett plays to the screen, the Beckett Film Project, using *auteurs* like David Mamet (*Catastrophe*), Neil Jordan (*Not I*), Atom Egoyan (*Krapp's Last Tape*), Anthony Minghella (*Play*), and possibly Bernardo Bertolucci (*Come and Go*). It describes a fascinating recirculation of Beckett, the author, through a wide range of auteurist visions.

18 None probably exceeds the bad faith logic more than Al Pacino's narcissistic meta-drama *Looking for Richard* (1996): part documentary, part personal performance, the film describes Pacino's struggle to understand and stage *Richard III*, punctuated with tortured self-reflections and interviews with the greater performers of Shakespeare, John Gielgud, Derek Jacobi, Vanessa Redgrave, Peter Brook, and of course Kenneth Branagh.

19 In a telling distinction, James Schamus (1991) notes that Orion Classics focused on "art cinema as opposed to avant-garde or even quirky independent." See Shatz (1993) on the so-called "mini-majors" and "independents" to emerge from the shake-up of the US film industry in the 1970s.

20 Tiu Lukk's (1997) *Movie Marketing: Opening the Picture and Giving It Legs* is a useful presentation of distribution strategies of a variety of contemporary films.

21 Miramax is one of many players in this business game. From *The Sixth Sense* to the television program *Survivor* the marketing of shared secrets may define much of the spirit of this cultural age.

22 "Art that hides the art" he calls this and distinguishes it from a precise textual approach that can appear "like a lecture" (Crowdus, 1998: 36–7).

23 Curtis Breight (1998) places this point in the context of Branagh's relationship with Prince Charles. Graham Fuller (1989) quotes Branagh's claim about *Henry*

V that "his great desire . . . to make it look like a film of today, to take the curse of medievalism off it, so that the *Batman* audiences could conceivably be made to see it."

24 Competing with Bloom but ultimately sharing the same contemporary ground, Frank Kermode's (2000) *Shakespeare's Language* takes a more circuitous route back to the human agency of Shakespeare by suggesting that Shakespeare's later texts struggle so dramatically with linguistic meaning that they make sense only as the reflection of the creative mind thinking. In a curiously appropriate essay that discusses both these works, Ron Rosenbaum (2000) sees these as part of a recent rejection of the textual deconstructions of postmodernism and cultural studies and the birth of "the post-postmodern," a renewed belief in fundamental human values and expressivity.

References

Andrew, Dudley (1984). "Adaptation," in *Concepts in Film Theory*. New York: Oxford University Press.

Astruc, Alexandre (1948). "The Birth of the New Avant-Garde: La Camera-Stylo." In Timothy Corrigan, ed., *Film and Literature: An Introduction and Reader*, Saddle Brook, NJ: Prentice-Hall, 158–62.

Bazin, Andre (1971). *What is Cinema?* vol. 1. Berkeley: University of California Press.

Belting, Hans (1994). *Likeness and Presence: A History of the Image Before the Era of Art*. Chicago: University of Chicago Press.

Bloom, Harold (1999). *Shakespeare: The Invention of the Human*. New York: Riverhead Books.

Boose, Lynda E. and Burt, Richard (1997). "Totally Clueless?: Shakespeare Goes Hollywood in the 1990s." In Lynda E. Boose and Richard Burt, eds., *Shakespeare the Movie: Popularizing the Plays on Film, TV, and Video*, London: Routledge, 8–22.

Breight, Curtis (1998). "Branagh and the Prince, or a 'Royal Fellowship of Death.'" In Robert Shaughnessy, ed., *Shakespeare on Film*, New York: St. Martin's Press, 126–44.

Clausen, Christopher (2000). *Faded Mosaic: The Emergence of Post-Cultural America*. Chicago: Ivan R. Dee.

Corrigan, Timothy (1991). *A Cinema Without Walls: Movies and Culture after Vietnam*. London: Routledge.

Corrigan, Timothy (1999). *Film and Literature: An Introduction and Reader*. Saddle Brook, NJ: Prentice-Hall.

Crowdus, Gary (1998). "Sharing an Enthusiasm for Shakespeare: An Interview with Kenneth Branagh," *Cineaste*, 24, 34–41.

Desnet, Cristy and Sawyer, Robert, eds. (2000). *Shakespeare and Appropriation*. New York: Routledge.

Fuller, Graham (1989). "Two Kings," *Film Comment*, 25, 6.

Giddings, Robert, Selby, K., and Wensley, C. (1990). *Screening the Novel: The Theory and Practice of Literary Dramatization*. Basingstoke: Macmillan.

Kermode, Frank (2000). *Shakespeare's Language*. New York: Farrar Straus Giroux.

Lukk, Tiu (1997). *Movie Marketing: Opening the Picture and Giving it Legs*. Los Angeles: Silman-James Press.

Murray, Timothy (1997). *Drama Trauma: Specters of Race and Sexuality in Performance, Video, and Art*. New York: Routledge.

Orgel, Stephen (1988). "The Authentic Shakespeare," *Representations*, no. 21 (winter).

Pearson, Roberta E. and Uricchio, William (1993). *Reframing Culture: The Case of the Vitagraph Quality Films*. Princeton, NJ: Princeton University Press.

Richardson, Robert (1969). *Literature and Film*. Bloomington: Indiana University Press.

Ropars-Wuilleumier, Marie-Claire (1970). *De la Literature au cinéma: genese d'une écriture*. Paris: Armand Colin.

Rosenbaum, Ron (2000). "The Play's the Thing, Again," *New York Times Book Review*, August 6, 12–13.

Schamus, James (1991). "Points of Light: Orion Classics Stays At the Top," *Off-Hollywood Report*, 6: 2, 20.

Shatz, Tom (1993). "The New Hollywood." In James Collins, Hilary Radner, and Ava Preacher Collins, eds., *Film Theory Goes to the Movies*, New York: Routledge, 8–36.

Shaughnessy, Robert (1999). *Shakespeare on Film*. New York: St. Martin's Press.

Stam, Robert (2000). "Beyond Fidelity: The Dialogics of Adaptation." In James Naremore, ed., *Film Adaptation*, New Brunswick, NJ: Rutgers University Press, 54–78.

Wagner, Geoffrey (1975). *The Novel and the Cinema*. Cranbury: Associated University Presses.

Whelehan, Imelda (1999). "Adaptations: The Contemporary Dilemma." In Deborah Cartwell and Imelda Whelehan, eds., *Adaptations: From Text to Screen and Screen to Text*, New York: Routledge, 3–20.

Further Reading

Donaldson, Peter (1990). *Shakespearean Films/Shakespearean Directors*. Boston: Unwin Hyman.

Higbee, Helen, Weimann, Robert, and West, William (2000). *Playing and Writing in Shakespeare's Theatre*. New York: Cambridge University Press.

Howlett, Kathy (2000). *Framing Shakespeare on Film*. Athens, OH: Ohio University Press.

Jackson, Russel, ed. (2000). *Cambridge Companion to Shakespeare on Film*. New York: Cambridge University Press.

Jorgens, Jack J. (1977). *Shakespeare on Film*. Bloomington: Indiana University Press.

McFarlane, Brian (1996). *Novel to Film: An Introduction to the Theory of Adaptation*. New York: Oxford University Press.

Naremore, James, ed. (2000). *Film Adaptation*. New Brunswick, NJ: Rutgers University Press.

Rothwell, Kenneth S. (1999). *A History of Shakespeare on Film*. New York: Cambridge University Press.

8

No (Popular) Place Like Home?
Jim Collins

Within the past decade the home has become not just a site, but a form of popular culture unto itself. In a certain sense, domestic space has been within the realm of popular culture for decades as a receiver of television and radio waves and as an archive for bestsellers, pop albums, magazines, and trendy fashion items, etc. Richard Hamilton's photo-collage, *"Just what is it that makes today's homes so different, so appealing?"* (1956) visualized this penetration of the domestic interior by popular culture four decades ago, a dwelling place where virtually everything that wasn't a television screen or a movie marquee was an icon or logo appropriated directly from comic books, muscle magazines, or advertisements. Yet the furniture is barely visible; it remains a mere support for the barrage of mass-media messages that circulate throughout this living room. As prophetic as Hamilton's vision of mass-mediated space might have been, he didn't foresee what would occur in the 1990s – that furniture would become a form of popular culture unto itself, as would the sense of "decor" needed to make a space a *home* reflecting one's personal sensibilities. We can make sense of the current popularization of home decor, in the form of the *good design* chain store (Crate and Barrel, Pottery Barn, Restoration Hardware) and as a highly marketable sensibility (Martha Stewart, Terence Conran, a host of shelter magazines, the House and Garden channel) only by rethinking some of the most hidebound assumptions concerning the relationships between craft and mass production, authenticity and simulation, popular and personal tastes.

Until quite recently *interior design* was conceived of as a class-specific phenomenon distinguished by a very high snob factor.

Furniture was thought of as a relatively permanent investment, the cost of the items precluding the kind of quick turnover one normally associates with popular culture. Because of the costs involved, furniture could never have the ability that clothing did to demonstrate one's personal style, particularly a personal style that had to change on a regular basis to make sure that it was genuinely stylish. Furthermore, interior decor had no institutional framework, like that of the fashion industry, to encourage a mass audience to see furniture as expressions of self-image. Magazines devoted to interior design like *Architectural Digest* and *House Beautiful* featured people, usually celebrities, who were able to realize this goal, but the pleasures they offered were largely vicarious ones for all but an elite audience that could afford to conceive of furniture as the finely tuned visualization of personal identity. By the 1970s, televison cooking programs like Julia Child's *The French Chef* had begun to provide access to the world of *haute cuisine* by making cooking into a spectator sport, but interior design seemingly had no such potential. Audiences were entranced by watching Julia make *coq au vin* but who would want to see her hang pictures, or paint a floor? As such, interior design was anything *but* a form of *popular* culture, bound financially and discursively to a realm of rarefied cultural pleasure with little or no mass-media play.

But all that has changed within the past decade. The *Wall Street Journal* describes the current situation as the Age of Disposable Decor:

> these days, it's hard enough keeping track of whether gray or brown is the "new black," not to mention whether this year's suit should have four buttons or three. Now, homeowners also have to worry about whether their ottomans, throw pillows, and bed sheets are staying ahead of the trend police. Spurred in part by the marketing departments of mass retailers such as *Crate and Barrel*, *Pottery Barn*, and *Pier 1*, the fashion half-life of home furnishings – particularly accessories – has been cut shorter than ever. Items that consumers once bought with an eye to handing down as heirlooms fall out of date in a season or two. (Fletcher, 1999: W12)

This trendification of interior design is attributable to a number of interdependent factors. One is undoubtedly the emergence of the *good design* chain stores, which have drastically reduced the price of quality furniture. Another is the direct attempt to gain a share of this market:

fashion designers like Calvin Klein, Liz Claiborne, Ralph Lauren, and Tommy Hilfiger have moved into the world of home decor, thereby closing the gap between clothing and furniture. According to Joseph Aboud, "The home has become a lot like an apparel closet. New things come out for it every three months." Designer Alexander Juilian calls his home furnishings line "wardrobe for the home" (both quoted in Fletcher, 1999). But the most profound change is the formation of an entire design infrastructure in the form of shelter magazines and advice mavens who have created a new popular design discourse which has turned home decor into a medium capable of expressing self-image with a high degree of both flexibility and precision for an enormous mass audience. *Architectural Digest* may still present the homes of the rich and famous and includes, as a matter of course, the name of the interior decorator responsible, but *Metropolitan Home* and *Elle Decor* maintain the impression that the home-owner is the decorator, and it is the inspired realization of their tastes which make it worthy of being featured in the magazine, even conducting an annual contest to deter-mine who has realized their dream house most successfully. The ad for Corian tile which appears in mass-market shelter magazines like *Met-ropolitan Home, Elle Decor, Wallpaper,* and *House and Garden* sums this up perfectly: "You Are How You Decorate, send for our brochure, 'Home as Self'." The good design chain store has made home-as-self possible financially, while the design advice industry has made it a fore-gone conclusion as a mentality.

The sheer size of the audience for whom the cultivation of the home has become a form of popular entertainment can be measured most vividly by the success of Martha Stewart. According to the *New York Times*, Martha Stewart Omnimedia is a conglomerate that includes "a monthly magazine *Martha Stewart Living*, with a circulation of 2.35 million; 110 1-hour television shows a year; daily 'Ask Martha' radio spots; *Martha by Mail*, the catalogue she rolled out last month; a website; and 26 books. This great big enterprise touches about 91 million people every month" (O'Neill, 1999: 145). Home-keeping has quite obviously become a very lucrative spectator sport which allows for varying degrees of audience participation. Viewers watch Martha not only hang pictures but make the frames and offer advice on how to make family photos into design accessories. She has also entered into the *good design* discount store competition with a massive product line at K-Mart stores. The enormity of that appeal made it especially attractive to investors during its initial public stock offering on October 19, 1999; by the end of the day Martha Stewart's share of Omnimedia was worth $1.2 billion, making her, according to a cover story in *USA Today*, the wealthiest woman in the entertainment industry (Straus, 1999: 1A). To return to John Frow's essential point about the convergence between the systems of signature and brand, Martha Stewart takes it up to the next level, making signature into brand into conglomerate through a finely honed synergy. Yet why has Martha become a conglomerate entertainment machine unto herself, more successful than Madonna or Oprah as a popular culture icon?

As Stewart herself has said: "I stepped into the void and have always been perfectly clear about my intention of filling that void" (O'Neill, 1999: 145). The void in question can be theorized in a number of different ways, but I think the most productive way to conceive of her impact is in terms of how she has legitimized the cultivation of a certain kind of domesticity for a massive audience, largely by operating as a supremely skillful taste broker who can gesture toward bygone hierarchies while creating a new one of her own that is both elitist *and* populist. She is, then, the quintessential embodiment of high-pop, activating the vestiges of elite class distinctions and, at the same time, functioning as a representative home-lover, without ever losing the carefully constructed aura that those vestiges bring in their wake. As such, she can still invoke the sanctity of *haute cuisine* when she writes the foreword to a new cookbook by Daniel Boulud (currently New York's reigning master French chef), but she also demonstrates the mass audience appeal of the contemporary cooking show when she invites Aretha Franklin to make dinner at her house on her network Christmas Special (1999). There is no better example of both the delivery of elite pleasure to a mass audience *and* the concomitant need to mark those pleasures as still somehow rarefied than when Martha says she can't believe that *Aretha Franklin* is in her kitchen, to which Aretha responds that she can't believe *Martha Stewart* is helping her make her ham.

According to Metropolitan Home,

The way of making things that critics have been calling Good Design since the last World War (by which they mean pared down, muted and slightly machined) has gone so mainstream that it's available at Target. The idea of good design was first promulgated by European Architects and designers in the 1920s. But for a long time, modernism was seen as appealing only to an avant-garde elite. Good Design is both high style and so mass market that you can't escape it even if you want to. (Betsky, 2000)

Yet what might seem to be the final realization of a Bauhaus dream has met with a conflicted critical response. In his analysis of the mass production of high style, Paul Goldberger expresses his ambivalence about the profound changes these stores have wrought in terms of making design affordable. He describes chains like The Gap and Pottery Barn as a "taste machine, a veritable assembly-line of esthetics that knocks off both the high-end, innovative design and eccentric subculture notions, that appeal to people with sophisticated taste but that are also priced within the reach of a huge segment of the population" (Goldberger, 1997: 58). He concedes that this machine has changed the way high style has been circulated; that formerly, progressive design was available only to decorators through showrooms, a period when the "whole system seemed organized to prove the point that high design was the province of an elite." But if this taste machine has made high design affordable, Goldberger insists that the price we have paid for accessibility is too high: "we pay the price in a gradual but very real loss of individual variation: our houses and our wardrobes, like our entertainment, become part of mass culture, wherein we all increasingly display and consume the same thing." Ubiquity is antithetical to high style because "truly creative design has almost always come from breaking molds or finding new patterns, from someone doing something different from what has been done before. My house isn't supposed to look like your house. After we shop at Pottery Barn, however, it probably will" (ibid: 60).

To anyone familiar with the work of Theodor Adorno, Max Horkheimer, and their disciples, this argument will sound quite familiar because it contains all of the standard features of the mass culture critique, normally leveled at television, movies, or pop music: Mass Culture is diametrically opposed to Genuine Art, because the former is mass produced, which inevitably results in a rigid homogeneity of style, which in turn inevitably results in the homogenization of the audience that consumes it. Accessibility inevitably means diminished standards, a point that becomes particularly apparent when Goldberger, after saying that Mickey Drexler (president of The Gap) has had a greater impact on design than anyone else in the United States in the last twenty years, quotes him as saying: "I have never understood why certain things in America can't be available to everyone." The chief problem for Goldberger is the impact of this availability on taste, or more specifically, who has it and how we acquire it. He contends: "There was a time when good taste was something that signified a wordliness born of education and travel. These stores offer a shortcut" (ibid).

The issue of education in regard to taste remains a primary concern in popular discourse on style and it has crucially important ramifications for the study of popular places, because taste (no matter how explicitly or implicitly articulated) remains the lens through which all popular environments are viewed and, more importantly, judged to be authentic or inauthentic. In the introduction to this volume I argued that the shelter magazines and taste mavens presume to deliver the sort of education that the academy no longer provides, namely the refinement of individual sensibility in terms of personal taste. Design catalogues such as *Design Within Reach* now include, as a matter of course, museum catalogue-type explanations of the historical significance of the Nelson's Marshmallow sofa, or Yanagi butterfly stools, complete with photographs of the designer responsible. The popularization of interior design has made the question of the right sort of education a very visible concern, a point epitomized by the very title of the *New York Times Magazine* home design issue of fall 1997: "The Educated Eye." But what indeed is an educated eye at the end of the twentieth century, particularly one capable of understanding the nature of taste within popular places?

Design education involves the cultivation of a certain degree of design literacy, but *where* we acquire that literacy, *from whom*, and *toward what end* are the variables that have changed the basic terrain of the taste wars since the early 1990s. Goldberger is absolutely correct: there was a time when good taste signified a certain kind of education and worldliness. What has changed is the unitary quality of that "certain kind," a point made opulently clear by his own article – Drexler and Goldberger coexist as taste-makers, each articulating fundamentally different notions of taste, each imaging the other's elitism or populism as everything they work against, each one an opinion-maker, speaking from a position of authority and influence within their respective but nonetheless overlapping orbits of the marketplace and the *New York*

Plate 8.1   The Crate and Barrel flagship store on Michigan Avenue in Chicago.

Times. The current situation is defined then not by the abandonment of good taste as a category, but the proliferation of different notions of good taste which frame-up the same environments and phenomena in conflicting, often even contradictory ways, and have, to put it in Foucaultian terms, the discursive appartus to back it up. As I have argued elsewhere (Collins, 1995) what distinguishes taste wars in postmodern contexts is not a diminished interest in cultural value but an almost maniacal obsession with it, a situation in which different types of cultural authority jockey for position but none enjoys sovereignty *across the board*: no hierarchy of values or styles can be appealed to as a common cultural gold standard. The absence of such a consensus in postmodern cultures has been either celebrated or deplored by a variety of theoreticians, but I want to concentrate on how the absence of *a certain kind* of education and worldliness affects the production of both design and taste in popular culture.

In order to investigate the good design chain store as a site of popular culture unto itself, I decided to do some field work at the Crate and Barrel flagship store on Michigan Avenue in Chicago (plate

8.1). I want to make my discursive position clear at this point. I went not as a researcher armed with clipboard and pith helmet, venturing into the jungles of commerce intending to sniff out the rotten fruits of consumerism and lead the natives in a chorus of "Arise, Ye Prisoners of Simulation." Rather, I was a researcher who also needed a couch, who wasn't independently wealthy, but possessed some kind, if not a *certain* kind, of taste. After touring the site from top to bottom I decided that the best way to describe it in a manageable way for the readers of this chapter was to stand at the center of the furniture floor and detail the panoramic view, because it was here that space, design literacy, and popular taste-making coalesced. There were four different living room ensembles before me, each a *set* unto itself. Off to my left was "Loft," which featured the sort of Retro-modernism that has been one of the hallmarks of Crate and Barrel. But there next to the *colorized* minimalism was a Chippendale ensemble, complete with camelback couch and brocade. Off to the right was the "Morris" collection, a grouping which the card described as a "piece of art" with a "Mission" ensemble just behind it. Directly ahead was "Club," art deco complete with framed photo of the Brooklyn Bridge and martini glasses on the table.

Now what can be said about this wrap-around *mise-en-scène*? Taken together they form a postmodern space in the sense that they represent the simultaneity of multiple historical reactivations, all subject to random access as, at least in principle, co-equal options. Together they exemplify what Umberto Eco (1986) referred to as the force of the *already said*, which can be transformed into the *still being said*, or in this case the *still being designed*, with apparent ease. And together they are representative of contemporary forms of reservoir textuality like the cable box or the computer terminal: you can channel-surf through different historical revivals just by turning your head.

What sort of "educated eye" is called for by this particular popular place? Crate and Barrel undertakes a certain educational activity in the form of the museum-like cards which designate style and amplifies this through art historical accessories – the coffee table in the "Morris" ensemble features not martini glasses but copies of Barbara Mayer's book, *In the Arts and Crafts Style*. These touches obviously flatter the acquired design literacy the college-educated shopper brings into the store and offers to make furniture shopping into something more than brute consumerism; it can become an expression of your tastes formed by a college education — these are, after all, *pieces of art* that you can take home.

Yet the education of the eye at play here is more complicated than the simple appeal to traditional forms of education and wordliness. The explanatory sign over the "Club" ensemble begins: "A silhouette you'll find in vintage movies. With a purity of line that is a bit Deco in feeling, it conjures the sophisticated repartee of a bygone era." The reference to vintage movies suggests another dimension to education, namely popular culture, and another kind of worldliness, one that comes not from the Grand Tour or the junior year abroad but from the mass media, where easy travel to other cultures and other historical periods has literally been child's play for decades. This is also a certain kind of education, but, more importantly, the mass-media images which occupy our cultural literacy are part of the terrain, inseparable from our design literacy in electronic cultures. Charlie Lazor, designer and partner for Blu Dot (a design firm which has developed a new furniture line for Target intended for twentysomethings who are setting up their first apartments), has said of this new audience: "Their cultural landscape is media derived, whereas ours may have been defined by our parents' house or something we saw in a museum" (Marin, 2000). Style, as such, is seldom encountered in a pure state. It comes to us overlaid with associations that mediate our evaluation of it. This is what the Mickey Drexlers of this world have known for quite some time — the past (at least stylish bits of it like Marlene Dietrich) *wore khakis*. Crate and Barrel conjures the previous conjurings, envisions through the layers of envisionings that form an essential dimension of what constitutes worldliness at the end of the twentieth century.

The values that appear to be the basis of critical design literacy in the good design chain store are an interesting hybrid that reveal traces of disparate style ideologies gone by. The prominence of Arts and Crafts aesthetics, in both the "Morris" and "Mission" incarnations, throws a number of value distinctions into sharp relief. Ironically, the Morris in question and the movement he inspired, which defined itself as the enemy of mass production of the industrial age, has now become one of the most mass-produced styles of the post–industrial age. The valorization of craft, nevertheless, seems to be inseparable from the style despite its mass production. The museum card on "Mission" reads: "The Mission bed is made of solid black cherry in a bold, contemporary design. The flat slats proudly display the grain of this hand-oiled wood to its best advantage. Made by craftsmen in Vermont, the bed is available in queen size only." Here we find the privileging of natural materials whose inherent beauty is brought to the surface by hand (in Vermont, no less!). The values implied here are true to the original spirit of the Arts and Crafts aesthetic – even if the foregrounding of craft in this context seems a bit disingenuous, and the difference between "craft" and "mass-produced" is more a semiotic distinction than a matter of ontological status. The other intriguing terminological play concerns the designation of this historical revival as boldly *contemporary*. This unique sense of temporality is one of the defining features of the good design chain store and the basis of one of its most exhilarating pleasures: one's tastes are not only likely to be satisfied, they're guaranteed to be contemporary, even if they run to the Neo-Classical, Late Victorian or Early Modern.

But how do we judge this multiplicity of style options, this pageant of revivalist contemporaneity? As a Yuppie theme park in which all is simulation and inauthenticity? It would be easy to make such a sweeping value judgment, provided one's design literacy rested on ahistorical notions of authenticity and on entirely asemiotic notions of how any object takes on significance. If we judge Crate and Barrel's version of Arts and Crafts furniture to be mere revivalist simulacra, what then do we make of the medievalism so frequently incorporated in the original Arts and Crafts designs which presented a nostalgic vision of the Middle Ages when craft was the authentic expression of the human hand, yet conceived of that lost Eden in such whoppingly "inauthentic" ways? Was Morris *imagineering* a Disneyland Middle Ages before his time? One could easily pose the same question in reference to the Neo-Classical mania of a century before, a period when the fashion for all things Greek and Roman led to the mass production of pseudo-antiquities by John Cheere and company at his sculpture yards at Hyde Park Corner. In *Authentic Decor 1620–1920* Peter Thornton (1984) makes it overwhelmingly clear that the desire to furnish homes in the styles of other historical periods has been a defining feature of interior design for the past three centuries and the presentation of the historical as somehow contemporary has likewise been a recurring phenomenon.

Yet the historical revivalism we encounter now is not just the latest version of what has always been the case. It hasn't always been the case

because Modernism forms the immediate past and its mythologies –
specifically the sanctification of the "new," the dismissal of the historical revival as irrelevant if not downright immoral in the twentieth
century, the demonization of popular culture as inauthentic – linger
yet in the various forms of Retro-modern design, architecture and
criticism. The Retro-modern phenomenon[1] is distinguished by designers in a range of media who claim to embrace the future but insist on
envisioning it within the styles of the avant-gardes of the 1920s, which
they are determined to believe still represent a challenge to the status
quo (see especially the work of Peter Pran, Charles Gwathmey, etc.).
The rush to condemn popular places as inauthentic, as mere simulation, always takes for granted an unspecified past, before the Fall, when
things were authentic and there was no need for counterfeit versions
of the past – the past as theoretical theme park, a Never Never Was
the Case Land that nonetheless provides all sorts of thrills for the right
academic audience.

This ahistoricism is only part of the problem with the all-is-
simulation-the-world-is-becoming-a-theme-park argument. The chief
problem, theoretically speaking, is that the difference between simulation and representation is seldom if ever specified in either historical
or semiotic terms. If you want to make a Baudrillardian nervous, ask
him to delineate the relationship between representation and simulation. The answer usually goes something like this: "Simulation is well
. . . the mass cultural which *ipso facto* produces a fantasmatic reality full
of surrogate experiences, you know, then there was this realer used-to-
be that televison vaporized and now the masses can no longer recognize the really Real." The argument would be at least somewhat
convincing if it could determine when, in the history of representation, representation automatically becomes simulation. With photogra-
phy, film, or television? Or if it could determine whether it was a
matter of the raw material of signification; in which case, are all photographic media automatically simulation? Or if it was a matter of sig-
nifying intent; in which case, can any and all media be considered
simulation? Or a matter of desired effects; in which case, is it the profit
motive that is responsible for the inauthenticity? The all-is-simulation
approach clearly has nothing to do with the actions of the public as
receivers of the message because they're generally referred to as "the
masses," who are always duped into believing that the simulated real is
the really real. It is precisely this omission, this failure to grant the

receiver any agency in the communicative exchange, any voice or identity in the experience of popular texts, whether they be television programs or theme parks, that makes the simulation approach so unconvincing on both semiotic and ideological grounds.

It is beyond the scope of this chapter to do justice to the body of work that addresses the ways in which audiences make use of popular places like malls and theme parks and thereby make them vital players in the process of making those environments meaningful.[2] How we make sense of popular places depends on how we read the narratives that make sense of those environments. For Baudrillard, Soja, Michael Sorkin and company, evaluating the nature of public space means projecting a critical master-narrative that will counteract the duplicitous narrative of inauthenticity that lulls the masses into accepting the simulated as some sort of genuine experience. The game has two players (developer and critic) and two narratives (one which programs, the other which deprograms). What is left out of the equation is the multiplicity of micro-narratives projected onto these environments by the people who actually visit them, the personal narratives which give them significance, and measure their degree of authenticity, in reference to their own lives. It is in regard to precisely this question – who is empowered to project narratives which make sense of cultural space? – that we need to consider in reference to the popularization of the private home, because it is at this site that the relationship between design literacy, taste, and the narrativization of space interconnect in the most complicated ways.

At this point I want to return to Paul Goldberger's contention that after we shop at Pottery Barn and other high-style chain stores all our homes will become increasingly the same, since they've become yet another form of mass culture. It seems to me that we can accept this master-narrative only if we believe that individuals are incapable of constructing narratives that make sense of their own cultural existence. The need to make design choices that reflect one's *personal* history conceived of as the intersection of familial, ethnic, class, and educational influences is the engine that drives design literacy in the 1990s and serves as its chief distinguishing characteristic. The design literacy that was the foundation of taste amidst the swirl of the various historical revivals in the nineteenth century was undoubtedly a matter of establishing personal preferences, but those preferences were expressed through adherence to one style or another. That the construction of

personal style has become a higher priority than the choice of, or
fidelity to, any one historical style is nowhere more obvious than in
the introduction to Terence Conran's (1994) *The Essential House Book:
Getting Back to Basics*. The man who many see as the virtual inventor
of the good design chain store tells us that

> Home is where we feel at ease, where we belong, where we can create
> surroundings which reflect our tastes and pleasures. Creating a home has
> a lot to do with discovering those elements that convey a sense of place.
> Investigating these ideas relegates "style" to something of a side issue.
> . . . This is not to say that style isn't fun or even useful. But ultimately
> it is more important to find out what you really like. (Ibid: 11)

Selection and self-definition appear to be inseparable, at which point
a certain kind of connoisseurship becomes essential, a connoisseurship
conceived of, not in terms of abstract knowledge of the history of
art and design, but a far more specialized sort of educated eye whose
expertise is a matter of turning personal sensibility into domestic space.

This personalization of space depends on making the right consumer
choices and the anxiety over the rightness or appropriateness of those
choices has made design mavens like Conran and Martha Stewart into
extremely successful taste merchants. The complexity of that self-
fashioning process, however, cannot be understood with any degree of
subtlety if approached from the perspective of mere commodity
fetishism. The work of the new consumerism theorists such as Ann
Bermingham, Daniel Miller, and Colin Campbell is extremely useful
in this regard because it provides a different set of paradigms for appre-
ciating the relationship between consumerism and identity formation.
Since I've already discussed in the introduction to this volume the significance of this work for understanding high-pop as a phenomenon
which cross-cuts a variety of different media, I'll concentrate on just
two points here. The first is Bermingham's (1995) insistence that
gaining a fine-grain understanding of consumerism is made possible
only by rejecting the Modernist master narrative of culture, namely
that consumerism and genuine culture are diametrically opposed and
that the presence of the former only jeopardizes the purity of the latter.
She exposes the mythology that underwrites this narrative which, like
any myth, is enormously useful for easy moralizing but only counterproductive for historical analysis. For Bermingham, consumerism is

itself a form of *cultural* practice with a 400-year history, so examining the forces which animate it necessarily includes consideration of the functions it serves within specific historical contexts. Campbell (1987) also rejects that master narrative and presents a very different historical trajectory in which Romanticism represents, not a grand aesthetic alternative to consumerism, but the very basis of modern consumerism in its legitimation of the pursuit of pleasure. Campbell stresses that the Romantic theory of artistic creation emphasizes the "recreative" abilities of the reader as much as the original creative faculties of the poet, at which point "the reader is assumed to be a creative artist, capable of conjuring up images which have the power to 'move' him" (ibid: 189). This argument reveals a great deal about the nature of consumerism within high-pop phenomena because it provides a framework for understanding the process of self-fashioning in regard to one's domestic space, especially when that process is a matter of creating a personal *mise-en-scène* out of the signature styles of the right designers. What distinguishes the contemporary period, then, is the celebration of a uniqueness of style that rivals the Romantics, but the ability to realize that style has, in principle, been extended to a mass audience which now seemingly possesses the tasteful sensibility necessary to enact it, a point evidenced by the *Metropolitan Home* cover, "Shape Your Own Style GET PERSONAL" (July/August, 1999).

Reconceptualizing consumerism in regard to the historically contingent forces which animate self-fashioning requires at least a provisional theory of a *recreative* postmodern subject. Walter Benjamin's figure of the *flâneur* has become a widely circulated prototype of the modern consumer, but Daniel Miller has argued most compellingly that this has produced only counterproductive effects. Miller argues:

> I believe that if one is concerned about the political implications of shopping in the modern world, then the continued influence of this work of Walter Benjamin's has been little short of disastrous. . . . Benjamin appeals to the aesthetically inclined not only because of the brilliance of his style, but also because he maintained a deep – indeed mystical – sense of essence. . . . What Benjamin could not allow for, indeed what would have been his ultimate nightmare, is the acceptance of this world of shopping as mere reality. In Benjamin's notes there seems to be no attempt to understand the practice of those who used the arcades. (Miller, 1997: 35)

While Miller rightly questions the usefulness of the Arcades Project for understanding contemporary consumerism, he does suggest that another essay by Benjamin might prove useful for understanding contemporary consumerism. In "Unpacking My Library: A Talk about Book Collecting," Benjamin asserts that "ownership is the most intimate relationship one can have to objects. Not that they come alive in him: it is he who comes alive in them" (quoted in Miller, 1997). Benjamin sounds here like he could be writing the ad copy for a Mitchell Gold leather club chair. Collecting, especially used books, has a very different status than mere furniture shopping, but what is responsible for that discrepancy? Miller zeros in on the class prejudices of academics who subscribe to the Modernist disdain for the marketplace, but he poses a very suggestive question: what happens when we conceive of consumerism as collecting as opposed to mere shopping?

That question has profound ramifications for understanding interior design as a process of self-fashioning, particularly if we conceive of that personalized space as a series of choices in a collection unified not by particular type of item (say, art pottery) but a specific sensibility (the self-image of the dweller). It is not coincidental that one of the standard features of *Martha Stewart Living* is *Collecting*. While these feature stories conceive of collecting in a relatively narrow sense, the magazine's departments (Gardening, Restoring, Renovating, Homekeeping, Reading, etc.) all offer two types of interdependent expertise: lessons in specific techniques, coupled with how to *make it your own*. The expectation that underlies these articles is that readers are in the process of refining a coherent sense of self and are in the process of collecting the expertise needed to turn the various aspects of their domestic environments into a unified text, tied together not by a consistent style but, to echo Conran, a consistent sense of *what they like*. The *Reading* feature in the annual Special Decorating issue (September 1999) suggests a great deal about the model readers of the magazine. Entitled "Decorating Wisdom," the article surveys the history of the decorating books intended for an elite audience, beginning with Edith Wharton in 1897 and then moving through Elsie de Wolfe, Dorothy Draper, Billy Balwin, Sister Parish, and concluding with Mark Hampton. This history suggests that the readers of the magazine not only want to collect specific forms of expertise to expand their design literacy, but they're also keen to acquire a sense of historical context.

This notion of the individual engaged in a process of collecting disparate materials out of which are fashioned a relatively coherent sense of identity that has to be satisfying on a local level sounds like *bricolage*, a term used by anthropologists such as Lévi-Strauss to describe the formation of mythologies and rituals within primitive tribes. The *bricoleur*, like the *flâneur*, has been a widely used trope to describe the manner in which postmodern subjects make sense of their decentered existences. Yet conceiving of the readers of Stewart, Conran, and shelter magazines as *bricoleurs* is useful only if the proper adjustments are made for the massive differences in context. The process of self-fashioning through manipulation of domestic space is a matter of making the appropriate selection out of an array of widely disparate materials, but that process could hardly be less primitive, given the discourse of popular connoisseurship which pervades design discourse and the apparent need for taste mavens to aid that process. Nevertheless, comparing the *bricoleur* and the popular connoisseur can be a very productive exercise because it throws into sharp relief the critical categories and prejudices that are brought to bear in evaluating this self-fashioning. If we deny the authenticity of the desire to construct a personal sense of *place* when it becomes too *informed*, too dependent on consumer choices, then the limitations of cultural studies pop to the surface. Within the ethnographic sense of culture which has been one of the defining features of cultural studies, the authenticity of unsophisticated practices has seldom been an issue; if anything, the lack of sophistication serves as a guarantee of authenticity. Within the traditional mass-culture critique, mass culture can never be authentic because the sophistication of the modes of production and distribution guarantee only the inauthenticity of everything and everyone involved. If cultural studies is to come to terms with the need to fashion a meaningful sense of place out of the consumer whirl of popular culture, it must develop a way of accounting for the authenticity of that need without automatically invalidating it because it depends on consumer choices for its articulation.

The central question should be, if cultural studies wants to remain genuinely ethnographic, what cultural needs are addressed by the popularization of interior design? Whether the personalization of domestic space is a bogus homines or a *good thing* cannot be determined across the board, by the class of people involved or the amount of disposable income they do or do not possess. There is no better example of the conflicted nature of cultural authority and the absence of consensus about taste than the varying responses to Martha Stewart, since she appears to inspire equal measures of devotion and vituperative hatred, generating bestselling design books as well as parody issues of her magazine (*Is Martha Stewart Living?*), tell-all biographies and exposés in society magazines like *Spy*. The Martha Stewart phenomenon is undoubtedly part of the mass production of the pursuit of personal taste and, as such, it will inevitably be judged authentic or inauthentic by different audiences. But why have these questions about taste become the very stuff of popular entertainment?

One of the recurring themes of poststructuralist and postmodern theory has been the fragmentation of a coherent sense of identity. While a great deal of theoretical work has been devoted to the philosophical and psychological dimensions of a decentered subjectivity, and a significant amount of literary and film analysis has traced its impact on the structure of narrative, its impact on how we forge some sense of identity in terms of domestic space, our most personal space, remains largely unexplored. Popular culture has always been especially good at turning widespread anxieties into rousing entertainment. Like it or not, Pierre Bourdieu and Martha Stewart are responses to the same perceived crisis – the need to identify some sort of *habitus*, where one makes all that stuff out there, into one's own localized, cultural space. The Martha Stewart phenomenon could be thought of as the successful realization of the desires Bourdieu identifies, a kind of *Habitus Inc.*, something I suggest only somewhat facetiously since the name of Terence Conran's high-style chain stores that started it all was *Habitat*.

The current popularization of interior design then is about domestic space, but it revolves around the *domestication* of the excess of postmodern culture, a domestication which makes fashioning a sense of place possible despite the excess of images, messages, style choices and authorities about what to do with it all. The postmodern context is frequently conceived of in terms of an ever-increasing globalization; both theoreticians and computer commercials tell us that traditional geographic and historical boundaries have been erased by information technologies, mass communication, and transnational corporations. The image of the home as information depot that has become so commonplace in computer advertising bears a remarkable resemblance to the home envisioned by David Hamilton in 1956. Yet that image of the globalized home is only half the picture because the image of the home without walls is countered by another vision in which the home becomes refuge from that excess, a closed set where the *mise-en-scène* of one's private life takes shape. Both forces, the centrifugal drive toward globalization and the centripetal drive toward the maximum personalization of space, have become part of popular culture – we see Martha Stewart's house on the same box as CNN, we encounter the decor equivalent of world music at Pottery Barn. The home is alternately unavoidably public and relentlessly private. An "educated eye" at the turn of the twenty-first century is one which can domesticate that sort of *worldliness*, at which point authenticity would indeed seem to be a matter of taste.

Notes

An earlier version of this essay appeared in *Harvard Design Magazine* (Winter/Spring 1998).

1   For a more extended discussion of Retro-modernism see chapter 4 of my *Architectures of Excess* (1995).

2   See, especially, Rob Shields, ed., *Lifestyle Shopping* (New York: Routledge, 1992) and Michel De Certeau *The Practice of Everyday Life* (Berkeley: University of California Press, 1984).

References

Bermingham, Ann (1995). "Introduction." In Ann Bermingham and John Brewer, eds., *The Consumption of Culture 1600–1800: Image, Object, Text*, New York: Routledge.

Betsky, Aaron (2000). "When Good Design Goes Bad," *Metropolitan Home*, November–December.

Campbell, Colin (1987). *The Romantic Ethic and the Spirit of Modern Consumerism*. Oxford: Blackwell Publishers.

Collins, Jim (1995). *Architectures of Excess: Cultural Life in the Information Age*. New York: Routledge.

Conran, Terence (1994). *The Essential House Book: Getting Back to Basics*. New York: Crown Trade.

Eco, Umberto (1986). "Postscript to *The Name of the Rose*." San Diego: Harcourt Brace Jovanovich.

Fletcher, June (1999). "Staying Ahead of the Furniture Fashion Police," *Wall Street Journal*, November 19.

Goldberger, Paul (1997). "The Sameness of Things," *New York Times Magazine*, April 6.

Lovell, Amanda (1999). "Decorating Wisdom," *Martha Stewart Living*, September.

Marin, Rick (2000). "The Rush to Feather the Gen Nest," *New York Times*, February 24.

Miller, Daniel (1997). "Could Shopping Ever Really Matter?" In Pasi Falk and Colin Campbell, eds., *The Shopping Experience*, London: Sage.

O'Neill, Molly (1999). "But What Would Martha Say?" *New York Times Magazine*, May 16.

Straus, Gary (1999). "Living Well," *USA Today*, October 20.

Thornton, Peter (1984). *Authentic Decor 1620–1920*. New York: Viking.

9

Style and the Perfection of Things
Celia Lury

One walks in and out of shoe shops, jewelry stores, and art galleries, and the shoes, the jewelry, and the art don't seem any different from one another as objects. This is No-brow – the space between the familiar categories of high and low culture. (Seabrook, 1999: 104)

Choice – the most bewildering thing to the consumer – is rendered magically simple. Everything looks (and is) acceptable, and almost everything goes with everything else. The white shirt goes with the sweater, which works with the khakis, which look fine with the denim shirt, all of which sits nicely on the slip-covered sofa next to the forger-iron coffee table, which looks good beside the metal picture frame and the brushed-metal lamp. (Goldberger, 1997: 59)

The ingenious blend of approximate identities out of which the Cairo Chest is constructed has made it oddly impervious to any individual act of taste. It is as though taste, formerly in the eye of the beholder, had been built directly into the table itself. (Seabrook, 1999: 110)

Introduction

In these comments, dismay is expressed at a decline – or perhaps more accurately, a displacement or disorganization – in taste. In what follows I want to suggest that the processes that provoke this reaction are at least as much a matter of style as they are of taste. The suggestion is that, as Daniel Miller puts it,

style has achieved a certain autonomy in contemporary industrial society, going beyond its capacity for ordering to become itself the focus of concern. . . . In this new world, all architecture, furnishing, clothing and behaviour are intended to relate to each other in a visibly coherent fashion. This works to break down all frames into a universal order of good design. (Miller, 1991: 129)

The development of this stylistic autonomy is closely connected to the role of objects in the mediation of the economy. On the one hand, production is increasingly design intensive; and design has a new visibility, both in terms of the self-presentation of consumer goods companies such as Nike, Philips, Ford, Sony, and Apple and in the emergence of name designers such as Phillipe Starck, Jasper Morrison, and Marc Newson. On the other hand, consumers are adopting an increasingly reflexive relation to objects (Lash and Urry, 1994). This reflexivity is in part linked to the understandings of products provided by the growing numbers of lifestyle experts, but is also a consequence of the less fixed and more flexible relations between objects and spaces that characterize some aspects of contemporary life (Margolin, 1995). However, the significance of contemporary design for contemporary culture is hard to evaluate. While the implications of shifts in the world of objects may be – and indeed frequently have been – understood in terms of the rise of particular classes and the judgments of taste (Bourdieu, 1984; Featherstone, 1991; Lash and Urry, 1994), the comments above suggest that the vocabulary of distinction with which such developments are commonly discussed is, momentarily at least, inadequate.

In considering what might be involved in the disorganization of taste the work of Georg Simmel (1990) is of obvious relevance, for it considers the uneven interrelationship between objective and subjective culture. Indeed, Simmel seems to have anticipated the phenomenon that is the cause of concern in the comments above:

The more objective and impersonal an object is, the better it is suited to more people. Such consumable material, in order to be acceptable and enjoyable to a very large number of individuals, cannot be designed for subjective differentiation of taste, while on the other hand only the most extreme differentiation of production is able to produce the objects cheaply and abundantly enough in order to satisfy the demand for them. (Simmel, 1990: 455)

For Simmel, while any society is characterized by both an objective and a subjective culture, these cultures are not necessarily either symmetrical or analogous. Indeed, Simmel argues that in modern societies objective culture has become in some sense autonomous from subjective culture. He writes:

> Obviously there can be no subjective culture without objective culture, because the development or condition of a subject is culture only through its incorporation of the cultivated objects which it encounters. In contrast, objective culture can be partially independent from subjective culture, insofar as "cultivated" – that is, cultivating – objects have been created whose availability for cultural purposes is not fully realized by subjects. . . . Particularly in periods of social complexity and an extensive division of labour, the accomplishments of culture come to constitute an autonomous realm, so to speak. Things become more perfected, more intellectual, and to some degree more controlled by an internal, objective logic tied to their instrumentality; but the supreme cultivation, that of subjects, does not increase proportionately. (Simmel, 1971: 234)

For Simmel, the gap between objective and subjective culture is always mediated, more or less successfully, by the practices of consumption. During the eighteenth century, he argues, objective culture was developed in relation to the ideal of the *individual*, by which he means an internal, personal value. By the nineteenth century, however, it is organized in terms of the concept of *education* in the sense of a body of objective knowledge and behavioral patterns. Importantly, although the individual may still define him or herself in terms of learning, and the acquisition of an educated sensibility, he or she is at a distance from this body of knowledge. What I want to suggest is that the situation described above is one in which the recognition of the partial independence of objective culture is, temporarily at least, forcing itself upon us as a style of life; that education, taste, and reflexivity are no longer the means by which objective culture is organized; that they are displaced by information, operationality, and technique. Or, to put this more strongly, there is no longer a means by which objective culture is organized; rather it is a medium. Subjects are no longer at a distance from objective culture, but are instead within it, immersed in the flow of objects in a discontinuous time and space.

Simmel identifies a number of tendencies to explain how a partially independent objective culture might arise in modern industrial societies. The first of these is that the *sheer number of objects increases* to such an extent that any individual is incapable of comprehending the system of objects as an ensemble or totality. Second, with the *intensification of the division of labor*, exchange relations become increasingly complicated and mediated with the result that the economy necessarily establishes more and more relationships and obligations that are not directly reciprocal. The producer and the consumer lose sight of each other, with the consequence that no individual (neither producer nor consumer) is able to comprehend the status of knowledge embodied by and as objects. As Simmel puts it,

> Just as our everyday life is surrounded more and more by objects of which we cannot conceive how much intellectual effort is expended in their production, so our mental and social communication is filled with symbolic terms, in which a comprehensive intellectuality is accumulated, but of which the individual mind need make only minimal use. (Simmel, 1990: 449)

The third tendency identified by Simmel is that the *specialization of objects themselves* contributes to the process of their alienation from human subjects. This appears as an independence of the object, as the individual's inability to assimilate it and subject the object to his or her own rhythm. Simmel offers the example of furniture here, a case which he uses to demonstrate a growing estrangement between the subject and the products that ultimately invade even the more intimate aspects of daily life. He writes:

> During the first decades of the nineteenth century, furniture and the objects that surrounded us for use and pleasure were of relative simplicity and durability and were in accord with the needs of the lower as well as of the upper strata. This resulted in attachment as they grew up to the objects of their surroundings. . . . The differentiation of objects has broken down this situation. (Ibid: 459–60)

The number of very specifically formed objects makes a close and, as it were, personal relationship to each of them more difficult.

Here Simmel points not only to the rapidity of the consecutive differentiation of objects (a differentiation which he analyses in terms of fashion), but also to their concurrent differentiation. As a consequence of the latter, the suggests, objects increasingly present themselves in terms of an interconnected enclosed world that has fewer and fewer points at which the subjective individual can interpose his or her will and feelings. Together, he suggests, these tendencies help explain the stylization of life. In what follows, I want to develop these rather general points, focusing on the paradox that while objects may be said to be more and more design intensive, they are less and less a matter of taste. In order to do this, I will first consider some general accounts of the object, before moving on to some more particular stories about how objective presentation might be changing. Such changes do not concern all objects, neither is the transformation described here complete; nevertheless, the shift in objective presentation has implications not only for objects but also for subjects.

The Presentation of Objects

In his influential book *Material Culture and Mass Consumption*, Daniel Miller (1991) addresses what he calls the most obvious implication of the object: its materiality or physical nature. As a physical thing, he argues, an object may always signify its own material possibilities and constraints and thereby the more general world of physical practices. This is not, he says, to see physicality or matter as some ultimate constraint or final determining factor, but rather as the manner in which objects continually assert their presence, the manner in which they present themselves to us. And this notion of presentation is important to Miller; indeed, he distinguishes presentation from both discourse and representation. Language, he says, is a discursive process from which a series of independent component parts derives meaning through sequential articulation. A presentational form, such as an object, however, has no natural divisions; in assimilating a presentational form we have to take it all in at once, rather than in an ordered sequence, over time.

Similarly, Grant McCracken (1990) argues that the expressive properties of material culture are better understood as a puzzle than as language or discourse. Reporting on the findings of an empirical study of clothing, he concludes that material culture has no genuine syntagmatic aspect; that is, there is an absence of any principle of combination and thus of the generative freedom this principle affords. Instead, he argues the communication of material culture is to be understood in relation to the transmission and creation of cultural categories and principles. McCracken further suggests that material culture is inconspicuous, while Miller argues for the humility of the object. Miller suggests that since it tends towards presentational form, the object has a particularly close relation to emotions, feelings, and basic orientations to the world. Rather than being perceived, the object is assimilated in a process of apperception. As such, the object is the basis of discriminations that tend to remain outside of consciousness and language.

However, while Miller implies that material characteristics are definitive of the object as such, he does not directly consider differences over time in the manner in which objective presentation may occur. But objective presentation should not be perceived as an historical given; indeed, a number of writers have recently argued that we are witnessing a crisis of objects. The design theorist Ezio Manzini (1989) provides one such account. He argues that objects are now capable of offering more than a single "sincere" image of themselves. This identity crisis is in part a consequence of the development of new materials which has eliminated the possibility of intrinsically endowing any material with identity.[1] There are now combinations of materials and processes that completely lack references with which to connect:

> In a period in which techno-science manipulates the extremely small and manages the enormously complex, matter no longer appears to the scale of our perception as a series of given materials, but rather as a continuum of possibilities. . . . In this new world, we seem to perceive only surfaces, only local and momentary relationships. (Manzini, 1989: 31)

Manzini believes that the emergence of new materials shows that the references by which people made sense of matter were always the result of convention, of the accumulation of experience, the memory of a material's predictable performances in set conditions. As a consequence of these developments in "the matter of invention," he concludes, objects now share a kind of universal transitivity of form. For Manzini, this contributes to the increasing importance of the production of an image as one of a material's possible performances.

Jean Baudrillard, too, has argued that the "objective status of objects itself is threatened" in contemporary society. In *The System of Objects* (1996) the threat derives from the rise of a cybernetic imaginary mode "whose central myth will no longer be that of absolute organicism, nor that of an absolute functionalism, but instead that of an absolute interrelatedness of the world" (Baudrillard, 1996: 118). Within this cybernetic mode of information, objects lose the substantiality and individual presence that was previously the source of their objective status; furnishing transmutes into interior decor. It is now space, and in particular the ability to communicate across the space of a distributed system, which has become the function of objective relationships. Consequently, the value of objects resides no longer in their individual presence or substance, but in "information, in inventiveness, in control, in a continual openness to objective messages" (ibid: 118).

For Baudrillard, the changing status of the modern object (and he suggests, the modern subject) is dominated by the producer's manipulation of the model/series distinction. By this he means that a key dynamic of innovation in production involves the emergence of a model, or exemplary product, which is subsequently developed and produced as a series of products. According to the terms of this distinction in the contemporary economy, the series "hews ever more narrowly to the model, while the model is continually being diffused into the series" (ibid: 139). While the distinction is dynamic, it is also stable:

> There is no prospect of a model entering a series without being simultaneously replaced by another model. The whole system proceeds en bloc, but models replace one another without ever being transcended as such and without successive series, for their part, ever achieving self-transcendence as series. (Ibid: 154)

Historically, the basis of the introduction of a model was sometimes related to technical innovation within the production process, but was also often an ad hoc process of trial and error. Now, as Baudrillard remarks,

> A single function of an object may in turn become specific in a variety of forms – which brings us into that realm of "personalization," of

formal connotation, where the inessential holds sway. Indeed, the characteristic of the industrial object which distinguishes it from the craft
object is that in the former the inessential is no longer left to the whims
of individual demand and manufacture, but instead picked up and sys-
tematized by the production process, which today defines its aims by
reference to what is inessential (and by reference to the universal com-
binatorial system of fashion). (Ibid: 9)

The contemporary culmination of this is that, whereas the model conventionally refers to a transcendence *internal* to a series of objects, it
may now be deployed in terms of a transcendence *across* series. Thus
the classification of objects is now highly dynamic, continuously in
movement, and the distinction between object classes itself is not stable.
In many cases the very distinction between consecutive and concurrent differentiation seems to break down. So, for example, it is argued
that the contemporary system of objects is more like a system of flow
than a system of categories (Wood, 2000). This is a development closely
(but not exclusively) associated with the rise of the brand: for example,

> WiLL is a shopping concept created by five of Japan's premier compa-
> nies – Aashi, Kao Corp, Toyota and Matsushita, along with the splen-
> didly named Kinki Nippon Tourist Co. Together, the five have produced
> WiLL, a spanking new brand – identified by its trademark orange – that
> crosses all boundaries of consumer culture. You can buy WiLL-branded
> beer, bikes, deodorants, computers and cars . . . all neatly packaged with
> cute designer curves. Targeting young, active consumers, there are even
> overseas tours to complete the WiLL lifestyle. (*Wallpaper*, 2000: 53)

Previously existing object categories are redefined, as the performance
of an image comes to be the basis of objective classification.

A final perspective provides further insight into changes in the
organization of space in which objects may now present themselves.
This is the perspective outlined by Norman Klein in a discussion of
the history of animation (Klein, 1993). Klein points to the ways in
which, in animation, an abstract surface of metamorphic possibility
continually intrudes into the object or figure. He describes this in terms
of "a war of surface and object," a conflict surrounding how an object's
properties or qualities emerge and are made recognizable in its surface
appearance. Rather than functioning as a limit, he argues, forgoing
the dimension of depth has opened up the possibility of occupying
an abstract surface as the very condition of the object in animation.

Moreover, the war between surface and object is now increasingly able to draw on the imaginative possibilities afforded by the (computer) screen. Here the abstract surface that intrudes into the object is not understood in contradistinction to perspective, depth, and inwardness, but rather in relation to an abstract space of extension, of unlimited finitude. The exploration of this new surface space thus further contributes to the making of the contemporary object a matter of play, of calculation and control, not only in animation or computer games but also in everyday thinking with things.

To sum up: interconnecting with shifts in the economy that foreground design, rapid prototyping, and short production runs are a series of changes in the very materials of design resulting in an almost unlimited potential transmutability of form. At the same time, the rise of animation, alongside the widespread use of personal computers, means that the space of the object is being reconceived: we have moved from the depth of a vertical field to the extension of a horizontal one. In this space the object is constituted not so much in relation to inwardness, substance, and durability, that is, as a fixed, discrete, and stable entity, but rather in relation to externality, connection, and inventiveness, as open, receptive, and incomplete. In other words, there is a shift in the manner in which objects present themselves, and in this shift the stylistic autonomy of objects becomes newly visible. Objects are no longer understood in terms of the quality of the body of a product, but rather as a system of relations, a set of performances. Formal properties such as flexibility, heaviness, and heat- and stress-resistance are less and less determining. Instead, a complex, somehow informational logic comes to structure the designed object such that its properties are understood by both producers and consumers in relation to communication, or, more specifically, as media. As the philosopher Vilem Flusser suggests, there is a shift in the nature of objects: objects are no longer just objective, but also inter-objective, not just monologic but dialogic as well. As he puts it, "Objects of use are . . . mediations (media) between myself and other people, not just objects" (Flusser, 1999: 59).

Transparency and the Mediation of Objects

An understanding of objects in terms of communication is not, of course, new. However, such communication is often seen to be relatively crude, especially when compared with that afforded by language. McCracken, for example, argues that, "unlike the [advertising] director, the designer does not have the highly managed, rhetorical circumstances of the advertisement to encourage and direct" the transfer of meaning from world to good (McCracken, 1990: 82). As a result, systems of material culture such as clothing have to "specify in advance of any act of communication the messages of which the code is capable. . . . These messages, come as it were, prefabricated" (ibid: 67). There is a certain truth to this claim, if you think of T-shirts that sport slogans: "Soap star," "In your dreams," "resolution #15 TREAT FAMILY LIKE FRIENDS," "What are you looking at?" or spaghetti forks which display a smiley face, ice-cream scoops that have eyes, the "Tim" dish-brush which stands on its own legs, or even high-tech training gear, such as the Nike "Personal Sport Audio" (a portable player) that transmit prerecorded messages or information. And, of course, merchandised goods, in which there is a licensed use of figures, icons, and slogans in the design of objects, also contribute to a limited form of communication by objects, often being little more than an "application" of a preexisting message. But the communication of the object becomes more sophisticated when the message does not simply precede the object, but is rather produced, enacted, or performed in the use of the object; that is, when objects are able to present themselves as media. But what has made this possible, or rather, more possible?

I want to suggest that this mode of presentation has recently been enhanced by the ways in which the use of objects may now draw upon a transformed understanding of transparency. The shift in the meaning of this term is identified and outlined by Sherry Turkle in her study of the use of computers (Turkle, 1995; see also Schlossberg, 1998). For Turkle, it is a transformation associated with the use of Macintosh's iconic computer interface, but it is also "part of a larger cultural shift" (Turkle, 1995: 42). In describing the relationship between person and machine that occurs by means of the interface, Turkle suggests that users have to learn to communicate by manipulating "a system whose core assumptions they don't see and which may or may not be 'true,' but which can be navigated by means of experimentation." They have "learned to learn through direct action and its consequences" (ibid: 35). For Turkle, when people say that something is transparent, they mean that they can easily see *how* to make it work. They don't necessarily mean that they know *why* it is working in terms of any underlying process. (ibid: 42; my emphasis)

The suggestion, then, is that rather than presenting itself in terms of cause-and-effect or "why?" thinking, the object today is able to present itself in terms of "how?" thinking. That is, the object increasingly does not show "why" it has the uses it has, but "how" it is to be used. It does not present itself as a means to an end, but instead presents itself as a medium, a medium for effects that will be discovered in use.

To explore the notion of transparency further, let us take the case of the Nike brand. This brand enables a transparent relation to products in both the senses that Turkle identifies. It is transparent in the sense that it enables one to see "why" Nike shoes and apparel are fit for particular sports activities. Promotional and advertising materials explain the technology and scientific rationale for the shape, size, materials, and styling of specific items; they explain *why* you should use Nike products. "F.I.T.," for example, is "Functional. Innovative. Technology", it is the acronym that describes a range of materials which direct air, water, and heat in ways that are supposedly appropriate for different activities. "DRI F.I.T.," for example, is a "base layer" material:

> High performance microfiber polyester that manages moisture and dries quickly. Acts as a wicking layer next to the skin in cold or warm weather to keep you cool and provide warmth when needed. This soft, cotton-like jersey fabric is ideal as a technical replacement for 100% cotton polos.

At the same time, other components of the Nike logo are transparent in the sense that they show you not "why" but "how" the branded products work. For example, the Swoosh is iconic, comparable to the icons of the interface communication of the Macintosh screen; it mediates the product. It is a medium that shows how to move and how to see movement.

Consider, for example, the beach on which I saw two boys playing in the waves, both wearing Nike shorts, the letters, NI and KE on each leg of their matching shorts. One was bigger, one was smaller: the shorts were what united them; the boys were larger and smaller versions of each other. Their shorts gave a flickering message as they ran in and out of the water. This was a visual message, but it also had a rhythmic accompaniment: a bit like a football chant, a crowd chant. NI-KE, NI-KE. What the branded object communicates here is not an exclusively visual message; instead it draws on the tactual mode of perceiving described by McLuhan in relation to television:

> It is not a photo in any sense, but a ceaselessly forming contour of things limned by the scanning-finger. The resulting plastic contour appears by light *through*, not light *on*, and the image formed has the quality of sculpture and icon, rather than of picture. (McLuhan, 1997: 313)

In this and other occasions and events, the branded object communicates a dynamic, affective experience of immersion in the multiply-mediated spaces that transparently overlap and refigure the places of everyday life.

And while the Nike brand makes use of both notions of transparency, it is the second sense that seems to predominate in the presentation of products. Nike publicity sustains the view that Nike shoes and clothing are designed with the athlete or sportsperson in mind ("To all athletes and the dreams they chase, we dedicate Niketown"; "Nike is a shoe company. Excuse me, an *athletic shoe company*"; "This is not a shoe for shopping. This is not a shoe for gardening. This is an athletic shoe with maximum-volume Nike-Air® cushioning."), but 60–80 percent of purchases are recognized to be for leisure or everyday use. In these uses, the "why" of the product is unnecessary and unimportant. In any case, the technical description of different F.I.T. fabrics is supplemented by the use of iconic diagrams. Most poignantly, the use of special (inert gas-based) materials in the sole of their shoes which is supposed to give them properties of cushioning and traction did not contribute to their success until it was made visible as "air" through a window or bubble in the sole of the shoe. In response to a recent downturn in sales, Nike are introducing the Shox system that will work on the same principle as a simple spring. This range has a "spring" visibly displayed in a bubble in its heel: the Nike head of design calls it "the shoe as caricature" (quoted in Hill, 2000: 9).

The general point here is that the shift in understandings of transparency is such as to lead to the presentation of objects in terms of the performance of effects that are accomplished in use and may be elaborated in terms of "how" thinking. Consider, for example, the following description of the transparent or "clear" style of Benetton clothing:

> If we really want to define the Benetton style we can say that it is a "non-style"; a positive identification or, better, a "clear" style. It doesn't hide you. It shows you off. (Mattei, n.d.: 4)

This emphasis on "how?" encourages play, experimentation, or "tinkering" with objects. It encourages the relations of externality, connection, and inventiveness described above. In many cases, of course, the communication of objects is restricted to the capacity that Heath describes as receptivity and Baudrillard describes as "responsibility," in which one object merely "responds to," "goes with," "looks fine with," or "sits nicely by" another. At its minimum, then, the acquisition and use of objects by individuals become no more complex than "tuning in" to a style, becoming receptive to a series of signals, a more or less straightforward process of selection from a set of options organized not only in terms of a choice of colors, shapes, sizes, or features and limited only by restrictions as to compatibility between products, across both space and time.

But in other cases the responsibility of objects is extended such that they are not only responsive but also responsible. Indeed, the stylized autonomy of the object may be such that it organizes the interrelationship between objects and/or between the subject and what he or she wants to do selectively and sequentially. Think, for example, not only of the computer screen, of sequences of movement on the World Wide Web, of selection and sequence on programmable video recorders and mobile telephones, but also of the use of other "smart" or "proprioceptive" products. In this world of "smart" things, what an object does is increasingly something that is discovered in use, rather than in the context of habitual patterns of behavior or by following instructions. At a time of increasing mobility, there is an increasingly variable relation to context, with the result that the established temporal horizons and habitual spaces of object use are displaced, and are continually renegotiated in use. ("Swatch is a colorful timepiece that is as versatile as everyday life, perfectly suited to any mood, outfit, or occasion.") This under-determination of context contributes to the emergence of product interactivity. In interactivity, the product is, in some sense, "closer" to the consumer as the object makes visible different facets of user participation; it underlies the contemporary description of many objects not simply in terms of user-friendliness but use-ability. Most frequently, however, the new object is respons*ible* insofar as it presents itself in terms of the articulation or performance of an image. No longer simply the container of meaning, the object comes to be able to articulate its own content. The respons*ible* articulates an image in terms of the stylization of "how?" thinking, through the manipulation of the elements of line, shape, color, feel, and sound.

The transformation in the meaning of transparency itself builds on the notion of receptivity that was afforded the (surface of the) object by the television screen. As Stephen Heath remarks in relation to the latter:

> The hierarchy of message and medium on which notions of communication habitually depend here shifts: what is transmitted is important, but it is the realization and maintenance of the function of reception that is *all*-important, everything else then to be seen as simply something like the minimum required to allow that realization and maintenance, to guarantee the fulfillment of the function. (Heath, 1990: 270)

In this respect the mediation of things described here is intimately related to what might be called the "thingification" of the media. It is a relation that is further elaborated in the multiply-mediated presentation of the object in packaging, as an advertisement, on the computer screen, or within a three-dimensional retail environment. The latter in particular – both niche and mass market – now offer a highly elaborate set of scenarios in which objects present themselves as media. During the last ten or so years, for example, a number of lifestyle boutiques and stores have been established, including DKNY in New York, Corso Como in Milan, and Colette in Paris. Such stores are an alternative to department stores: products are no longer categorized in terms of type, but style, and specifically in terms of their responsiveness to each other: "Department stores are such a headache, going up and down those escalators" (quoted in Freeman, 2000: 9).[2] In these cases, objects afford an experience that Turkle describes as immersion. This experience – of what Baudrillard calls, not aura, but "atmosphere" – is most intense in dedicated retail environments (what are sometimes described as "complete lifestyle environments"). In addition, however, a number of consumer service spaces – hotels, restaurants, and bars – offer the experience of designed, objective space. Guests at St Martin's Hotel in London, for example, may alter the color scheme of their room by adjusting a switch next to their bed, while diners at restaurant 44 in New York City visit the toilets to view the work of Phillipe Starck. More widely, the effectiveness of this notion of transparency is supported by the development of what Klein calls consumer cubism:

> The door of a refrigerator (or any appliance) became the ultimate grid for consumer gratification, opening like a little diorama into the new highway or the new airport. By cartoon logic, the consumer object arrived (or was packaged) to the happy consumer at right angles. (Klein, 1993: 210)

Klein argues that cartoon memory entered into real space, in the grid of the new suburbs and shopping centers in 1950s USA, and has recently been extended in themed environments across the globe. This spatial organization produces "pleasure designed off a short, grid-like menu." This is a system "based on coordinated pauses" (ibid: 211) in consumer space, what Klein calls the architectonic spaces of cartoon nostalgia.

Taste, Style, and Virtuosity

But how are we to understand the implications of the mediation of objects for contemporary culture? Turkle suggests that the shift in the meaning of transparency described above has gone some way to overcoming the low regard in which "playful," "experimental," or "concrete" ways of thinking have conventionally been held. She points out that while this way of thinking with objects has long been acknowledged in Euro-American culture, it has been marginalized by its designation as merely a stage in the development of thinking. As such, it has been delegated to children and so-called primitive peoples and should supposedly be superseded by abstract thought as "propositional logic liberates intelligence from the need to think with things" (Turkle, 1995: 55). So, for example, she argues that the psychologist Jean Piaget's discoveries about the processes of children's thinking – a developmental stage that we are all supposed to leave behind – point to a cultural amnesia as profound as that identified by Freud:

> While Freud discovered the forgetting of infantile sexuality, Piaget identified a second amnesia: the forgetting of concrete styles of thinking. In both, our stake in forgetting is highly charged. In our culture, the divide between abstract and concrete is not simply a boundary between propositions and objects but a way of separating the clean from the messy, virtue from taboo. (Ibid: 55)

Rather than a *stage*, however, Turkle argues, concrete thinking must now be seen as a *style*, by which she means an aestheticized mode of conjecture.

Certainly it is possible to argue that a particular social group – young professionals, perhaps especially those associated with the new information and media sector – have adopted concrete thinking as a style of their own. And they have done so by elaborating a playful relation to objects in which the graphic elements of the object – color, size, line, and shape – are animated. This playful relation to objects is facilitated by this group's familiarity with animation, the new hybrid media, and the acquisition of the virtuoso skills of game-play. Indeed, as Dan Fleming argues in his fascinating account of toys as popular culture, the subject position of *player* must now be placed alongside that of *spectator* in any analysis of contemporary culture. He writes:

> It is the former that now keeps the latter alive, since to be a spectator without the resources of a player is now to have little purchase on the fragmentary accumulations of a culture which has itself become unremittingly playful and piecemeal. (Fleming, 1996: 171)

Similarly, on the basis of his analysis of new media, Andrew Darley argues that, "no longer merely a viewer, the player also becomes a doer" (Darley, 2000: 158). In this respect, then, this looser understanding of style might well be said to coincide with a new formation of taste (if only in the sense that this group lays claim to the ownership of this stage in the stylization of life).

However, while this may be so, this formation of taste is continually being undercut – or overridden – by the contemporary dynamic of style, in which the signals of objects are continually on the verge of degenerating into noise. There are a number of points to be made here, which both draw on and extend the arguments made by Simmel to explain the stylization of life – the overwhelming number of objects, the complexity of the division of labor, and the specialization of objects. Perhaps most important, however, is the way in which the contemporary communication of objects is as much with other objects as it is with subjects; that is, what is at issue here are, increasingly, a set of relations between objects, rather than between objects and subjects. Think, for example, of the incredibly rapid regularity with which objects are updated, and the many other ways in which objects have complex technical and stylistic dependencies on other objects. This is a point which is powerfully made by Karen Knorr-Cetina (2000) as she shows how many objects – scientific and technical objects as well as consumer goods – are now (designed to be) unfinished, simultaneously things-to-be-used and things-to-be-transformed. It is further elaborated by Andrew Barry (2001) in his discussion of the importance of standards and conventions in the ordering and reordering of technological connections and borders; establishing what can be used where, by whom, and in what situations.

The examples of computer hardware and software and technological goods more generally are obvious examples in relation to the argument being developed here, but consider also the example of the rise of the accessory. This is now to be understood not simply as a limited class of goods (of hats, gloves, and bags), but in relation to a movement in which more and more goods can be defined as accessories. In the chain of shops called Accessorize, for example, goods are designed to demonstrate the verb, "to accessorize." An article in *Time* on the rise of design claims that "Shopping for household items is no longer dutiful; it's part of a person's articulation of his or her personal style. Everything is an accessory" (Gibney and Luscombe, 2000: 54). An unrelated feature in the same issue has the heading, "Wheelie good fun. Shiny, compact and cool, scooters have become Europe's ubiquitous accessory" (Labi, 2000). An advertisement for a dinnerware company asserts "Accessories? A great way to forget your salad came in a bag. We know your life is often one big time crunch. So we do what we can to make things easier. Like offer you more matching accessories, in more patterns, than any other dinnerware company." In these and other cases, style produces a world of its own, but one which is highly conditional, linked to the setting and maintenance of conventions and standards. Such conditions transform the under-determination of use described above. In interactivity, objects may have an increasingly flex- ible relation to context, but, simultaneously, they are more able to produce – and indeed require – their own context, and that is other objects.

Importantly, interactive–objective communication occurs across an extended field within an ensemble of objects that is distributed not only in multiply-mediated space but also in discontinuous time. For example, Adidas recently reissued a 1984 shoe in very limited numbers (600 pairs in the UK), while at the time of writing Nike was promis- ing, but not yet delivering, a shoe designed in collaboration with Junya Watanbe of Comme des Garcons. It had only been sighted "in Japan and on the web (www.mars.dti.ne.jp/~motonike/index.html#new)" (Hill, 2000: 9). Similarly, a column in a British newspaper gives details of products under the headings: "Most popular," "Most wanted," "Most everywhere." In relation to this dynamic field, individuals may seek to establish their own position through their ability to intervene in a shift- ing map–territory relation in a way that is purposive, but cannot be intentional (or may only retrospectively be so). As a consequence, while the appropriation of this stage in the stylization of life may perhaps be understood in terms of an *aesthetics of ephemerality* (Appadurai, 1998: 83–5), it might better be understood in terms of the ability to make use of the *degree of play* afforded by a distributed ensemble of objects. The style of a system of objects is both unitary and dynamic: it is a field of possible or legitimate transformations (Gell, 1998). Within the contemporary system described here, it is the ability to identify the potential of "protentive" or "retentive" transformations – anticipating the appearance of cult objects, dropping apparent successes before they become widely popular, tracking down lost "classics" – that is valued in this new stage in the stylization of life. And while this identification may be done in a variety of ways – individuals can be stabilizers, con- densors, satirists, interpreters, samplers (Johnson, 1997) – such stylists are not exercising their taste. Instead they are feeding off information, navigating the bewildering sensory overload of the contemporary object world. They are operators, demonstrators, switching points of connection, translation, and manipulation.

From this point of view, the communication of objects outlined above makes possible a latitude in strategy or game-play, but it does not allow the kind of subjective investment that the notion of taste implies. As Simmel foretold,

> Through the differentiation of styles each individual style, and thus style in general, becomes something objective whose validity is independent of human subjects and their interests, activities, approval or disapproval. (Simmel, 1990: 463)

Operators act not so much in relation to modes of experience based on symbolic concerns and interpretive models, but rather in terms of modes linked to information and models of reaction. And while technique may facilitate an individual relation to style it also exerts a kind of compulsion, exerted through objects, towards integration into a repertoire with no syntax, that is, into a constantly changing system of categories that is distinctly not a language. What matters in this system are switches in modalities of attention, shifts in levels of boredom and engrossment and intensities of sensual stimulation, and movements in a transformed and transforming environment. Move and click. Such relations result in loyalties that are both highly charged and apparently inconsistent; they exist in relation to a scattered time and space:

> Fanship, brandship, and relationships are all a part of what the statement "I like this" really means. Your judgment joins a pool of other judgments, a small relationship economy, becoming one of millions that continually coalesce and dissolve and reform around culture products – movies, sneakers, jeans, pop songs. Your identity is your investment in these relationship economies. . . . The reward is attention and self-expression (your identity is in some way enhanced by the culture product you invest in); the risk is that your identity will be overmediated by your investment and you will become like everyone else.
>
> These cultural equities rise and fall in the stock market of popular opinion, and therefore one has to manage one's portfolio with care. No value endures. (Seabrook, 1999: 109)

In sum, the suggestion is that at the beginning of the twenty-first century it is no longer education, reflexivity, and taste that mediate our relations with objective culture, but rather *information*, operationality, and technique. More concisely, we are increasingly in a transitive relation to objects. Just Do It. And in this transitive relation it is not simply the distinctions between form and matter, means and end that dissolve, it is also the very opposition between subject and object.

Conclusion

Such a relation to objects may easily be criticized as being without either aesthetic or moral value (Borgmann, 1995). Certainly in contradistinction to the formation of taste in which objects (and subjects) are valued in terms of inwardness, substance, and duration, this relation to objects may appear to fail to give them respect, integrity, or aesthetic value. But such judgments in some sense miss the point. They fail to recognize that in this stylization of life, objects have intense – if often temporary – holding power; they do not acknowledge either the concrete, sensory possibilities or the distinctive limitations of an objective culture that is increasingly constituted as a medium. What needs to be recognized, so it has been argued here, are the ways in which, in the contemporary stylization of life, we are drawn into, and not at a distance from, objective culture.

Turkle provides an optimistic analysis of the possibilities of our use of the transitive relation, but other considerations would indicate that the terms of immersion are limited. So, for example, the ends of objective interactivity are often pre-given. That is, while interaction may be described as mutual and simultaneous activity in which the participants are usually, but not necessarily, working toward some goal, in much interactivity the goal is typically a foregone conclusion, one of a limited number of options. Similarly, while on the one hand, it may be that the object is brought closer to the subject insofar as it is presented in terms of use-ability, on the other, the dimensions of style and the conditions of objective classification are simultaneously being disembedded from the everyday life of the individual. More generally, while the object is the message, it is a message that is profoundly shaped by the characteristics of mediation as they are informed by the complex requirements of the economy:

> The artifact is something other than a controlled transformation of the
> object for the purposes of knowledge: it is a savage intervention in
> reality, at the end of which it is impossible to distinguish what in this

reality arises out of objective knowledge and what results from the technical intervention (the medium). (Tort, quoted in Baudrillard, 1993: 64)

This is especially clear in relation to the development of brands, themselves a consequence of the more consumer-driven[3] basis of contemporary product innovation, in which innovation is understood in relation to the consumer as interpreted by the discipline of marketing and its use of socioeconomic, cultural, and psychographic data.

So, for example, in seeking to develop their *Vision of the Future* (1996), the electronic goods company Philips made use of practices of modeling or simulating everyday life. Multidisciplinary teams were brought together to develop "scenarios," that is, "short stories describing a product concept and its use." Such scenarios were then evaluated in relation to four "domains" that supposedly "represent all aspects of everyday life": the "personal," the "domestic," the "public," and the "mobile." New products were then proposed for production in the form of "tangible models, simulations of interfaces and short films." This is a very common process of research and development for major corporations. Another example is the process of product development described by Gary Friedman, the chief merchandising officer for Williams-Sonoma (which owns the US retail chains Hold Everything and Pottery Barn):

> "We travel the world, looking for inspiration," Friedman says. "Then we edit it down to what we think is most appropriate for our customer. But it's what we like – we are all the customer."
>
> "We sit around a table and talk about what we see, what's happening in design, what any of us have seen that's excited us," he says. "Then we try to boil that down to a target. Someone will say a modern thing is happening. Someone else will interrupt to say, "But everyone still cares about being soft and comfortable." And we will distill all of that into a general product development." (Goldberger, 1997: 56)

Eventually this "general product direction" becomes a set of products, organized in compatible combinations that are photographed for the catalogue and displayed in the stores in carefully planned arrangements intended to enable stylized interobjective communication.

Such examples suggest that concrete thinking is being channeled in forms of regulated, conventionalized play. Another way to put this might be to say that in contemporary culture, the principles of play are subject to processes of instrumentalization. The individual and collective memory and imagination necessary to sustain its more subversive, anarchic aspects are being displaced by the brand and replaced with routinized, standardized expectations, with the mobilization of culture as a construct or as a technology. This is not so much a technology that organizes "why" things work, but a technology that organizes "how" they work. Take the example of Levi's engineered or twisted jeans. Their design is a brilliant example of concrete thinking, of imagineering, in Disney's classic phrase. But it is also an example of the ability of the brand to anticipate and imitate the required responses of the consumer, to foreclose the uses of products.

In relation to the brand then, the individual is doubly immersed in objective culture; that is, the role of the brand in objective culture is non-subjective in a double sense (Rabinow, 1992). First, the brand coordinates the interobjective communication of things through the application of information, that is knowledge that is objectively arrived at through techniques of data manipulation. Second, it does not apply to a subject of representation, a deep self whose interior life is developed in terms of learning, taste, and judgment, but to an individual who operates techniques of selection, connection, and transformation. In other words, in the contemporary stylization of life as it is organized by the brand, in which information moves in the opposite direction to products, the mediation of objects is a matter of "directional signals on maps of power and knowledge" (Haraway, 1997).

Notes

1   In his use of the term "new materials" Manzini does not merely refer to a limited number of "artificial" materials, but rather to a set of qualities that are appearing throughout the whole range of materials, both old and new, "natural" and "artificial," and to their relationship to manufacturing.

2   This recognition is not lost on the managers of department stores. The text for an advertisement (from 1998) for the department store Selfridges in London asks: "How do you get from Paul Smith to Helly Hansen in under 2 minutes? Visit our new menswear department. At Selfridges, we've got over 100 brands and a whole range of services to choose from. You'll find restaurants, bars, personal shopping, men's grooming and a car park." Recently publicized development plans for Selfridges include not only more restaurants, but also clubs, a gym, a spa, and a cinema,

as well as a new hotel and more than 100 apartments, serviced by both the store and the hotel.

3 Note that consumer-driven is not the same as user-led.

References

Appadurai, A. (1998). *Modernity at Large*. Minneapolis: University of Minnesota Press.

Barry, A. (2001). *Political Machines: Governing a Technological Society*. London: Athlone Press.

Baudrillard, J. (1993). *Symbolic Exchange and Death*, trans. I. Hamilton Grant. London: Sage.

Baudrillard, J. (1996). *The System of Objects*, trans. J. Benedict. London: Verso.

Borgmann, A. (1995). "The Moral Significance of the Material Culture." In A. Feenberg and A. Hannay, eds., *Technology and the Politics of Knowledge*, Bloomington: Indiana University Press, 85–96.

Bourdieu, P. (1984). *Distinction: A Social Critique of the Judgement of Taste*. London: Routledge and Kegan Paul.

Castells, M. (1996). *The Rise of the Network Society*. Oxford: Blackwell Publishers.

Darley, A. (2000). *Visual Digital Culture: Surface Play and Spectacle in New Media Genres*. London and New York: Routledge.

Featherstone, M. (1991). *Consumer Culture and Postmodernism*. London: Sage.

Fleming, D. (1996). *Powerplay: Toys as Popular Culture*. Manchester: Manchester University Press.

Flusser, V. (1999). *The Shape of Things: A Philosophy of Design*. London: Reaktion Books.

Freeman, H. (2000). "One life. One shop," *Guardian*, June 16, 8–9.

Gell, A. (1998). *Art and Agency: An Anthropological Theory*. Oxford: Clarendon Press.

Gibney Jr., F. and Luscombe, B. (2000). "The Redesigning of America," *Time*, June 26, 48–55.

Goldberger, P. (1997). "The Sameness of Things," *New York Times Magazine*, April 6, 56–60.

Haraway, D. (1997). *Modest Witness @ Second Millennium*. London: Routledge.

Heath, S. (1990). "Representing Television." In P. Mellencamp, ed., *Logics of Television*, Bloomington: University of Indiana Press, 267–302.

Hill, A. (2000). "Sport Culture," the *Guardian*, August 4, 8–9.

Johnson, S. (1997). *Interface Culture: How New Technology Transforms the Way We Create and Communicate*. San Francisco: HarperEdge.

Klein, N. (1993). *7 Minutes: The Life and Death of the American Animated Cartoon*. London: Verso.

Knorr-Cetina, K. (2000). "Post-social theory." In G. Ritzer and B. Smart, eds., *Handbook of Social Theory*. London: Sage.

Labi, A. (2000). "Wheelie Good Fun," *Time*, June 26, 62.

Lash, S. and Urry, J. (1994). *Economies of Signs and Spaces*. London: Sage.

McCracken, G. (1990). *Culture and Consumption: New Approaches to the Symbolic Character of Consumer Goods and Activities*. Bloomington: Indiana University Press.

McLuhan, M. (1997). *Understanding Media: The Extensions of Man.* London and New York: Routledge.

Manzini, E. (1989). *The Material of Invention.* London: Design Council.

Margolin, V. (1995). "Expanding the Boundaries of Design: The Product Environment and the New User." In V. Margolin and R. Buchanan, eds., *The Idea of Design: A Design Issues Reader,* Cambridge, MA: MIT Press, 275–80.

Mattei (n.d.). "A Matter of Style," *News: United Colors of Benetton,* 4–5.

Miller, D. (1991). *Material Culture and Mass Consumption.* Oxford: Blackwell Publishers.

Poster, M. (1990). *The Mode of Information: Poststructuralism and Social Context.* Cambridge: Polity Press.

Rabinow, P. (1992). "Artificiality and Enlightenment: From Sociobiology to Biosociality." In J. Crary and S. Kwinter, eds., *Incorporations,* New York: Zone, MIT Press, 178–90.

Schlossberg, E. (1998). "Interactive Environments." In S. Heller and E. Pettit, eds., *Design Dialogues,* New York: Allworth Press, 239–44.

Seabrook, J. (1999). "In Pursuit of Status," *The New Yorker,* September 20, 104–11.

Seremetakis, C. N. (1994). *The Senses Still: Perception and Memory as Material Culture in Modernity.* Chicago: University of Chicago Press.

Simmel, G. (1971). "Subjective Culture." In D. N. Levine, ed., *Georg Simmel: On Individuality and Social Forms. Selected Writings.* Chicago: University of Chicago Press, 227–34.

Simmel, G. (1990). *The Philosophy of Money,* ed. D. Frisby, trans. T. Bottomore and D. Frisby. London: Routledge.

Turkle, S. (1995). *Life on the Screen: Identity in the Age of the Internet.* New York: Simon and Schuster.

Vision of the Future (1996). Eindhoven: Philips Corporate Design.

Wallpaper (2000). July–August.

Wood, J. (2000). "Towards an Ethics of Flow: Design as an Anticipatory System." Paper presented at Fourth International Conference on Computing Anticipatory Systems, Center for Hyperincursion and Anticipation in Ordered Systems, Liege, Belgium.

Index

Aaker, D. A., 72
Aboud, Joseph, 184
Ackerman, C., 168
Adorno, T., 186
Age of Innocence, The (1993), 157, 165
Alagna, Roberto, 8
Alloway, Lawrence, 6
Almereyda, Michael, 157
Almodovar, Pedro, 170
Amsterdam, 97
Andrew, Dudley, 160–1
Ang, Ien, 24
Anna Karenina (1999), 160
Anthony's Morocco, 85
Appadurai, A., 24–5, 218
Architectural Digest, 183–4
Art Institute of Chicago, 129, 135
Astroff, R., 109
Astruc, A., 166
Audience for the American Art Museum, The, 120–1
Ault, G., 142
Austen, J., 8, 10, 166
Authentic Décor, 191

Babbo, 9
Bakeer, W., 81
Baker, Billy, 196
Baking With Julia, 81
Bamberger, L., 139–40, 144, 149
Barber of Seville, The, 33

Barnes and Noble, 1
Barr, A., 21, 146–7
Barry, A., 217
Battali, M., 9
Baudrillard, J. L., 193, 207–8
Bazin, A., 155
Becky Sharp (1935), 162
Being John Malkovich (1999), 168
Benjamin, W., 195–6
Bennett, T., 15, 80, 90–1
Berenson, B., 28
Berlin Alexanderplatz (1980), 168
Bermingham, A., 22–5, 194
Betsky, A., 185
Bloom, H., 176
Bocelli, A., 8
Bocuse, P., 83
Book-of-the-Month Club, 7–8
Booker, C., 5
Borges, J., 161
Borgman, A., 220
Boulud, D., 185
Bourdieu, P., 19, 37, 76, 114–17, 120–1, 136, 202
Bozza, A., 79
Branagh, K., 26–7, 163, 169–78
Braque, G., 142
Brontë, E., 165
Brooker, K., 85
Brown, J., 75, 85
Browning, D., 17

Calvin Klein, 184
Cahiers du Cinéma, 166
Camerata, 32
Campbell, C., 26–7, 194–5
Campion, J., 157
Captive, The (2000), 168
Carlton Food Network, 77–8, 85–6
Carrier, R., 83
Carson, M., 68
Channing, W. E., 18
Cheere, J., 191
Chez Bruno, 85
Child, J., 75–7, 80–6, 183
Church, C., 8
Clausen, C., 177
Clueless (1995), 157
Coiner, C., 108–9
Collins, J., 1–31, 182–200
Conran, T., 194–6, 198
Cooper, G., 81
Corrigan, T., 26–7, 155–81
Cowley, M., 149
Crate & Barrel, 182–3, 188–90
Crowdus, G., 175
Crying Game, The (1992), 172
Cyr, D., 75

Dallas, 24
Dana, J. C., 21, 133–42, 144–7
Danes, C., 159
Dangerous Liaisons (1988), 167
Darley, A., 216
DeForest, R., 143
Derrida, J., 71
Design Within Reach, 187
Dewey, J., 18
de Wolfe, E., 196
Dickinson, E., 8
Dictionary of Cultural Literacy, The, 94
DiMaggio, P., 4–5, 35–6
Disney, 170–1
Don Giovanni, 33
Don Quixote, 161
Drama Trauma, 159
Drexler, M., 187, 190
Dru, J. M., 70

Duncan, C., 19–20, 129–54
dwell, 27

Elle Décor, 184
Emily Brontë's Wuthering Heights (1992), 26, 165
English Patient, The (1996), 2, 172–3
Erendira (1981), 171
Essential House Book, The, 194
Ethnic Canon, The, 93
Europa, Europa (1991), 170
Evans, D., 43–4

Fantasia, R., 80
Fassbinder, R. W., 168
Featherstone, M., 202
Feeling for Books, A, 7
Fiennes, J., 156
Fine, B., 76
Finkelstein, J., 78
Finley, J., 143
Fleming, D, 216
Fletcher, J., 183
Floyd, K., 83
Floyd on Africa, 83
Flusser, V., 209
Food Network, 77–9, 85
Foucault, M., 75
Frank, J. M., 9–10
Franklin, A., 185
Freeman, H., 215
French Chef, The, 8, 80–1, 183
Friday, 161
Frow, J., 9, 14, 19, 56–72, 91, 185

Gaines, J., 69, 71
Gandelman, C., 58, 63
Gap, The, 186–7
Gehry, F., 9
Gell, A., 218
Getting Opera: A Guide for the Cultured But Confused, 38
Getty Museum, Los Angeles, 13
Gheorghiu, A., 8
Gibney, J. F., 217
Godard, J. L., 163

Godfather, The (1972), 157
Goldberger, P., 186–7, 193, 201, 221
Golden, A., 16, 95–110
Gone With the Wind, 8
Gorris, M., 157
Grassl, W., 65
Graves, M., 1, 10
Greenaway, P., 159, 178
Guterson, D., 16, 92–110
Gwathmey, C., 192

Haigh, D., 65
Hall, Stuart, 51
Hamilton, R., 182
Hamlet (1996), 174
Hamlet (2000), 157, 169
Haraway, D., 222
Harris, L., 171
Hart, S., 67
Hawke, E., 169
Hawke, R., 77
Heath, S., 214
Hebdige, D., 5–6
Heckerling, A., 157
Hemingway, E., 2–3
Henderson, W. J., 34
Henry IV Part I, 165
Henry V (1989), 162, 174–6
Higginson, H. L., 4
Hirsh, E. D., 94
Holland, A., 170
Horkheimer, M., 186
Hornby, N., 14–15
Horowitz, V., 4
House and Garden, 17–18, 184
House Beautiful, 183
Howard's End (1992), 170
Hunt, J., 140

In the Arts and Crafts Style, 189
Iron Chef, The, 86

Jacobson, A., 11
Jauss, H. R., 69–70
Jaws (1975), 157
Jervons, W. S., 132

Johnson, S., 218
Jordan, N., 172
Joy Luck Club, The, 90–1, 93
Juilian, Alexander, 184
Julia Child and Company, 81
Julia Child and More Company, 81
Julia Child and Jacques Pepin: Cooking at Home, 81
Julius Caesar, 162
Just Another Girl on the I.R.T. (1993), 171

Kaiser, M., 45–6
Kammen, M., 29
Kapferer, J. N., 67
Kerr, G., 83
Kimmelman, M., 2
King Lear, 162
King Lear (1987), 163
Klein, N., 208–9
K-Mart, 184–5
Knorr-Cetina, K., 217
Kuhn, W., 142
Kurosawa, A., 163

L. Bamberger and Company, 139
Lagasse, E., 11–12, 84–5
Lash, S., 63, 202
Last Metro, The (1980), 170
Last Year at Marienbad (1961), 167
Lauren, Ralph, 70, 184
Leach, W., 150
Ledbetter, J., 75
Lee, A., 157
Lee, R., 95
Leopold, E., 76
Levine, L., 33–7, 44–5
Levi-Strauss, C., 197
Life is Beautiful (1998), 171
Lippman, W., 136
Liz Claiborne, 184
Lord & Taylor, 142
Los Angeles County Museum of Art, 129
Love of Art, The, 111–17, 122
Love's Labors Lost (2000), 174

Lucretia Borgia, 33
Luhrmann, B., 158
Lury, C., 28–9, 60, 65, 69, 201–24
Luscombe, B., 217
Lynes, R., 8

McClary, S., 32
McConachie, B., 33–4
McCracken, G., 205–6, 210
Macdonald, D., 7–8
McGrath, D., 157
Macintosh, 210
McLuhan, M., 212
Macy's, 133, 143–4
Made in Newark, 140–1
Making of Middle-Brow Culture, The, 7
Mansfield Park (1999), 166
Manship, P., 113
Manzini, E., 206
Margolin, V., 202
Marjorie Morningstar, 8
Marshal Fields, 133
Martha by Mail, 184
Martha Stewart, 1, 7, 28, 182, 184–5,
    194–5
Martha Stewart Living, 184
Marx, K., 23
Mary Shelley's Frankenstein (1995), 165,
    174
Mastering the Art of French Cooking, 81
Material Culture and Mass Consumption,
    205
Mayer, B., 189
Meier, R., 13
Memoirs of a Geisha, 95–110
Merchant–Ivory, 170
Metropolitan Home, 2, 184–5, 195
Metropolitan Museum of Art, New
    York, 114–15, 119, 143
Middleton-Meyer, K., 16, 90–113
Midsummer Night's Dream (1935), 162
Midwinter's Tale (1995), 174
Miller, D., 194–6, 201–2, 205–6
Miller, T., 11–12, 75–89
Ming Tsai's East Meets West, 86
Minghella, A., 2

Miramax, 1, 23, 155–7, 169–78
Mona Lisa (1986), 172
Mondavi, R., 86
Moran, J., 73
Morgan, H., 68
Morris, W., 191
Moser, C., 45
Mrs. Dalloway (1998), 157
Much Ado About Nothing (1993), 163,
    174, 176
Murray, T., 159
Museum of Fine Arts, Boston, 2, 130,
    139
Museum of Modern Art, New York,
    146–9
My Beautiful Laundrette (1986), 170
My Own Private Idaho (1991), 165

Naremore, J., 181
Nasty Girl, The (1990), 171
National Gallery of Art, Washington,
    114, 116, 119
Newark Museum, 130–9, 146–8
Newson, M., 202
New York Times, 2, 10, 184, 188
New York Times Magazine, 28, 34, 187
Nike, 210–11, 218
Notting Hill (1999), 2
Nunn, T., 157

Oedipus Rex, 160
Ohmann, R., 73
Oliver, R., 76, 80
Olivier, L., 162, 174, 176
Ondaatje, M., 63
O'Neill, M., 184–5
Opera, 43
Opera: A Crash Course, 38–40
Opera For Dummies, 38–40
Opera: The Rough Guide, 40
Orlando (1992), 170
Oscar and Lucinda, 97
Othello (1995), 174

Palumbo-Lui, D., 93
Pavarotti, L., 41–3

PBS, 80–3
Pepin, J., 81, 84
Philadelphia Inquirer Magazine, 77
Philippines Lifestyle Network, 78
Philips, 221
Picasso, P., 142
Pier I, 183
"Pierre Menard," 161
Popkin, Z., 142
Portrait of a Lady (1996), 157
Postman, The (1994), 171
Potter, S., 157, 170
Pottery Barn, 182–3, 186, 193, 198
Pran, P., 192
Prichard, M., 118–19
Prospero's Books (1991), 159
Puccini, G., 41
Pulp Fiction (1994), 171

Quo Vadis, 160

Rabinow, P., 222
Radway, J., 7–8
Raynor, H., 33
Reiter, E., 79
Reinhardt, M., 162
Rensi, E., 80
Restoration Hardware, 9, 182
Ritzer, G., 88
Robinson Crusoe, 161
Romanelli, D., 28
Romeo and Juliet (1968), 155, 163
Rondine, La, 9
Rozema, P., 166
Rubin, J. S., 7, 18
Ruiz, R., 168
Rushdie, S., 9

Said, E., 94–5, 109–10
Saint Laurent, Yves, 70
Sargent, J. S., 2
Scarlet Letter (1995), 166
Schlondorff, V., 168
Schmitt, B., 73
Schuster, M., 20, 120
Scofield, P., 174

Scorsese, M., 157, 165
Seabrook, J., 201, 219
Seinfeld, 9
Sense and Sensibility (1995), 157, 165
Sex, Lies, and Videotape (1989), 171
Shakespeare, 155–78
Shakespeare in Love (1999), 26, 155–6, 171, 177–8
Shakespeare: The Invention of the Human, 176
Shall We Dance? (1997), 171
Shaughnessy, R. J., 66
Shepard, S., 169
Simmel, G., 202–4, 217, 219
Simmons, L., 11
Simonson, A., 73
Simonson, L., 143
Sister Parish, 196
Smith, D., 83
Snow Falling on Cedars, 92, 95–110
Snow, Mrs. G., 143
Soderbergh, S., 171
Soja, E., 193
Sorkin, M., 193
Springsteen, B., 17
Stam, R., 161
Stark, P., 9–10, 202
Stathis, P., 10
Steinmetz, C., 136
Stella, J., 142
Stephenson, P., 80
Stewart, D., 81
Stirling, A., 80
Stoppard, T., 156, 178
Storey, J., 25–6, 29, 32–55
System of Objects, The, 207

Tait, T., 63
Tan, A., 90, 96
Tarantino, Q., 170–3
Target, 1
Taymour, J., 157
Teach Yourself Opera, 38
Tempest, The, 162
Ten Things I Hate About You (1999), 157
Thanhouser, E., 162

That's Life, 83
Thompson, E., 174
Thornton, P., 191
Throne of Blood (1957), 163
Time Re-Gained (2000), 168
To Kill a Mockingbird, 8
Tommy Hilfiger, 184
Tournier, M., 161
Truffaut, F., 166, 170–1
Turkle, S., 210–11, 215–16, 220
TV Dinners, 86
Twelfth Night (1997), 157

Ulysses, 161
United Artists, 170
Urry, J., 63
USA Today, 185
Utrillo, 142

Vadim, R., 167
Valmont (1989), 167
Van Sant, G., 165
Vanity Fair, 162
Veblen, T., 135–6
Verhoeven, M., 171
Vickers, J., 40
Victoria and Albert Museum, 130–1,
    137, 141
Vintage Books, 97, 110
Vitagraph, 162

Vogue Magazine, 143
Voortman, J. J., 66

Wagner, G., 161
Wall Street Journal, 183
Wallach, A., 19–20, 114–28
Wallpaper, 208
Waters, A., 9
Watson, R., 82
Webster, J., 177
Welles, O., 173
Wenders, W., 170
Wharton, E., 8, 196
Wheelright, P., 11
Wilkins, M., 64
William Shakespeare's Romeo and Juliet
    (1996), 26, 158, 165
Williams, R., 13
Williams-Sonoma, 221
Wings of Desire (1988), 170
Wolf, J., 4–5, 36–7
Women on the Verge of a Nervous
    Breakdown (1988), 170
Wong, S. L. C., 96
Wood, J., 208
Woolf, V., 84
Wright, F. L., 22

Zahler, K. G., 70
Zeffirelli, F., 163
Zelochow, B., 33